HEROES
OF
LAMSDORF
Lest We Forget

COMPILED BY
KEN SCOTT

Fortis
Publishing Services

ISBN 978-1-913822-29-3

Fortis Publishing
Kemp House
160 City Road
London
EC1V 2NX

This book is dedicated to Prisoners of War everywhere, in every war ever to have taken place, to those who died in captivity and those who survived.

Contents

PREFACE

Over the years as a ghost-writer, I have been introduced to many incredible stories relating to the very real personal trauma and torment of those who found themselves thrust into a war that most of them wanted no part of.

WWII, as we know, was the bloodiest conflict the world has ever seen with up to fifty million military and civilian deaths worldwide. But they weren't they only victims. As well as the maimed and injured, there were those who Philip Baker (in his excellent foreword that follows) rightly calls 'the survivors', the military men and women who were captured by the enemy and thrust into the toughest battle of their lives.

My first foray into a prisoner of war (POW) book was *Do the Birds Still Sing in Hell?*, nearly twelve years ago. I felt very honoured and yet humbled to sit down and speak with the late, great, Horace Greasley, then aged 89, who had spent five years at Lamsdorf VIII-B, (later renumbered Stalag-344), and the surrounding work camps.

The two years I spent with Horace changed my life as he opened up and spilled raw emotion each and every time I sat with him. We shed tears of laughter and sadness and became great friends, we shared a gin and tonic every Friday right up to the day he died.

Horace told me stories of love, respect, suicide, revenge, torture and torment, boredom and frustration. He described how evil and how kind and compassionate the creature known as Man can be.

As soon as the book was published I received another POW book commission and then, a few years later, another. I wrote further books on WWII and the Spanish Civil War. This was followed by a book about the war in the former Yugoslavia, about an 18-year-old girl taken prisoner by the Kosovan Liberation Army and then, as the war neared its conclusion and she managed to escape, how the Serbian Army imprisoned her again.

I quickly realised that POW books interested me more than any subject I had covered, the research alone can consume you for days on end.

When the opportunity arose to co-author another Lamsdorf prisoner's book, I did not hesitate to give it a thumbs-up, and in late 2021 John West's book, *The Psychiatrist*, was completed.

John and I made the journey to Lamsdorf and the surrounding area in December 2021. It was cold, with snow on the ground. Only by visiting those bleak surroundings at that time of year can you appreciate just how hard the battle to survive really was.

I consumed POW books voraciously and more than twelve months ago, on a whim, I posted on the Lamsdorf Facebook group, asking how many more unpublished POW stories were out there. The response was overwhelming and this book was born.

I'd like to think there are still more untold stories to be unearthed and I look upon it as my duty to humanity to keep digging, and to keep these stories alive in order that the younger generation appreciates what these prisoners went through. I also like to think that there may be future politicians who will read these stories of fortitude, sacrifice and survival and that, somehow, authors like me may just have a small influence on how the future is shaped.

If you have a story that you think is worthy of a book, please do not hesitate to contact me.

Ken Scott
www.kenscottbooks.com
kenscottbooks@gmail.com

FOREWORD

In May 1945 a group of recently liberated British former prisoners of war were lodging with British troops in Lübeck whilst awaiting repatriation. One evening they decided to watch an Entertainments National Service Association show being held in this former German Army camp. A sergeant at the door refused them entry, as the show was, 'only for fighting men'.

In their few days there, the men had become dispirited by being on the receiving end of this sort of ignorant attitude from other soldiers, including remarks about white feathers and the colour yellow, which they hadn't expected at all. Luckily for them the incident was witnessed by an ATS (Women's Army) sergeant, who angrily told the man on the door that, unlike these former POWs, he had never heard a shot fired in anger, particularly as he was only a signaller, well behind the lines. She propelled them into the show and explained to an officer what had happened. He immediately cleared space in the front row for them and treated them with great respect.

These were fighting men indeed, having been captured in combat on land, sea or in the air and they had seen many of their comrades fall in action. Having become prisoners of war, they then had to spend the next few years in another fight, one for survival.

But what was it actually like to be a prisoner of war? Something that I have discovered in more than twenty years of researching and recording the history of prisoners of war, is that it is impossible to generalise at all about what life was like at Stalag VIII-B/344 Lamsdorf and its working parties, or indeed about any POW experience anywhere. Some years ago I was able to talk to a few of the former POWs who were still alive. I have read many books written by ex-inmates of Lamsdorf and other camps, many other books on the same subject and very many personal accounts sent to me by former POWs or by their relatives. All this comprise a vast amount of information and opinion, and this has convinced me that is very difficult to sum up the 'POW experience' briefly and to remain fair and accurate, simply because the experience was so complex, involving many differing experiences, reactions, and impressions from different people. For anyone to say that 'this camp was like this' or 'the working parties were like that' or 'the guards behaved in such-and-such a way' cannot convey the whole truth because there were so many widely-varying experiences and recollections.

Stalag VIII-B/344 was a vast camp. Its size varied through the years, but at its peak in 1943 it contained just over 31000 men, not including the thousands who were in hundreds of working parties scattered over a large area. Just like any town, different parts of this huge camp had their own characteristics. All branches of the armed forces were represented and there were men of many nationalities, often in separate compounds. The perceptions and experiences of one man in one hut, perhaps with people he didn't get on with very well, perhaps bored, miserable, lonely, apathetic, or depressed, might have been hugely different to another man in another compound or even in the next hut, who was among good friends, who was involved in sporting or cultural activities and whose morale was generally higher.

Multiply this by the tens of thousands of men there and you can see how accounts of what life was like as a prisoner of war can differ considerably.

It is also true that the camp changed very much in the course of time. One POW arriving at Lamsdorf in 1940 described it as a depressing place with 'lads ambling about like lost souls with nothing to do all day'. He subsequently spent eighteen months away on a working party, and when he returned he found that, 'Lamsdorf had changed beyond belief. It was like a small town, with institutions, a sick bay for minor ailments and an efficient organised, equipped, and staffed hospital. There was also a school, and orchestra, various bands, concert parties, drama groups and sports of all descriptions. There was now no excuse to amble about like zombies'.

After a spell away at another working party, he returned to Lamsdorf towards the end of the war. He could hardly believe how it had changed again: 'It was like a Persian market. The enterprising had set up stalls where, for the price of cigarettes, one could obtain clothing, books, toilet requisites and items from food parcels'. Commenting on recent arrivals at the camp of POWs from all over the world he wrote, 'this cosmopolitan crowd certainly added colour and entertainment.'

A certain perception of life as a prisoner of war was created by films and books that, even when they told some of the truth, rarely told the whole truth, wanting to portray the more sensational aspects. In the years immediately following WWII, as well as the films, there was a plethora of books written by or on behalf of former POWs. A number of these gave sensationalised versions of the prisoner-of-war experience, where all Germans were jack-booted, bayonet-wielding monsters and where the prisoners, though brave and determined to escape, were held in "hell camps" and were in daily fear for their lives. I have often had newspaper and magazine articles sent to me, some dating back to the 1940's, that loved to use dramatic headlines, huge generalisations, and unchecked evidence. These rarely conveyed the truth. Clashes with guards did take place of course, but these did not define the POW experience. The experiences of capture and transportation to POW camps certainly featured harrowing incidents of cruelty and inhumanity and in the camps the men were held, some for more than five years, in very crowded conditions. Food was inadequate, there was little comfort and poor sanitation. Clothing, particularly in winter, was inadequate and there was little in the way of heating. All this put a tremendous strain on the inmates and reflected badly on their captors. Despite many of the camp guards behaving reasonably well towards the prisoners, there were enough examples of atrocious behaviour by some guards to increase the unpleasantness of life. In the latter years of Stalag VIII-B/344 Lamsdorf, and especially in 1943, overcrowding became an extreme problem. For most, the possibility of escape was completely unrealistic.

But none of this really defined the whole experience of being a prisoner of war. Being a prisoner of war at Lamsdorf or anywhere else was rarely about an on-going battle of wits with vicious guards. Even without the deprivations, the mere fact of being a prisoner would have been bad enough. Sir Winston Churchill was a prisoner of war in the Boer War and described it as being a melancholy state.

He wrote, 'Companions in this kind of misfortune quarrel about trifles and get the least possible pleasure from each other's society. You feel a sense of constant humiliation in being confined to a narrow space, fenced in by railings and wire, watched by armed men and webbed about with a tangle of regulations and restrictions.'

The biggest battle was to maintain their mental health, although in those days they would not have thought of describing it as such. However, Trevor Gibbens, a medical officer at the Lamsdorf POW hospital who later became a distinguished specialist in psychiatry, treated many in the psychiatric ward there and after the war he published a treatise on the effects of imprisonment on the mental health of the prisoners of war. There were many cases of prisoners becoming 'Stalag happy', the POW slang for someone who displayed eccentric behaviour due to borderline or actual mental health problems.

A former Lamsdorf POW, Ted Lees, wrote, 'As the months passed uneventfully, it became fairly obvious that we should in time become utterly fed up with one another's company. Week after week, month after month, year after year, the same old faces, the same mannerisms, the same conversations. All this played on one's nerves and one felt that one would go mad. I was desperate sometimes and as I gazed out of the window there was nothing to see but barbed wire. There were no prospects in the immediate future; one could see no end to the war and no end to our own captivity. What was the remedy? Just to stick it out, have a sleep and try to dispel all thoughts from one's mind. There was no other way. It was that or insanity.'

To the men's great credit, most of them did not give up on the fight for survival, whether mental or physical, and they created and participated in a range of activities that was astonishing, considering the conditions of deprivation in which they lived. There were sports of all kinds, theatre productions and musical shows, church services and much more. It was noted in 1943 that 2400 men regularly attended the Lamsdorf School. Many of the working parties also organised activities. On the whole, the main role of the guards was to police the perimeter fence and the POWs were left to organise themselves.

After the war it was not unusual for former prisoners of war to be reluctant to talk about their experiences, and at a time when those returning servicemen who had never been prisoners were full of exciting stories of war, it must have been particularly difficult to explain that for them the battle had been to overcome the oppression of confinement and that their main enemies were hunger, separation from loved ones, boredom, irritation with one's comrades, uncertainty and helplessness as months and years drifted by so very slowly. It was undoubtedly easier to relate any more dramatic incidents that they had experienced or witnesses, even though these probably didn't happen very often, and easy for listeners to believe that such were typical of day to day POW life. But the prisoners of war had as much need for courage and perseverance as any others engaged in war, and heroism manifests itself in many ways.

Despite their best efforts, imprisonment took a heavy toll on many of these men, the effects often lasting for the rest of their lives. Little did they know whilst at Lamsdorf that the worst was yet to come. The Long March began in the terrible winter of early 1945 when Lamsdorf and other camps were evacuated westwards as Soviet troops advanced from the east.

As the accounts in this book illustrate, the whole picture is like a vast jigsaw and each of the many thousands of pieces is an individual, and each of these individuals has a story which is unique, complicated, fascinating, perhaps distressing in parts, and many of the stories demonstrate the strength and goodness of human nature that can emerge in severe times of trial. Here we have a few more pieces of the jigsaw. These were men who, in the service of their country, left all that was dear to them, endured hardship, faced danger and suffered imprisonment in the cause of freedom.

Let those who come after, see to it that their names are not forgotten.

Philip Baker
Curator, The On-Line Museum of Prisoners of War

THE STORIES

Lest We Forget

FUSILIER JAMES GARNER

Compiled by Jim's daughter Lynne, in collaboration with her brother, also called Jim. They were both born and brought up in Swinton, Lancs. Jim joined the Royal Navy at the age of 15 and served 35 years until his retirement; he lives in West Sussex. Lynne trained as a nursery nurse, then proceeded to qualify as a State Enrolled Nurse, but returned to childcare after marriage and two children. Having moved around a few times due to her husband's medical pathology career, she currently lives in Berkshire, enjoys researching her family tree and singing with her local Rock Choir.

Fusilier James Garner, 1/8th Battalion, Lanc Fusiliers was born in Salford Lancashire, in 1919. Jim, as he was known, was one of seven children. Two had died in very early childhood, before Jim was born. He had the chance of a scholarship to Manchester Grammar School, but family circumstances dictated otherwise and he went to work at a local butcher's shop when he left school. He enlisted in the Territorial Army on 2 May 1939 and was called up for active service on 2 September 1939, after which he was transferred to the 1/8th Lancashire Fusiliers on 1 Nov 1939.

At the time he was going out with his future wife's sister, Beatrice and they became engaged on 2 December.

On 12 April 1940, the battalion sailed on the *Archangel*, landing at Cherbourg the following morning at 9 a.m. On the 26 April, he received a "Dear John" letter from Beatrice, breaking off the engagement.

On 10 May the battalion marched into Belgium and saw action against the Germans at Wavre. A little over a week later they were at La Bassée where they were blown up by their own artillery. A couple of days later Jim injured his right foot during the action but failed to report sick. At 3 a.m. on 27 May, the battalion was trapped by crossfire and mortar fire in a sewerage ditch. It went on for four long hours during which time Jim's rifle was smashed by shrapnel. By 9 a.m. they were overpowered and taken prisoner on the outskirts of Bethune, France, on retreat to Dunkirk.

After three days on the captive march along with other regiments who had also been taken prisoner, Jim discovered that there were men from the Royal Artillery, so he was able to meet up with his cousin, Gunner John Goring.

According to the 1/8th Battalion Lancashire Fusilier War Diary entry for 26 May, there were leaflets dropped in the area.

'British soldiers, you are surrounded.'

'German troops invaded Courtrai, Tournai.'

'Why do you fight further? Do you really believe this nonsense that Germans kill their

prisoners? Come and see yourselves the contrary.'

'The match is finished, a fair enemy will be fairly treated.'

Despite this, several massacres of Allied prisoners took place shortly after capture, such as the Le Paradis massacre, and Jim and his fellow prisoners were also rounded up into a field at one point with machine guns trained on them. Fortunately for them a German Wehrmacht senior staff officer happened to pass by on a motorbike, saw what was going on and put a stop to it. Had he been an SS officer, things might have been very different.

The captured men arrived at Stalag XXI-B, Schokken, on 11 June and registered as POWs two days later. Jim's 21st birthday was on 31 July, and he wrote this in his war log.

'July 31st. 21st birthday. Work road breaking – rain all day – no hat, overcoat or blanket. Rations bowl of soup, 3 biscuits, jam – no smokes – holes in boots – a marvellous birthday!'

Towards the end of November 1940, Jim started receiving his first letters from home. The first one was from Ruby, his ex-fiancée's sister, who he had known previously. A month later, then based at Schildberg, the first Red Cross parcels arrived and would be received on a fairly regular basis. The men were also supplied with new English greatcoats.

The two cousins were transferred to several camps, where Jim would be put to work as a brickies labourer and John did some navvying, but there was recreation time too, and they attended some of the concerts and plays put on by their fellow POWs. In one letter home to Ruby in June 1942, Jim mentioned there was to be a dance that night and that his dance partner was a very good boxing chap!

Later in 1942 Jim and John would see themselves finally transferred to Stalag VIII-B Lamsdorf and put to work on the oil refinery at Blechhammer, working in all weather and having to wear leather gloves so their hands would not to stick to the ice-cold steel. While there, Jim reported that he had a week off work due to getting a piece of steel in his right eye, but with no lasting damage. Later there was another incident in which he described his moustache getting somewhat singed after trying to light a cigarette in the wind.

Again, entertainment in the camp was put together by the men themselves; one such stage performance was entitled *Mexican Madness*, described by Jim as, 'Quite a good show, but the biggest laugh was to see them tripping across the stage, not one under six feet and weighing about fourteen stone …'

There was a wealth of talent and resourcefulness amongst the men putting on these shows and eventually Jim and John became involved in one themselves. Jim appeared as Sally Hardcastle, the leading lady in *Love on the Dole,* and John played the part of the young brother.

There were also sports events organised such as athletics and football which John got involved with as well as boxing matches, which Jim must have been interested in as he appears as a spectator in one of the many camp photographs.

The first Allied air raids took place over the Blechhammer area in early July 1944. Bombs landed all around the shelter although no casualties were reported. Usually when these air raids occurred the men working in the factory would run into the nearby woods, but on 2 Dec 1944 there was yet another Allied air raid over the area and John had just recovered from appendicitis and could not run. He and Jim went back to camp shelter. They crouched down, but John wasn't finding this comfortable and asked Jim to swap sides.

This time a stray bomb hit the camp and the shelter Jim and John were in. Jim was one of many badly injured; John and 29 others were killed. As soon as it became known that a shelter had been hit, several men left their own shelter and before the aircraft had left the area, worked unceasingly until the last of the injured and the last body had been brought out from the debris. One of these workers was Albert 'Happy' Eckersall who used a tractor to drag away a huge slab of concrete that was pinning Jim down. Initially it was thought Jim was also dead, because when Happy carried him out, he was like a rag doll. But then they realised that Jim was still alive, Happy helped carry Jim to hospital on a stretcher through the snow. When Happy asked Jim if he was okay, he asked him to look in his mouth from where Happy removed a piece of concrete from his gum.

They never saw each other after that day as a month later the camp was evacuated because of the approaching Russian forces.

Jim's injuries were described as including a large horseshoe-shaped laceration of the scalp requiring 20 stitches, fractured ribs, haemothorax, fractured right wrist, loss of blood, cuts to leg, hips and face. And shock. He was unconscious for a long time, taken to Reserve Lazaret at Cosel, and told of John's death on 8 December.

Jim was subsequently transferred to the *revier*, Stalag 344, Lamsdorf and the convalescent block, where he remained until the evacuation of the sick and injured in cattle trucks on 2 March 1945. They passed through the Sudeten foothills, Prague, Muisberg near Munich, Regensburg, Linza and Salzburg ending up at Stalag XV11-A, Kaisersteinbruch, Austria. The journey took seven days and the men were in the cattle trucks the whole time, 45 men per truck with very little food and the weather throughout very cold with snowstorms.

Their evacuation march began on 1 April and being so badly injured and with very few rations, Jim was weak. He inevitably began to lag behind. A fellow soldier who was from New Zealand stayed back with him, told him he would have to keep walking and encouraged him to keep going by saying, 'You want to see your mother again, don't you?'

People from the villages they passed through would leave out boiled eggs on walls for the soldiers and they would also scavenge for turnips. Not all the men survived but defying all the odds Jim and the rest made it through and were finally liberated by US troops on 4 May at Neukirchen.

The freed POWs were given cigarettes and what food the US troops had with them in emergency rations. Jim was finally able to write home for the first time in three months.

On 9 May, the day after VE Day, Jim and the rest of the men left Neukirchen by truck, arriving at Ulm Bavaria the following day. Five days later they flew from Bavaria, arriving in Brussels a couple of hours later.

While waiting for the flight back to England Jim and his fellow soldiers were in line to get cups of tea from a NAAFI van. One of the girls serving also came from the Manchester area and was telling them what had been going on back home, which resulted in the men missing the call to get their plane. There was also a pilot in the queue who was taking his Dakota plane back to England. He said if he couldn't help out his fellow comrades, then it's a poor show, so Jim jumped on his plane back to Dunsfold Aerodrome in Surrey. There a grand reception with tea and cigarettes awaited the men, given by the Red Cross. Jim was taken to the reception unit at Paxhill, Haywards Heath in Sussex afterwards.

Jim married Ruby in January 1946. He returned to work at the butcher's shop, but as meat was still on ration there wasn't enough money in the business, and he joined the bus service in 1949. He stayed with them until his retirement in 1984.

Jim and Ruby's first home was, in fact, a former army hut. Ruby, was who was pregnant with their son at the time, climbed the gates of the army hut camp with Jim, and like others in many parts of the country, claimed squatters' rights.

A policeman came by some time later and said it was trespass, but as he walked away he wished them good luck. In August of that year the War Office decided to take no action against squatters moving into former army huts across the country. A Northern Command officer is quoted as saying, 'The invasion is on, but we do not intend to take any action. The last thing we want to do is put these homeless people out.'

Jim and Ruby eventually went on to buy their own home where they brought up their son and daughter and got on with life. But Jim's experience in the POW camp would take its toll from time to time, more so when he was tired or unwell and he would have bad dreams where he was back in the shelter. On one occasion, for a lark, someone threw a firework into a hall they were in, which unnerved him tremendously.

In 1990 Jim was reunited with Albert 'Happy' Eckersall. He had never seen Happy again after that fateful day where he'd rescued him, until Jim's son came across a reference to the camp at HMS Dolphin, Gosport some 46 years later. They met up again at Gosport submarine museum, where their story made the local paper. Jim and Happy remained friends until Jim passed away in 1995. It was also discovered that there was a family link by marriage between the two men.

Jim was a quiet, unassuming person, with a great sense of humour, a hard worker, a loving father, and a true 'gentle' man. But as his story shows, he was also strong, determined, and resilient. We're proud to have had him as our dad.

In memory of James Garner, John Goring, Albert 'Happy' Eckersall and all the POWs at Stalag VIII-B.

SIDNEY WATERFALL

By Sonia Waterfall

Sonia Waterfall was born and bred in the Yorkshire Dales before leaving home for university in Norwich, Newcastle and finally Sheffield where she gained an MA in Librarianship.

She emigrated to New Zealand with her husband in 1972 and spent the next fifteen years there, living and working in both the North and South Islands.

In 1987 she went as a volunteer to Tokelau, a New Zealand dependency in the South Pacific, where she worked for two years after which she moved to Australia with her new partner and lived there for almost thirty years.

Sonia retired in 2007 and after ten years of spending half the year in the UK and half in Australia, she settled permanently near her sister in

Rothbury, Northumberland. She started writing on retirement and has self-published two books, Escape to Auschwitz: Hulda's story, *an account of her grandmother's life and death during World War II and 'Choices and Opportunities: Memories of a Baby Boomer', her memoir.*

Sidney (Sid) Waterfall, from a Quaker family, was a conscientious objector who agreed to take a non-combatant role and was enlisted in the RAMC as a medic. After training at Beckett Park in Leeds he was assigned to the 7th (British) General Hospital, 18th Company and shipped out to Crete, via South Africa and Egypt, arriving there on 19 April 1941.

For the first four weeks there he worked at establishing the hospital at Galatos, helping to treat the sick, wounded, and exhausted troops that had been evacuated from mainland Greece. 25000 men had arrived on Crete by the end of April.

During the Battle of Crete, beginning on 20 May, the 7th (British) General Hospital worked in tandem with the 5th and 6th (New Zealand) Ambulance Units. They moved from one site to another along the north coast and then inland trying to keep one step ahead of the German troops landing at Maleme airfield and advancing east. During this period the medics were treating German as well as Allied troops and Sid maintained that he treated Max Schmeling, the world famous boxer, while he was working in caves on the north coast.

On 27 May it was decided to evacuate the walking wounded and medics, and along with the majority of the Allied troops they started the trek over the mountain pass to Sfakia where the navy was waiting to evacuate them to Egypt. They moved at night and took cover during the day while German planes strafed the road in an attempt to halt the retreat. To escape the strafing, Sid, being an experienced rock-climber in his former life, led a group of ten men down the cliffs into the gorge below where they met up with a group of Layforce troops (the precursor to the SAS) taking cover in a cave in the gorge.

From here they made their way down the gorge until they hit the south coast and re-joined the main force who were waiting to be evacuated.

Sid was captured and marched back to Galatos where a POW camp had been established with a hospital. He spent the next four months there and then was shipped out, first to the hell-hole that was Salonika for a couple of weeks, then overland by rail in cattle-trucks to Stalag VIII-B.

He arrived at the end of October, completed his POW card on 2 November and became POW No. 24321 for the next three years and five months.

Medics were put to work in the wards, the barracks, the laboratories, dispensary, and theatre as well as staffing a large out-patient clinic which dealt with the sick referred from the medical inspection rooms in the barracks. Other medics found work as sanitation orderlies attending to the condition of the latrines, staffing the camp delouser, or organising the use of the bath-houses. Others worked on a daily fatigue party of cleaners and gardeners to keep both the inside and outside areas of the camp in a clean and healthy condition.

There are only a few hints in Sid's letters about his medical work – he mentioned that he preferred 'Surgical' to 'Medical' and on three occasions said he'd been very busy working six days a week because of an influx of new POWs from other camps or from new theatres of war.

From October 1943 unto early 1944, he was working in the out-patient clinics which he found very interesting because of the wide variety of cases that came through.

For most of 1943 Sid was on the outside fatigue party and, as well as trimming the grass edges and keeping the ditches clear, he also helped maintain a vegetable garden and mentioned growing tomato plants, lettuce, radish, onions, and peas. Later in the season he mentioned that he has had 'four or five dozen' tomatoes and was hoping for a few more if the sunny weather continued.

He liked the outside job because it got him 'out and about' the camp. He had been brought up as an outdoorsman and his father had taught him all he knew about the natural world – the wildflowers, the birds and the 'fruits of the forest'. Sid remembered what he had learnt in his youth and told his parents about a couple of skylark nests he found – each with five eggs which all hatched safely. A week later he mentioned them again, saying that the nests were still safe but that he was expecting them to be empty soon as the young birds fledged.

Later in the war (mid-1943 onwards) medical staff were allowed out for a walk, courtesy of the Geneva Convention. Sid describes a walk of about four miles to a lake where they had a swim. They were also allowed a double ration of letters and cards to write and Sid made good

9

use of that perk too. Letters were important, not so much because of what they said but because they reminded the POWs that there was a life outside the camp and the families at home knew they were still alive and functioning.

Unfortunately, letters could bring bad news as well as being a comfort, and Sid was the recipient of a 'Dear John' letter when his fiancée, Amy, wrote to tell him she was going to marry someone else. The disappointment must have been a blow to Sid, but he didn't blame Amy and in a letter to his parents he acknowledged that it was difficult for young people to be apart for long periods, especially as there'd been a six-month period of no communication between them immediately after he'd been captured. He kept hoping that she would change her mind but found, when he arrived home in 1945, that she was married, and had a child.

A year later came the news of his father's death which he heard about two months after the event. It wasn't totally unexpected as he'd been ill for six months with cancer and Sid's brother had written to him warning him of the probable outcome. It was a sad-happy time because the first member of the next generation had been born around the same time and Sid's father had managed to hold his new grandson in his arms before he died. It still hit Sid hard as he'd been very close to his father. He wrote to his mother that he felt he'd let his father down as he was the only one of the family not there at the funeral.

The ongoing possibility of repatriation gave Sid an element of hope for the future. Repatriation was the exchange of troops, both Allies and German, who were allowed to return to their home countries according to rules set down by the Geneva Convention. Only long-term sick and wounded were exchanged but medics travelled with them to care for them on the journey home.

In October 1943 Sid wrote his parents, mentioning the possibility of 'walking through the front door' and surprising them. And again in 1944, not long after his father had died, he was hoping he'd be able to get home to his mother and help her out. Both times he wasn't chosen and both times he had to apologise for raising the hopes of his family. The hope of 'repatting' raised everyone's spirits for a time, but for most of the medics those hopes would be dashed when they realised it wasn't to be their turn. There was always a gap in his letters during these periods as once again he had to come to terms with the dashing of his hopes and the disappointment. 'Everything is at sixes and sevens,' he wrote and said he'd had to resign himself to staying where he was 'for the duration'.

What mainly kept Sid sane while at Stalag VIII-B was football. He'd played for the First XI while at school and for local teams pre-war but it was while he was a POW that it became the most important thing in his life. His letters are full of matches played, the scores, the pitch conditions, where his team was placed in the league and how fit he was becoming. It was 8-a-side in early letters until a new pitch was built in 1943 and it became 11-a-side. He played at centre half and wrote that he only managed to kick goals if the defence was poor.

Apart from football, he read a lot – mainly books set in Yorkshire. The family business was a bookseller/stationer's shop and many books were sent from home in book parcels. He studied as well, gaining a qualification in shorthand. He also continued his interest in Law as he'd been a solicitor's clerk pre-war. He also seemed to attend every play, musical event, and art/craft exhibition available – other interests that had started at school. He had no performing or artistic talent personally but enjoyed watching those who had.

In June 1944 Sid was moved to Tost to help establish a new hospital there – the Tost Reserve Lazaret. Living conditions were much improved there – four men to a room, more privacy, and views of a normal world from the windows. No football though, but two-hour walks were allowed twice a week. It was while he was at Tost that he met a young woman from the German offices that ran the hospital in tandem with the British staff. He and Elisabeth Wieland were friends from then until the evacuation six months later and she wrote to him until 1946.

In January 1945 evacuations began as POWs were moved away from the Russian advance.

In an interview for the local paper when he returned in April 1945, Sid said that all hospital patients who were fit to move were certified by the British Government and the Germans accepted their ruling without question. He also said that those remaining in the hospital were later liberated by the Russians and repatriated via Odessa.

The first stage for Sid was a train journey, lasting two weeks, which took medics and moveable patients form Tost to Stalag VIII-C at Sagan. It was expected that they would continue by train to Spremberg and then change trains again to take them further west. This didn't happen as the Russian advance had already cut the train lines so they had to continue by foot. They left Sagan on 8 February in a group of 2000, about 250 from Tost Reserve Lazaret.

All 2000 seemed to have walked the same route but the Tost group were the last to arrive at Bad Orb, presumably because they were unwell or carrying wounds when they set off and could only travel at the speed of the slowest of the group.

Sid drew the route of his Long March on a map of Europe when he returned home in 1945 and this is confirmed by a hand-written daily record kept by one of the patients from the Tost group.

In an interview after the war, he said that throughout his POW years he was always grateful for his upbringing as an outdoorsman and particularly during the Long March when the habits he'd learned on some of the long treks he'd made in his youth came in useful. In the same interview he said that there was a serious lack of medical equipment on the march and also that the Tost group lost about one man per day. He blamed some of the deaths on the men's addiction to cigarettes. He said that when the food parcels were distributed by the Germans, those with a cigarette craving bartered their food for cigarettes which then meant they starved themselves.

The Tost group arrived at Stalag IX-B at Bad Orb on 14 March 1945 and were liberated by the Americans on 1 April. Sid was transported back to England on 8 April and arrived at No 92 Reception Camp at Pipers Wood, Amersham, Bucks on 9 April.

For Sid his war was over.

For more details about Sid and his war, as well as his life pre- and post-war, the complete story is available in A Pacifist's War: Sid's story *by Sonia Waterfall from the publishers, FeedARead at www.feedaread.com or from the author at waterfallsonia@gmail.com.*

DR DAVID LIVINGSTONE CHARTERS

M.B.E., M.B. Ch.B. (Glas), D.O.M.S

By Kerstin Hinkley

Kerstin is the eldest of David and Margaret Charters' seven grandchildren. She lives in Surrey with her husband and foster son. At least some of her current interest in buying and selling antiques stems from her grandfather's own interest in Georgian glass and 18th and 19th century furniture. At the age of 18, Kerstin moved to Birkenhead to live with her grandmother Margaret Charters. She recalls the regular trips to the nursing home that were made to visit David Charters in the last months of his life, during which time he suffered from severe Alzeheimers. Kerstin has fond memories from her childhood, of many trips to stay with her grandparents. These always involved a much

13

anticipated visit to a sweetshop to be treated to Lindt chocolates by her Grandpa.

Dr David Livingstone Charters was a major with the Royal Army Medical Corps. He was born in Stirling and came from a Scottish Presbyterian background. His ancestors included a long line of Scottish missionaries (he was named David Livingstone after the most famous of his uncle's colleagues).

Dr Charters set up his medical practice in Birkenhead where his social conscience earned the name 'the poor man's doctor', as he so rarely charged his more needy patients (before the days of the NHS). He was one of the few doctors to earn the trust of dock workers during the General Strike of 1926 when he was allowed to cross the picket line.

Nothing could have prepared Dr Charters for the severity of sickness and injuries that he ended up treating in the POW medical camp systems that he experienced. His specialism was ophthalmic, so little in his pre-war medical practice prepared him for the reconstructive plastic surgery work that he was later called on to perform.

He was in charge of the 26th General Hospital R A M C Crete, when they were captured by the Germans in April 1941. Most of the following information is taken from a medical pamphlet that Dr Charters produced for a medical journal after the war titled: *Medical Experiences as a Prisoner of War in Germany* by D. L. Charters (Liverpool, 1946). He described this publication as a personal narrative: 'The few facts and figures I can give you are drawn largely from memory, because any statistical records I had were taken from me by the German authorities and are now irretrievably lost.'

This followed the bombing of the central medical archives in Berlin.

Following the capture of Crete by the Germans, evacuation of the POWs (via Athens) commenced in November 1941. After spending three weeks in terrible conditions in Salonika, Dr Charters was amongst those 'Ex-Creta' POWs moved into Germany by rail. The journey lasted eleven days.

The captured 'Ex-Creta' prisoners travelled via the Varda Valley to Belgrade and then through Vienna, Regensburg, Augsburg, Nuremberg, Chemnitz, Dresden and Breslau. They eventually reached Stalag VIII-B in Upper Silesia near the German, Czech and Polish borders. During the rail journey the men were locked in cattle trucks with no sanitary arrangements, although many of them had dysentery. The officers travelled under crowded conditions in wood-seated workmen's carriages. 'To sit for eleven days on a narrow wooden seat has to be experienced to be understood.'

For the last 36 hours, they had no food or water. Several of the men escaped during the journey by cutting a hole in the floor in their carriage while they were in the mountains of Yugoslavia, and this probably accounted for the harsh treatment the others received on their journey. They were severely punished because they had not prevented the escapes. Many of the men were ill on the journey. The more seriously ill were taken off the train and left at civilian hospitals in various towns on route.

On arrival at Stalag VIII-B in late 1941, Dr Charters described it as an organised POW camp of up to 30000 men, most of whom had been taken prisoners in France in 1940. It was quite well built brick and concrete standardised military huts. The men slept in three-tier bunks, even in hospital. There were facilities for bathing and delousing and reasonable sanitation. There was, of course, the usual barbed wire fencing with sentry towers, complete with machine-guns and searchlights at regular intervals.

The POW standard daily diet amounted to 800 to 1000 calories and was composed of black bread (frequently stale and mouldy), turnips, potatoes (frequently bad). There were minute quantities of meat, cheese, margarine and ersatz (i.e. substitute) jam or ersatz honey. They were also allowed ersatz coffee (such as ground roasted acorns and chestnuts), which at least had the merit of being hot.

One Red Cross parcel was received every third week: thus bringing total calories up to about 1600 a day. Most men were working in neighbouring quarries, mines, farms, or factories, with slightly better conditions being offered by the Germans to encourage them to do this. Since the Germans had control of their Red Cross food parcels, the working parties received the more generous supply.

The men were supplied with captured British clothing and boots or with Red Cross clothing from home. The winter of 1941-42 was exceptionally cold and the temperature averaged about 20 centigrade below zero. Fuel for heating was very limited. Water froze in the rooms at night. Dr Charters recalled how, one morning, a New Zealand surgeon tried to thaw out his false teeth from a glass full of solid ice. To do so, he used his entire breakfast supply of ersatz coffee. One post-diphtheritic patient developed frostbite in both big toes while in bed in hospital.

This severe cold was the cause of an unforeseen tragedy in connection with the delousing plant, which utilised cyanide gas. The men stripped completely and all their clothing and blankets were put in sealed chambers filled with cyanide. Meanwhile, the men shaved, had warm showers, and then waited in the drying room for the return of their clothing. On this occasion, the arrival of a large party of Russians, all of whom were lousy, caused the staff to hurry the drying-out process. The Russians got quickly back into their clothing and marched back to their hut. Being inexperienced, they used all their fuel trying to cook food, with the result that later their hut became bitterly cold. Most of these new arrivals went to bed fully clothed, wrapping themselves up in their great coats and blankets and fell asleep. In the morning, eight of them were dead. They were the men that had slept with their heads inside their blankets. The cyanide had not been driven out at the delouser but had become gaseous again as their beds warmed up.

The hospital (lazaret) at Stalag VIII-B had 400 beds, which David Charters described as reasonably, if sparingly, equipped. There was a medical and surgical team, and the work followed the usual hospital routine except for the following unusual types of cases: Diphtheria and nutritional oedema (abnormal fluid retention in the tissues resulting especially from lack of protein in states of starvation or malnutrition). At first, nutritional oedema was little understood, and many of the cases were diagnosed as nephrosis, while others were put down as beriberi. Most of the cases of nutritional oedema recovered, or nearly so, when Red Cross parcels came in normal quantities. The Red Cross parcels contained Bemax, Marmite, Aluzyme and Ascorbic Acid *et cetera*, as well as usual protein foods. Chronic dysentery was not rare and tended to aggravate the tendency to nutritional oedema. Dr Charters' own oedema lasted well into 1944.

In John Borrie's book *Despite Captivity: A Doctor's Life as Prisoner of War*, fellow doctor John Borrie described David Charters at one point as 'being unrecognisable from acute oedema of face and hands, his eyelids tense, the size of bantams' eggs, his cheeks and hands huge and blotched.'

POWs lived almost exclusively on vegetables, mainly turnips. Much of the food that they were forced to eat was mouldy and the soups were usually contaminated by semi-rotten potatoes. At this time, practically everyone in the camp had polyuria (frequent urination), and most POWs visited the urinal twice or more between 10 p.m. and 7 a.m. Every night there was a continuous tramping of ammunition boots on concrete, as men shuffled back and forth to the latrines.

During Dr Charter's time at Stalag VIII-B, there was an epidemic of typhus fever. The medical team didn't recognise it at first because none of them had ever seen typhus and the cases presented themselves in a very misleading way. Also, they had no books of reference. The source of the infection was the Russians, who used the same delouser as other POWs. The epidemic was small amongst the British prisoners, but the Russians' experience was very bad, with their death rate varying from 40 to 150 a day. Many other Russian deaths were, however, due to exhaustion and starvation.

Dr Charters left Stalag VIII-B in May 1942. Following several months of petitioning the authorities, the German War Office granted him permission to set up a central 500 bed eye hospital and braille school for British prisoners in Western Germany. As well as eye patients, there were 240 leg amputees (12 of them double). This new hospital became the centre for the most seriously injured (*les grands blessés*) awaiting repatriation. The hospital lasted until October 1943, when the patients were the first to be repatriated to the UK. After he turned down the offer of being repatriated himself, Dr Charters was then moved to Stalag IX-B near Frankfurt-on-Maine. The Daily Mail reported on his decision, referring to him as *One Man Who Stayed Behind*. At Stalag IX-B, Dr Charters performed 300 plastic surgery operations for airman with burned faces, using instruments selected by Archie McIndoe at Victoria Hospital, East Grinstead, and supplied by the Air Ministry. David Charters' work was described by blind MP Sir Ian Fraser as 'performing veritable miracles'. The International Committee of the Red Cross 'admired the skills with which Major Charters has performed difficult plastics operations, grafting skin etc. Some of the results are astonishing'.

One of David Charters patients later in the war was Marmaduke Hussey, Baron Hussey of North Bradley, who went on to become Chairman of the BBC. Lord Hussey described Dr Charters as 'a remarkable man and whose great devotion to the wounded and fellow combatants has been widely under-estimated ...I owe my life to his insistence that I should have the best care possible in those circumstances'. David Charters had a reputation of having an ambivalent view of authority and Lord Hussey recalled he took 'his responsibilities as a senior officer in our camp with great skill, courage and understanding. All of us were in his debt and the course he steered, refusing to yield one jot to the Germans, was one of strength and dedication.'

Dr Charters remained a POW until the end of WWII and continued to look after many thousands of injured and sick POW servicemen of all nationalities. He was finally able to return to his wife Margaret and three young daughters Mavis, Ruth, and Eve in Birkenhead (his son David was born after the war), after being liberated by the American Third Army on 31 March 1945.

Dr Charters was a truly selfless man and a remarkable surgeon who put the needs of his fellow serviceman ahead of his own. A quiet man before the war, he became more austere on his return deploring any kind of ostentation, triviality and most specially any waste of food. He rarely mentioned his POW experiences, although his family realised that his imprisonment was the most overwhelming event of his life.

E.R Mayhew devotes several pages to David Charters' medical and surgical work during his later time as a POW in her book *The Reconstruction of Warriors: Archibald McIndoe, the Royal Air Force, and the Guinea Pig Club*. In her book Dr Emily Mayhew says of Dr Charters 'Many of his colleagues in the post-war period never realised his history, but when they were contacted as part of the research for this book, none of them was surprised at Charters' courage and determination, or by his ability to adapt his surgical skill in the most testing or environments. Charters had clearly been greatly admired – even loved – by all who worked for or with him for his gentleness, his clinical abilities and flair (despite his skills being somewhat old-fashioned) and his quiet Christian convictions. Charters' reluctance to capitalise on his war experience led to him declining an invitation to

Buckingham Palace to collect his MBE which was instead sent to him by registered post.'

JOHN MACAULAY

Stornoway, Outer Hebrides, Scotland

By Iain and Mairi Macaulay

Iain lives in Stornoway in the Western Isles of Scotland and is married to Amy. Iain runs a Mortgage business and, amongst other hobbies, enjoys playing chess and hill walking. His sister Mairi is a Teacher and is married to William. They also live in Stornoway and enjoy gardening and walking their 2 Springer Spaniels!Both couples are followers of the Lamsdorf, Stalag V111B facebook page and look forward one day to visiting Lambinowice and the Museum there.

John was from the Isle of Lewis in the Western Isles of Scotland. He joined the Territorial Army as a seventeen-year-old and did a lot of training and sentry duties on the island. He often talked about the day he left the island to go to war, how he said goodbye to his parents, telling them he would be back on leave very soon. And then he would give a half laugh, sadness in his eyes. It took him over five years before he got back home, he would say.

John was with the Seaforth Highlanders' Battalion who was sent to Newcastle, as part of the 51st Highland Division, then on to France in 1940 where they spent long days and nights retreating and digging trenches. They knew they weren't going to win. While moving up a large slope in Fécamp, they discovered the Germans were on the inside of them, instead of being on the outside. The Germans fired at the truck in the front and it went up in flames. Two men were lost there.

The battalion made it to Lille the next day and were walking on the pavement with their boots tied on their backs so that they would not make a noise. But a German picked them out with a torch and they were captured. They joined the prisoners marching to Germany.

Going through Holland some men managed to put their names and addresses on pieces of paper and gave it to locals. The notes would make it to the Red Cross and John's parents were notified he was alive.

In Holland the Dutch people tried to give them food but the Germans would not let them. But they did manage to throw bits of bread and cheese and packs of cigarettes to the men. The prisoners were also extremely thirsty and the Dutch left buckets of water for them. Often, the German guards would kick over the buckets and the men had to watch the water they longed for seeping into the ground.

The journey continued some distance on crammed coal barges. John hated this since it was terribly cramped and coal dust suffocated them when the roof hatches were closed.

Then they were marched thousands of kilometres in the direction of Lamsdorf. They were hungry and tired and needed water, knowing that they could survive a while without food but not without water. They took every opportunity they could find to drink water.

During their time on the march to Stalag VIII-B, John and a few friends tried to escape twice. One time they deliberately fell behind the other prisoners, getting away from the guards, travelled at night and slept through the day. John's cousin, Neil, also a POW from the Isle of Lewis, had a small Bible and they used to read it together. It would pass the time and give them comfort. They would fall asleep in the early morning, only to be woken up by the planes flying overhead.

After several days, passing through a village one night, a German guard appeared, shone a torch on them and whistled. A dozen soldiers appeared from a house across the road and John and Neil were captured.

A good while later, still exhausted from marching and having very little food, they were taken into a barn along with about 200 other prisoners and guards. John, Neil and two friends decided to escape. It was autumn and the oats were ready to harvest, and the men hid in the oat field until the march passed by.

Then later they hid in a brick factory, some of it was underground. A little French boy came around and they signed to him they were hungry. He brought them three pieces of bread. Then the boy's father came and gave them civilian clothes to put on, on top of their battle dress. They then felt more confident that they wouldn't be spotted.

At night they walked through the woods and during the daytime they went into hiding. One morning there was a farmer nearby and they approached him. He gave them a loaf of bread to share and they rushed back to the shelter of the woods.

The farmer called them back. They thought he was going to offer them more food and but as they approached him there were German guards waiting for them. John and Neil raised their arms. That was their last attempt at escape during the journey to the camp.

The camp at Stalag VIII-B was just dreadful. John was sent to work in a paper factory with 30 other men. They had to offload three meter long logs of wood when these arrived in wagons, load it onto trolleys and take it to the saws, which they would feed one log at a time.

It was very repetitive, heavy work with little food at the end of the day to sustain them. After some weeks of doing this, the Germans wanted ten volunteers to join a work party in the coal mine. John volunteered, but was there for only two months, when they asked if anyone could repair boots. He stepped forward because when they were young his father had shown them how to give each other hair-cuts and repair their own shoes. John was kept in the camp repairing shoes for the other men. Little did he realise then how significant this job in the camp would become. Every month the Red Cross sent replacement leather soles to the main camp and John would regularly go collect these at a train station, accompanied by a guard. John wouldn't take many replacement soles back with him, so he could get away the next month to collect more and get a break from the camp.

Three months before they had to go on the forced march, John got new boots and put quite a few extra soles and heels on them. He did this for some of his friends as well, and the boots were thus well-layered. John's boots had just a small hole in one of them after marching for approximately 700 kilometres. They definitely helped him through the arduous journey.

After the war he kept these boots in a cupboard in the house and they would be taken out every so often and shown to visitors who asked about his experiences.

We still have them today and show them to friends who are amazed at their provenance.

The thing John missed most in the camp was food, always food. Whatever they would talk about together, it always came back to food. Whatever they were doing, they would think of food. Most days food was the sole topic of conversation in the camps. They talked about where they were going when they were released, what food they were going to have when they reached home, and how they were not going to stop eating till they burst.

They talked about what was going to be in the soup that day, potato soup, cabbage soup or pea soup. Pea soup has sustenance. Sometimes there was vegetable soup. But potato soup was not great; one basin of potatoes in the boiler for 500 men. It was boiled so brash that the potato went to mush.

When they got a piece of meat it was horse meat. The boys in the cookhouse would throw the bones to them. Once they got this really long bone and when they asked where it had come from, the response was a horse's neigh. The men sucked on those tasty bones, then broke it to get to the marrow. Horse or cow, it didn't matter

John used to send a letter home and say, 'Acras (Gaelic for "hunger") is here'. As his parents didn't know anyone called Acras, they realised he was hungry. Once he was so desperate that he stole potatoes. He knew where a cellar was and several steps down were the stores. The Germans guarded the store but the prisoners did the cooking. John tied a piece of string around the bottom of his battle dress trousers. His plan was to go down into the cellar and fill his trousers with potatoes. He did this and on the way back up the steps, a guard caught him and opened his jacket. The potatoes all went bouncing down the steps. Then the guard butted him on his forehead with a rifle and pushed him down the steps. Neil was waiting for him and after the guard had walked away laughing, dragged him back up the stairs. John told Neil in Gaelic, 'He may have gotten the ones in my jacket but not the ones down my trouser legs.'

That haul kept them fed for several days.

The prisoners were outside in the campgrounds for some of the time. Twice a week the guards would suddenly make them go inside and tell them to lie flat on the ground. They couldn't understand why, until one day they realised that every time they made them lie on the ground a train passed. John slept on the upper floor where there was a hatch in the roof.

Once when they were ordered to lie on the floor they got a small man to stand on the shoulders of two men, and peek through the hatch. All he saw was a train of cattle wagons, but the wagons had small openings in the sides and there were human hands waving out of each opening. One of their own men who worked in the mines with the Poles, explained what he had seen. He said that these were the Jews and Poles on their way to their death at Auschwitz.

John would sometimes talk about how it was so good to get letters from home even though they didn't tell them much. Neil and he would exchange letters and read them dozens of times. It became the only excitement they had. Any spare moment they had, they would lie down and take their letters out.

It was such a comfort for John to see the address on the letter, such a comfort to know the letter had come from home, that his family was in touch with him, that they knew where he was, and that they were safe.

There was a man in Breasclete, John's home village on the Isle of Lewis, called Angus Macphail, whose nickname was *An Russanach*, Gaelic for 'The Russian'. One day towards the end of the War, John sent a letter home saying, 'I am glad that Angus MacPhail is here helping us to get the job done'. He was aware that all the mail was censored but was confident their captors wouldn't have a clue about his code for letting his family know that the Russians had joined in.

Often they would feel that all hope was lost, especially when they heard of the ships that were sunk and that the Germans were advancing.

But when the Russians came into the war, that gave them hope. At the end of the war, the skies were full of Russian and British planes and they knew that a lot of men were lost with all the planes that went down. But they didn't know if they were German or British.

There was a huge barn with a corrugated roof near the camp. Once the boys heard loud bangs and crouched down by the walls. When they emerged the corrugated iron sheeting was full of holes.

They had often seen many people going into that barn but amazingly no one was killed.

John had made friends with a lad who sadly did not get any letters from home. He said he had no home, was brought up by a couple, joined the army and hadn't been in touch with them. John started thinking about him and how he could help him. At that time, you got a form for writing home. So he gave the lad's name and address to his sister Chrissie. She wrote to him and he was delighted to get a letter. He would regularly ask John, 'Is there any word from Chrissie?' John felt sorry for him and said he would take him to Lewis for a holiday to meet his sister after the war is over. Unfortunately the day after the barn had been strafed, it was attacked again and the lad had been in there. He was killed. John always said that if he had survived, they would have become good friends.

A lot of the boys died on that Long March. One of the men on the march was in real pain as his boots were in ribbons. John saw this and, along with another friend, Archie, wondered if they could help him. So they decided to ask if they could go to a farm to be able to repair this man's boots. They were allowed to go with a guard. There was a huge barrel outside the house with rotting apples and suet, that the farmer was going to feed the pigs with.

In Gaelic, John and Archie discussed how they could get to the food in the barrel. The plan was that before John finished repairing the boots, Archie was to tell the guard he wanted to go the toilet. When he did, he filled his pockets with the rotting apples, suet water and all. Archie said afterwards that he was soaked through, but he didn't care as they had a feast with the suet and apples that night.

One day they woke up and there were no guards, but they decided it was too dangerous to move from there. They were on a big farm and heard the noise of a tank coming in.

The Americans had arrived.

One of the soldier's first words to them were, 'We've been a long time coming boys, but we sure made it'. In later years John would smile broadly retelling his family about this moment. He would show them a book by Charles Morrison from Aberdeen, which was titled after that greeting from the soldier.

John had a recurring dream during captivity, in which he saw a man with a board on this back. The date 10 May was written on it. John was trying to get past the man, but he would turn around and get ahead of John again. John would continue trying to get past the man with the placard but he wouldn't let him past. All he could see was, *10 May, 10 May, 10 May*.

He remembered the dream so vividly that one day and said to his friend Archie, 'I know the date we will get home, but I don't know which year it will be. The 10th of May'.

Time passed and he then forgot all about the dream, until they arrived back in Britain. They got new uniforms and had to sign for them. He asked the storeman what the date was.

'10th of May'

Archie was in the queue behind him and John shouted to him, 'What's the date today?'

'I don't know, ask the sergeant,' came the reply.

'I know what the date is,' John said. 'It's the 10th of May.'

Archie was amazed. 'My goodness. You told me years ago that it would be on the 10th of May that we'd be free!'

How that happened he didn't know, but he always looked forward to 10 May ever since. Everyone in the family was aware of the special date each year. It was welcomed as an old friend and the story of John's dream was recounted to those around him.

John would also talk of how there were so many people in Stornoway when he got back. One day he visited his sister, Mary, at the restaurant on the quay where she worked. Mary asked John if he wanted some tea and she also gave him a scone. Instead of eating it, John asked for a newspaper. He wrapped the scone in it and put it in his pocket. A week later his mother found the scone and asked him why it was in his pocket. He replied that he was keeping it in case he was hungry the next day. He found it difficult to believe that there was going to be enough food the next day, that everything was plentiful back at home. It took him some time to realise he was free and that he could eat something anytime he wished.

On another occasion he was walking on the road and kept looking behind him all the time. Someone asked him why he kept looking back.

'Just checking there are no Germans.' It took time, but he overcame that fear as well.

The only things John brought back home with him with were his precious boots, his POW identity disc (17003) and bad memories. He would often think about his experiences, particularly when he would see people starving on the television. He would rarely talk about these experiences except with fellow POWs when they would meet up.

Remembrance Day was always a vital part of his calendar when he would parade with other former soldiers and attend the services. He would stress the importance of us all remembering and to reflect on the peace we now enjoy and those who gave their lives. He would stress how thousands of them had been killed in many ways, to ensure that we are well off and free to travel the world on a whim.

When John returned after the war he was employed for a while as an attendant lighthouse keeper, visiting remote islands and later as the keeper at Stornoway's Arnish Lighthouse. He also worked as a designer and weaver of Harris Tweed.

John married Jessie, also from Stornoway, and had two children: Mairi Charlotte and Iain Macaulay.

John passed away in October 1999.

BERT LILLY

By Jane Lilly

Jane Lilly is from Clevedon in North Somerset, where her family has lived for several centuries.

I have compiled this account using diaries and letters written by my father during the war, and information supplied to me by his companion in Canada when air training, Leslie Bond. A few letters from relatives have survived, but not many, as he could carry very little away from his last camp at Stalag III during evacuation.

My dad, Bert Lilly, joined the RAF in October 1940, leaving his job at his father's grocery shop in Kenn Road, Clevedon, in Somerset. After initial training at Newquay, he set off in January 1941 for Canada to do his air training in Avro Anson aircraft.

Travelling for twelve days by boat was tedious, and his diary entry on 21 January is, 'Hope rising' followed by, 'Sighted land in the morning' the next day.

At weekends Bert visited Windsor, Ontario with Leslie Bond, 'Lucky' Humphries and Bob Russell, where they met and were befriended by the Wilkinson family. Many weekends were spent with the Wilkinsons. With their assistance the RAF lads were able to visit Detroit, just across the border with the USA, with a police escort who treated them like royalty. The Wilkinsons kept in touch during the war, and in a surviving letter of 1942 Mrs Wilkinson remembers Dad singing, 'Happy the day, the airman gets his pay'!

In July 1941 Dad got his 'wing and stripes', becoming Sergeant Lilly, and later that month came back to Britain. In October he married Selma Johansen, from Portishead, and they had a brief honeymoon in a far from sunny Minehead.

By December Dad was in the Mediterranean, reaching Cairo via Gibraltar and Malta, and carried out seven 'ops' with 148 Squadron as a navigator before his plane came down over the desert with engine trouble. He and the rest of the crew walked for three days, covering 80 miles with only three bottles of water. They were captured on 25 February, within sight of the British lines. As Dad put it, 'We waved to the wrong army'.

Eighteen days later, he was in the *dulag* (German Air Force transit camp) at Frankfurt-am-Main for a month, then moved by train on a two day journey to Stalag VIII-B at Lamsdorf in Germany. The coach was packed, with no room to sleep, arriving on 15 April. There were no fires and it was snowing. Without Red Cross parcels, this was what Dad called the 'menu': a pint of tea at 7 a.m., soup at 11.30 a.m., potatoes at 1 p.m., bread at 3.30 p.m. and lastly, fat, if any, at 4.30 p.m. (I assume that you kept the bread until the fat arrived). Later in his diary he noted that their rations provided 1500 calories a day, a starvation diet being 1400 calories. The vital Red Cross parcels provided a crucial additional 300 calories, bringing the total to 1700 per day – in peacetime 2000 to 2500 calories per day was a healthy intake. However, he comments that the 'Germans seem badly off for food, a good sign'. POWs cooked their Red Cross issues for themselves, queuing for their turn at the wood stoves.

Sanitation and drainage caused a big problem, with latrines built over seldom emptied trenches. There were limited and primitive showers, and nowhere to throw the water after you'd washed. During parts of the winter the ground became a quagmire, making exercise difficult.

My mother heard late in March that Dad was missing and he was confirmed as being a POW weeks later. Dad first received post from her late in June, four months after he'd been captured, and the first he'd heard of her in six months, due to the state of the post during the war. When you consider that they'd been married less than three months when he crashed and didn't see each other again until he came home in May 1945, three and a half years later, it's no surprise that when they met again at last, they felt like strangers.

During his time in Stalag VIII-B, Dad found ways of making the time pass. Reading was a boon, and he was always grateful for his parcels of books, and letters from family and friends. He was allowed to send two letters and two postcards per month, though at times this was reduced or stopped. He kept a brief diary in Stalag VIII-B. From this and his letters we found that he joined a choir at the camp, sang in church and in theatrical shows, played bridge, cricket, quoits and tennis. Best of all for him, being a keen swimmer, he could swim in the pool of water maintained in case of fire. There were classes available too, which provided relief from boredom – when they weren't cancelled by the Germans.

Occasionally life took a brighter turn when he met someone from home, like a chap called Mayne who lived in the Down Road in Portishead. Rather often this was tempered by bad news – his best man and old friend, Lin Dorney, was killed in 1942. Another friend, Chris Russell, was killed later during the war.

When the weather was bad in the winter, camp life must have been painfully tedious and depressing.

Many items had to be posted to Dad, and there are requests in his letters for 'razor blades, clothing, a toothbrush, sewing materials and gum'. Cigarettes were always welcome, and of course, as many books as possible.

In October 1942 Dad and many other POWs had their hands tied together for a number of hours every day, as German reprisals for the tying of their men at Dieppe and the Channel Islands. The rope was replaced by chains or manacles over the next five months, until the practice ceased in March 1943. Dad's 1942 Christmas card, showing a

POW watching a snow scene, has chains pencilled in between the POWs hands – it seems that this has escaped the censors.

Life was also affected by the fact that Red Cross parcels were stopped, then resumed and finally reduced.

From Stalag VIII-B and later from Stalag III, Dad was able to send occasional photographs of the shows he was in, one of which ran for twenty three performances, touring the many compounds within the camp. The men wrote their own revues as well as performing plays as varied as *As You Like It* and *French without Tears*. Dad persuaded the choir to include popular songs from shows in their repertoire, which went down well.

When escapes happened, the whole camp was called out on parade while searches and identity checks took place. Many of these were in cold weather, but in August 1942, Douglas

Bader escaped from Stalag VIII-B where he'd been in hospital waiting for his spare false leg to arrive from England. He shortly afterwards walked out in a work party in spare overalls but was recaptured and put in Colditz.

In July 1943, Dad was part of a group which was moved to Stalag III in Sagan in Poland, where conditions were far better than those at Stalag VIII-B. He remarks upon the fact that he was issued with a knife and fork, as well as spoons, basins, jugs, and bowls.

Dad also took classes in calculus and trigonometry in Stalag III to keep his mind and time occupied. Early in 1944 the guards began to take POWs on escorted walks outside the camp, and for the first time in over two years Dad had a view unobstructed by barbed wire. The general tone of his Stalag III letters is more cheerful and optimistic, partly due to better conditions, partly to the good news about our progress in the war filtering through from new POWs arriving and from illicit radios. Mail from home, however, was taking up to three months to arrive, and was occasionally stopped altogether if German POWs weren't getting their letters through satisfactorily.

In March 1944, the Great Escape took place at Stalag III, followed by the recapture of 73 escapees and the shooting of 50 of them under direct orders from Hitler. None of my father's letters mention this, and no diary survives from Stalag III, but he always said that those who escaped from

31

the camps caused great problems for those left behind, in the way of reprisals.

The Germans began to evacuate the camp in January 1945, and over a period of two days in freezing conditions, 2000 POWs were marched 50 miles to the west, to Spremberg. In February they left their warm quarters there and were moved by train to Nurnberg on a four day journey. There were 48 men and eight guards in each boxcar, which measured eight feet by twenty feet. After a day, eight men were taken out and moved to extra boxcars, but it was a relief after arrival to be able to stretch out.

There was little food, and only wet straw mattresses were supplied for sleeping. The prisoners were later moved again, to Moosburg, northeast of Munich, another forced march for those fit enough. Dad was one of the 'non-marchers', who together with those too sick to walk, travelled by train. He was lucky, as the marching column was caught up in air raids and some were killed or injured. As it was, the engine of the train had holes in it. At Moosburg, the men slept in four barracks and two tents in very crowded conditions.

Under pressure from the Swiss, the Germans agreed not to move any more POWs, and Dad was liberated from Moosburg on 5 May. A week later he telegraphed my mother, 'Here at last see you soon'.

In November 1945, he was discharged from the RAF and took up his peacetime occupation for a few more years, until he was able to take a post as design draughtsman at B.A.C. at Filton where he worked on various aircraft including Concorde.

MAC PIERCE

The Broken Rosary

By Lee Mylne

Lee was born and raised in New Zealand, and now works as a journalist and author based in Brisbane, Australia. She is the author, co-author, or contributor to more than a dozen books and lectures in journalism at the University of Queensland. She specialises in travel writing and has travelled to more than 60 countries, but no trip has meant more to her than her visit to the Site of Remembrance at Łambinowice in 2017.

Like his ten siblings, my father was given three names. These were the names that he would use when he enlisted for the great adventure that was World War II: Cecil Albert Clarence. But to everyone in his large family and the rural village in New Zealand in which he was born, he was simply Mac.

The origins of that nickname were long forgotten, even to him. Perhaps it had to do with his Scottish forebears who had travelled across the world from the Highlands and then from Nova Scotia to settle near the top of New Zealand's North Island in a place called Waipu. Whatever the reason, no-one ever called him Cecil, and for similarly forgotten reasons, his army buddies always called him Max. He'd answer to both versions of the name for the rest of his life.

Mac Pierce was 19 when he became a soldier. In December 1939, lying about his age – you had to be 21 to join up – he was soon in the Papakura Military Camp in the south of New Zealand's largest city, Auckland. It was late January 1940 when his first letter home arrived from camp where he was a private in the NZ21 battalion (5th Brigade), along with his older brother, Thomas Clifford George (always called Cliff).

A small collection of correspondence charted Mac's progress through training, being sent to England in readiness for action in the Middle East and then three-and-a-half years in prisoner of war camps in Italy and German-occupied Poland.

The letters are frustratingly short, determinedly cheerful, written on thin and fragile pieces of paper, in Mac's firm, distinctive copperplate handwriting. They don't say much, leaving us to read between the lines.

In the beginning, of course, it was all fun. The training camp was not hard for a young man from a family of 11 children, and already used to physical work as a farmhand. The first letter is upbeat, looking forward to final leave before shipping out.

'I have been having a hell of a good time…it is just like one big holiday. Cliff and I are in the best Company in camp. We have an over-strength of fifteen and only the best of men. We went out to the range today…I can put a hole in the target now…'

And a social life too, that this handsome young man was not going to let go to waste. He writes that some others question his age, 'but I told them I was 23'.

Then the real adventure starts. An undated missive from HM Transport, sometime in March 1940: 'Just a few lines to let you know we are alright. We called at our first port and had a good time, but we don't know where we are going because the army won't tell us. There is plenty of water around us now. I don't think I have ever seen so much water before. We have seen quite a few shoals of flying fish. I have also seen a swordfish and a whale.'

There's a gap in the correspondence, the next letters dated August 1940, from Aldershot in England. His brother Cliff, he says, had been transferred to 6th brigade three weeks before and he hadn't seen him since. The letters are full of news about the places in the UK he's seen – and wants to see. There seems plenty of leave and it's still a big adventure. 'We are having a pretty easy week. We went out to see Windsor Castle last Friday and gee it's a thing to see. The two Princesses are staying there at present, the King and Queen came down on the weekend. It is wonderful inside. We saw where the king was buried. The castle itself only covers thirteen acres of ground so you can see she is some size. I'm going away for seven days leave shortly and I just don't know where to go as there are so many places I'd like to see.'

But then reality creeps in. Air raid warnings, bombers flying over 'all day long'. 'One night we counted 80 in two hours, and they were still going over.'

By September, Mac was in Leeds and the realities of war were coming thick and fast. 'There has been an air raid on here today and one Hun plane came down and machine gunned the street, but no one was hurt. One of our planes was brought down here this afternoon but the pilot got out safely.

'There is hardly a day goes by but what there are bombs dropped round us and at night the siren goes about five o'clock and you don't get all clear until about half past five next morning. It never keeps us awake now as we are used to it, and we know he never hits what he aims at. You should have been here on Sunday when one of our planes brought down a German bomber. It was only about a hundred yards away from our camp and we went down to have a look at it and all we could find of the pilot was his head and one foot and his plane was just a heap of tin.'

And to his older sister Irene Mabel Rita, known to all as Tottie: 'We are up an hour before daylight and in full battle dress. It is great to watch the dog fights that go on here but the only trouble is you have to look out for a stray bullet. When a plane is crashing is the worst time of the lot. If you can't see it you would swear it was going to come right down on you and you just don't know which way to go. We wear our tin hats pretty often now as it is a lot safer. We get quite a few bombs dropped around us now. There is hardly a day goes by but what there is a raid. Three of us tried to get into the Air Force as air gunners but they won't transfer from one to the other. I am just as pleased now after I have seen some of the crashes.'

And a few days later, another letter:

'Just a few lines to let you know that I am still alive and kicking. We had a bit of excitement here the other day. We were just coming home from a swim when they dropped a bomb about thirty yards in front of our bus. We all grabbed our tin hats and crouched down as near to the floor as we could. We were waiting for shrapnel to come through the roof, but none ever came. Two of our boys had their heads cut open. They dropped about fifteen bombs altogether and killed eighteen people and quite a few hurt but there wasn't much damage.'

For a couple of months, life seemed to settle into a pattern, including a week's leave in Wales, dates with local girls, great hospitality from the villagers, and 'the only trouble is it is too cold'. Christmas 1940 came, with a rum issue and a bottle of beer, parties, and the novelty of seeing snow for the first time. But soon it was time to ship out.

January 10, 1941. At Sea:

'Dear Mum

Just a few lines to let you know that everything is OK. We have left England for where I don't know yet but I suppose you will by the time you get this. This trip isn't as comfortable as the first one but there you are we have got to put up with these things. We are sleeping in hammocks, and it is alright. Cliff and all the rest of the old company are on this boat, so we see quite a lot of one another.'

By mid-year, the letters were coming from Crete in the Greek islands, and then Cairo in Egypt, where the Western Desert campaign was in full swing. The letters were full of reassurances that all was well, the countryside was pretty, the weather lovely and 'I have never eaten as many eggs and oranges in my life'. And that after being in the front line on Crete, where 'there are still a few of the boys missing', seven days leave was 'just the thing we needed' and 'I am feeling my old self again'.

On 28 November 1941, about six weeks after his 21st birthday, Mac was taken prisoner, one of 2042 men of 2 New Zealand Division captured during Operation Crusader at Sidi Rezegh in the Libyan desert.

An undated postcard, printed with a message but signed in Mac's handwriting, delivered this message home to New Zealand:

'My dear Mothe

I am alright. I have not been wounded/~~I have been slightly wounded~~. I am a prisoner of the Italians, and I am being treated well. Shortly I shall be transferred to a prisoner's camp, and I will let you have my new address. Only then I will be able to receive letters from you and to reply.

With love

Mac (signature: C. Pierce)'

After being held in Greece for about six months, the prisoners were taken to Italian transit camps. Another postcard followed dated 20 March,1942:

'Dear Mum, I am now in Italy. We have been shipwrecked. We were in Greece. I am in perfect health. I hope all are well. Remember me to all. With love from Mac.'

The shipwreck was the Italian cargo ship MV *Jason* which was torpedoed by British submarines off the coast of Greece on 9 December 1941, while carrying 2000 prisoners to Italy. Mac was lucky to get out alive. Travelling in the hold, he was one of about 1600 survivors who reached shore safely. He spoke about this to his children for the first time in 1983, when Spence Edge, another survivor from our hometown, co-wrote a memoir called *No Honour, No Glory*. Dad then revealed that he too had been aboard the *Jason* and this was the cause of the 'old war wound' he had joked about for years, the dodgy knees that caused him chronic pain and ultimately needed replacement.

There were more letters from the transit camps in Italy, dated throughout April and May 1942, with assurances that he was 'in the best of health' and 'perfect health' and receiving Red Cross parcels. It's hard to know if those letters arrived before or after the official telegram from the New Zealand Government to his mother, dated 15 July 1942:

MUCH REGRET TO INFORM YOU THAT YOUR SON 21611 PRIVATE CECIL ALBERT CLARENCE PIERCE HAS BEEN REPORTED MISSING BELIEVED PRISONER OF WAR STOP THE

PRIME MINISTER DESIRES ME TO CONVEY TO YOU ON BEHALF OF THE GOVERNMENT HIS SYMPATHY WITH YOU IN YOUR ANXIETY + F JONES MINISTER OF DEFENCE +

For his widowed mother, knowing that two of her eight sons – Cliff was also a prisoner by now - were now incarcerated in a foreign country, would have been almost too much to bear. Another two had also joined up. The postcards and messages kept coming from Italy, as Mac and his comrades were moved from camp to camp: Campo PG 65, then 85, then 57 and finally 148 near Verona. The messages were formulaic, brief, and always reassuring. And each one proof that her son was still alive.

'Dear Mum,

Here I am again still in good health and hope you are the same. It won't be long now before we are altogether again. So, keep your chin up. Cheerio for now. Fondest love, Mac.'

There were other letters too over this time. Kind-hearted New Zealanders monitored radio broadcasts from the Vatican in which POWs were able to send messages home, and then wrote to the families, in case they had missed this further 'proof of life'. All were in a similar vein:

'Dear Mrs Pierce

In case you didn't hear or receive word of a broadcast tonight from Vatican City, I feel I must write and let you know that among others the name of Pt C.A. Pierce (21611) came over as a POW. There was also a message, which I got as near as possible. If you have not yet received letters I do hope it won't be long now. With kindest regards...

Message: 'I am in good health. There is no need to worry. I hope everybody is well. Fondest love to all from Mac'

Sincerely yours ...

By November 1943, Mac was in the notorious Stalag VIII-B/344 at Lamsdorf in German-occupied Poland, where he was one of more than 100000 New Zealanders and Australians who made up about a third of the prisoners held in this hell-hole. They arrived at the nearby village of Annahof (today called Sowin) in trains so cramped that prisoner spent days and nights standing, with little food or water and no toilet facilities. The new arrivals covered the last part of the route to the camp on foot. On the roadside outside Lamsdorf (now Łambinowice), row after row of identical stone crosses stand in the Old POW Cemetery where 50000 victims of deprivation, disease and murder were buried in a 1.8ha site. I can only imagine the impact that those lines of grey stone crosses – most of them from World War I – would have had on the prisoners as they rounded the corner and filed silently past, wondering if they too would end up there.

Postcards came intermittently now, for the first time bearing a prisoner number or *gefangenennummer*: 28787.

'Dear Mum, how is everything doing out there. The winter has started here with our first fall of snow. I must wish you all a Merry Christmas & a Happy New Year, & I hope to be back for the next. Love to all. From your loving son, Mac.'

That message, written on 20 November 1944, was the last from Mac as a prisoner. Little did he know that the worst was still to come. As the Allied Forces advanced and the war drew to a close, the Germans began to march their prisoners westward, away from the approaching Russian Army. In late January 1945, Mac and his fellow prisoners began the Long March that he later revealed extended for 900 miles and took nearly three months, from Stalag VIII-B in Lamsdorf to somewhere near Frankfurt in Germany.

Research tells me that January and February 1945 were among the coldest months of the 20th century in Europe, with blizzards raging and temperatures as low as -25 degrees Celsius. It is impossible to imagine the privations these men went through, poorly dressed and starving, scavenging for food at any opportunity. I do not know the exact route my father took, only that liberation by the Americans came on 8 April 1945. By then, Mac weighed just six stone (38kg). At some time, either in the camp or on the Long March, he contracted tuberculosis, something only detected later in life.

Within a week of liberation, my grandmother had received two telegrams:

URGENT TELEGRAM
VERY PLEASED TO INFORM YOU IT IS NOW REPORTED THAT YOUR SON 21611 PTE CECIL ALBERT CLARENCE PIERCE PREVIOUSLY PRISONER OF WAR IN GERMANY IS NOW SAFE IN THE UNITED KINGDOM STOP THE PRIME MINISTER DESIRES ME TO CONVEY TO YOU THE GOVERNMENTS SINCERE PLEASURE AT THIS GOOD NEWS

AND HOPES THAT IT WILL NOT BE LONG BEFORE REPATRIATION.

And no doubt the best confirmation of all, a telegram from Mac, on 16 April 1945:

FLEW FROM PRISON ENJOYABLE TRIP HAVE WRITTEN AIRMAIL HOPING TO HEAR FROM YOU LOVE TO ALL AT HOME ++ MAC

It was over. After six months in England, some of it in the repatriation centre set up by the New Zealand defence force in Kent, he sailed home to New Zealand, arriving just three days before Christmas 1945, as promised in that last brief missive from Lamsdorf.

Later in life, like many returned servicemen, my father only talked about his wartime experiences in fragments – usually after a few beers with his old army mates on Anzac Day (April 25). Anzac Day is a public holiday in Australia and New Zealand, a National Day of Remembrance that commemorates all Australians and New Zealanders who served and died in all wars, conflicts, and peacekeeping operations. My father marched in Anzac Day parades every year, with his family looking on. Later, the men would head to the Returned Services Association clubhouse to drink and reminisce.

I read my father's wartime letters now and try to marry them in my mind with the realities of what's not said. How would he have been different, without those horrific experiences... the bodies, the shipwreck, the privations of the camps, the long 'death march'? They were things seldom spoken of and never understood by others when he got home to the world he knew best.

My father never really told his story, leaving us with fragments of it to piece together as best we can. When we were kids, he'd tell us it was 'just like *Hogan's Heroes*', the television comedy that lampooned life in a German prison camp.

Mac was not a religious man. But in 1997, at my daughter's christening, he produced an unusual set of rosary beads. As his family came from Scottish Presbyterian stock, not Catholic, I asked him where they had come from. His voice shaking a little, he told me that while on 'the march' people came out onto the streets to watch the prisoners file past. As they passed through a village – he did not know where - a woman stepped from the crowd and put the rosary in his hand. Even in war, the sight of those skin-and-bone young soldiers trudging past on their way to who-knows-where, had touched her heart and her humanity. Perhaps something in his face told her my father needed that sign. He had kept this memento and his memory of that moment all those years but had never before mentioned it.

The rosary is broken; the crucifix is missing. But to me, it's still a miracle that it survived at all. And in late 2017, fifteen years after my father's death at the age of 82, I stood on the cobblestones of Chestnut Alley, the road on which he and his fellow prisoners set out from Stalag VIII-B/344 on what has become known as the 'Long March', holding the rosary in my hand. It was winter in Poland when I made my pilgrimage to the Site of Remembrance at Łambinowice. I was rugged up in thermals, a heavy winter coat, hat, scarf and gloves, thick woollen socks, and strong winter boots, but an icy wind nipped my face and I was still cold. I could not imagine what my father and his comrades went through as they undertook that epic march to eventual freedom, ill-equipped and already in poor health.

My fingers curled around the small wooden rosary beads in the pocket of my coat, I silently thanked that woman, whoever she was, for singling out my father's hand to press it into.

Mac's wartime experiences may be considered unremarkable; he does not stand out from any of the other hundreds of thousands of men who endured similar fates. He was a 19-year-old who went to war and returned a different man. I do not know what work he may have done as a prisoner or any of the details of his internment, except that at some time there were periods of solitary confinement. Survival was a matter of resilience, or perhaps luck.

My father's war story, as I know it, is a skeleton story, a mere outline of the real one. The real story is one I'll now never know, to my enormous regret.

DENNIS CHAMBERS

Rifle Brigade

By Sarah Sampson-Chambers

My father, Dennis Chambers, enlisted in the army on 11 May 1939. He was 19 years old at the time and needed his parents' permission which they refused to give. He really wanted to join up so he got a family friend to sign the papers for him.

On 22 May 1940 Dennis was sent to Calais with the 1st battalion Rifle Brigade to hold off the German Army. This later became to be known as *The Defence of Calais*.

At one time he was with two of his battalion crawling along the ground with their rifles, and the persons in front and behind him were shot and killed. Dad was wounded in the shoulder; it was a clean shot and the bullet came out the other side.

I remember Dad telling us that on another occasion he was up a tree protecting troops who were marching along the road. There was a large explosion and most of the troops were blown up. Dad ended up with 13 pieces of shrapnel in his leg. There was a lot of activity and the German troops were running along the road checking the trees and shooting anyone they found. He said he kept very still and was lucky they never saw him. The battle carried on and while t injured he made it back to the Citadel while trying to help hold back the German troops.

I understand from my dad that a French regiment was ordered to help them hold back the Germans. As the French marched towards the Citadel they said they were going to surrender. The British troops were so angry they told them they would shoot them before they would let them surrender. When Dad was captured he was taken to the hospital for attention to shrapnel and his shoulder wound. The medics poured iodine into the wound ... and Dad said he nearly hit the roof.

He was registered as missing, presumed dead, on 29 May 1940. He was registered as a POW on 7 June 1940. My nan never found out until 19 October of that year that Dad was actually alive, and a POW.

He was transferred to a field hospital and then to Stalag XX1-D Posen. He stayed in this camp doing engineering work with Norwegian soldiers until 7 June 1941, then was moved to Stalag XX1C for nine days, before being transferred to Lamsdorf on 16 June 1941.

When our dad arrived at Lamsdorf he was put into work party, E3, at Blechhammer, which was a chemical plant used to make synthetic oil. One day Dad and a friend escaped and managed to make it into Poland. It was winter, very cold, and heavy snow was falling. At one point they were running across the snow and my father realised his mate wasn't next to him. When he turned back he found that his mate had fallen down a big snowdrift. They couldn't stop laughing.

Eventually they came across a hut which turned out to be a small farmhouse. They knocked and a lady welcomed them in. She was with her son and asked Dad and his friend whether they would like something to eat. Of course they said yes and sat down to enjoy a decent meal. After a while they both realised that the boy was missing. When they asked where he had gone the woman said he had gone to play. My father said he felt uncomfortable and thought something was wrong. Not long after this they heard a truck pull up when they looked out the boy was with two SS guards.

Dad and his friend were arrested and as they were being walked to the truck, the guards relaxed and had their guns by their sides. Dad and his friend seized the opportunity, hit the guards, and killed them both.

They knew if they got caught they would be shot so they started running and kept running, down a hill and back into Lamsdorf camp.

The soldiers sat with my dad and his mate laughing about the incident as they were not fond of the SS either. The commandant of the camp took them to the office and not long after the SS turned up to take them away. The commandant of the camp was married to an Englishwoman and treated my dad and his friend quite well. He refused to let the SS take them as they did not have the correct paperwork and the guards had to leave.

As far as I can work out my father had to peel spuds for days on end after his work duties. He said he would not refuse as he saw men getting shot for doing so. Him and his pal were both very lucky and I believe if he was in any other camp he would have been shot.

Dad said that the guards they had were okay, had families and didn't want to be at war either. There was one guard who Dad became friends with who's name was Augustus. Dad always spoke fondly of him and said how he swapped the chocolate from his red Cross parcel with homemade cake made by his wife. Augustus also taught my dad German and my dad became fluent. In turn, Dad taught him English.

One evening one of the POWs stole some bread and for this they were all punished and made to stand outside in the snow all night. I was upset when Dad told me this but he said, 'Don't worry, your dad's made of strong stuff. The snow was melting all around me.'

The work party would throw food to the Jewish prisoners on a regular basis. At one point they cut a hole in the wire to get food to them, knowing they could have been shot themselves.

Once my dad was offered some bread, containing meat. He couldn't believe it when he was told by the Polish POWs that they had killed the German guard dog. He said this made him feel sick, and no matter how hungry he was he couldn't bring himself to eat it.

To keep his morale up Dad became a member of the theatre group. He helped make props for the shows and wrote the Christmas plays. One of the plays he helped to produce was called *Night Must Fall,* which was so successful that it was taken to Berlin for a performance.

Dad, like many others, left on the Long March but he never spoke about it and I only found out from newspaper clippings that he was definitely on it. It appears that at some point he escaped. I remember him telling me that him and his mate came across two children, a girl and boy, living on a bomb site. They were on their own so they presumed their family had been killed. They gave the children all their food and got them to hide it away from everyone and when they knew they were safe they left them.

Eventually my dad and his friend were picked up by the Czech resistance and hid below a café. I have a book with the Czech resistance names in.

Dad and his friend were eventually taken to an American airbase. Dad said they tried to feed him and his mate but years of not eating made it difficult to eat.

Dad finally made it home on 23 May 1945, flying back on a Lancaster bomber.

He was discharged from the army on 16 September 1946.

Dad trained as a precision engineer and ran the local T.A barracks. He played the guitar in a band, which he learned as a prisoner of war. He became a captain in the T.A. He retired from army life completely on 11 May 1951.

Dad met our mum, Joyce Tanner, the day after he got back to the UK. They were married for 59 years, until he passed away at the age of 88. He worked as an engineer all his life and was an amazing Dad and Grandad.

IAN ANDERSON

22nd Battalion, 2NZEF

By Michael Brown

Michael Brown is married to Ian Anderson's great-granddaughter, Kathryn. Michael has served as a New Zealand and British Army officer, including operational deployments to Bougainville, East Timor, Bosnia, Iraq, Afghanistan, and Somalia. Having a lifelong interest in history, he has edited and published Ian Anderson's war diaries.

Ian Anderson was a World War II infantryman in the New Zealand Army's 22nd (Wellington) Battalion, serving from 1940 to 1946. He was captured on Crete and spent three years in Stalag VIII-B.

Back in March 1918, just before his 20th birthday, Ian had gained his parents' permission and volunteered for service in WWI but did not serve overseas due to an enlarged thyroid gland.

Clearly determined to do his bit, he again enlists for overseas service on 6 January 1940 after seeing the First Echelon of the Second New Zealand Expeditionary Force (2NZEF) depart for Egypt. This time he is successful.

Enlisting shortly before his 42nd birthday, Ian creates a fictitious birthdate to be eligible for overseas service. In 1940 other ranks and non-commissioned officers eligible for overseas service have a maximum age of 35 years except returned soldiers or members of the Regular Reserve, neither of which apply to Ian. Reporting to the Buckle Street establishment in central Wellington on 25 January 1940, he is marched to the Wellington Railway Station with his fellow recruits, then 40 minutes north by train to Trentham Camp.

Ian is posted to the 22nd (Wellington) Battalion, a unit which will fight with distinction throughout the World War II. Until departure from New Zealand a few months later, he is at Trentham training as an infantry soldier. Ian is assigned to the Mortar Platoon (No 3 Platoon), which is part of the Headquarter Company. It is equipped with the British 3-inch mortar, an infantry close support weapon firing a 3-inch calibre bomb out to 1600 yards.

The time at Trentham is spent making recruits into soldiers, with foot drill, training on the various infantry weapons, and medical examinations. Ian has a reasonable amount of time off, being allowed home most weekends to be with his family and visiting the New Zealand Centennial Expedition near the Wellington Airport at Rongotai.

Ian bids goodbye to his wife Laura and his daughter Merlyn on 28 April, and on the train back to Trentham he 'sheds full tears'. 22nd Battalion, as part of the 5th Infantry Brigade, departs New Zealand on 3 May 1940 on the ship *Empress of Britain,* in convoy with several other ships. The sea voyage includes stops at Fremantle, Cape Town and Freetown, with shore visits at each. Ian and the other soldiers are hosted generously and welcomed by local people in each of these places. During the voyage the destination is changed from Egypt to the United Kingdom to bolster defences in the event of a German invasion, which is a real possibility at the time.

Arriving at Gourock, Scotland on 18 June 1940, the Battle of Britain is ongoing. The troops travel by train down to Mytchett in Surrey. Training activities ensue, including route marches to get the men fit after six weeks at sea. The famous Bisley, Pirbright and Ash ranges are nearby, so there is plenty of shooting practice.

Ian is on sentry duty reasonably often and witnesses a number of German air raids. Local people welcome the soldiers and entertain them in their homes. Leave is reasonably frequent, and Ian makes several visits, some to London and two to Lytham St Annes, a seaside town in Lancashire.

22nd Battalion next moves to Kent, near the Channel coast, to take up a defensive task in the event of German invasion. The battalion is based in the village of Hollingbourne, near Maidstone, and the troops are billeted in the village. They make good use of the local pubs including The Hook and Hatchet, which is almost disused but given new life by the soldiers. Again, people make them welcome, and friendships are formed.

The battalion's first casualty in action is Private Holms, killed by bombs jettisoned by a damaged German aircraft. Ian sees a lot of air battles over Kent during the key days of the Battle of Britain, and regular air raids at night.

On 4 November the battalion moves back to Camberley in Surrey, not far from the previous location at Mytchett. Christmas and New Year are spent by Ian in Camberley, being hosted by Mr and Mrs Houghton, local residents who Ian had got to know some months earlier. Ian has an early night on New Year's Eve because he departs early the next morning with the baggage party en route for Newport in Wales.

22nd Battalion and the 5th (NZ) Infantry Brigade embark on a ship bound for the Middle East to join the New Zealand troops there. After picking up the remainder of the 17 ships in the convoy near Belfast, the convoy proceeds all the way around Africa via Freetown, Cape Town and then up the East African cost to the Red Sea, arriving at Port Tewfik on 4 March 1941. The convoy takes this route for safety reasons; the air and U-boat threat mean the Mediterranean Sea is hazardous for shipping and use of the Suez Canal is restricted for most of the war. The troops disembark via barges, then proceed by rail to Helwan Camp via Cairo.

After two weeks at Helwan Camp training and occasional leave days in Cairo, the battalion moves to El Amiriya Camp on 17 March 1941. The transit camp comprises a number of Nissen huts with a lot of dust and flies, and the facilities are not well-regarded - all the more so after some Australian soldiers burn down the camp cinema in protest at the non-arrival of some promised films.

On 26 March 1941, the battalion departs El Amiriya Camp for the Port of Alexandria, where they board the *Hellas* bound for Greece.

The Battle for Greece is short; the Germans take the country in around three weeks. When Germany and Italy declare war on Greece on 6 April 1941, the New Zealanders are already in the town of Katerini, having arrived at the port of Piraeus (Athens) on 29 March 1941. The 5th Infantry Brigade takes up defensive positions at the Mount Olympus pass on 9 April. The 22nd Battalion positions are situated in rugged scrub-covered terrain bisected by a ravine on a two-and-a-half mile frontage between the 28th (Maori) Battalion on the left and 23rd Battalion on the right. The Mortar Platoon, of which Ian was a member, under its commander Lt E. J. McAra, is set up on a rocky outcrop named Gibraltar.

Here, Ian Anderson sees his first action. On 14 April (Easter Monday) the Germans carry out aerial and probing attacks. The next day it is announced that the Allies are withdrawing south, owing to the threat of being outflanked by Germans to the north-east. Under probing artillery fire, preparations for the withdrawal are made.

The Germans attack on 16 April with artillery fire and tanks. Ian's Mortar Platoon fires hundreds of rounds at the Germans on the approach road, the attack is broken up by the concentrated mortar and artillery fire. 22nd Battalion withdraws at night in inclement weather, over rugged terrain, in good order along with the rest of the Brigade. The route southwards is perilous, with bad weather, intermittent communications, conflicting orders, attack from the air and poor roads.

Different units become mixed up and parts of 22nd Battalion are lost for up to two days, including Ian. The next defensive position is at the narrow isthmus near Thermopylae, chosen for its defence-favouring terrain – as the 300 Spartan warriors had done 2300 years before against the Persians, where the battalion comes together again and digs in with the rest of the brigade.

The Germans are sighted but no attack eventuates. On 22 April Greece capitulates and orders are given for all Allied troops to be evacuated from Greece. After acting as a rear-guard, 22nd Battalion moves to the coast near Ay Konstandinos, then to an olive grove near Athens, awaiting evacuation to the island of Crete. Some other troops would go directly to Egypt. Stores and any equipment that cannot be carried are destroyed, rendered useless or buried. While 22nd Battalion has gone to considerable lengths during the withdrawal to keep hold of its weapons and equipment, confusion, and conflicting orders from beach liaison officers near the evacuation point cause key items to be lost.

Once on board the ships of the Royal Navy, the troops are given sandwiches, cocoa and rum, a welcome relief from the events of the past three weeks.

The 22nd Battalion, along with other New Zealand, British, Australian, and Greek troops, arrives on the island of Crete, ill-equipped to fight a hard battle against elite German troops.

Many are wounded or sick, and much equipment was lost during embarkation in Greece. 22nd Battalion lost most of its communications equipment and all but two of the three mortars in Ian's mortar platoon.

An additional rifle company is formed from HQ Company, consisting of three officers and around 60 administrative staff, drivers and storemen, and a number of surplus mortar platoon personnel. Lt E. J. McAra, Ian's mortar platoon commander, moves across to A Company as a rifle platoon commander and is killed on the day of the German landing on 20 May. Ian is one of those remaining with the remnants of the mortar platoon, which erects the two remaining mortars and 300 rounds of ammunition on the northern side of Hill 107, covering Maleme airfield. The role of these two mortars in 5th Brigade orders is to support an immediate counterattack from 21st and 23rd Battalions should the Germans land on the airfield.

On Tuesday, 20 May 1941 at around 10 a.m., Ian and his comrades emerge from their dugouts and trenches to make breakfast after the usual 'daily hate' aerial bombing. The air around the mortar position is thick with dust.

But today is different. Within minutes low-flying Junkers 52 transport aircraft appear and disgorge their cargos of paratroopers. The German attackers are the *Fallschirmjäger* - 'Hunters from the sky'; superbly equipped, highly trained and well-motivated airborne troops. The New Zealanders abandon their breakfast and grab their weapons, opening fire with everything in range at the descending *Fallschirmjäger*. Aided by numbers of Cretan civilians, the defenders set about the Germans on landing before they can even free themselves of their parachutes, using rifles, bayonets, agricultural implements, and fists. The 22nd Battalion war dairy relates how dead German parachutists lay in their hundreds, some still in their parachutes.

Ian stays at his post with the mortar throughout the 20th. At 11 p.m. that night a mortar baseplate moves during firing and the recoil crushes Ian's foot. Mortar platoon members Corporal Hack and Private Mitchell bid Ian good luck as he makes his way to the 22nd battalion's Regimental Aid Post (RAP), under Captain Longmore, in a location close to the airfield, several hundred yards north of the mortar position. But the RAP has moved to 23rd Battalion's lines after the 22nd's Commanding officer, Lt Colonel Andrew, ordered the 22nd Battalion to withdraw from the airfield a few hours earlier; an event that turns the course of the battle in the Germans' favour by enabling them to use the aerodrome to reinforce their hard-pressed parachutists.

The morning of 21 May found Ian and the other casualties camped in a clearing. The wounded made a white circle from RAP equipment to show it was a medical installation. German aircraft did not bomb or strafe the RAP during the 21st. By this stage the situation is very confused and attempts are made to get messages through. At 5 p.m. they are taken prisoner.

Ian is given medical attention and moved to a temporary hospital. He is treated well and stays there for a few days before being flown to Greece with other prisoners on 26 May 1941 on one of the Junkers 52 aircraft that had dropped the paratroopers. They see Athens from the air.

On arrival in Greece, Ian is sent to a POW hospital in Athens, known as Kriegsgefangen Lazaret Piräus – Kokina (Prisoner of War Hospital Piraeus – Kokina). He is treated for his foot injury, including an X-Ray, and moves to a convalescent hospital on 9 June. His German medical card states 'R Foot Crushed' in English and German.

Captain Longmore, the 22nd Battalion medical officer, is there too and gives Ian 100 drachmas.

In late June, his foot having healed sufficiently, Ian joins other prisoners in the main Athens POW camp, known as Dulag 183 (*Durchgangslager* – Transit Camp). He is given work in the cookhouse, and he recounts rumours of other prisoners travelling by ship being picked up by the Royal Navy. On 20 August he is in a group of prisoners marched through the streets of Athens to board a ship on the first stage of the long trip to Germany. The streets are crowded.

The Greeks show their appreciation and give the prisoners food on the way, which the German and Italian troops do not seem to obstruct.

After an uncomfortable voyage on a coal tramp steamer they arrive in Thessaloniki on 24 August and board a train for Germany a few days later. The prisoners spend nine days on a very uncomfortable journey travelling in goods wagons with 34 men in each. The men at Ian's end of the wagon are 'good chaps'. Ian manages to get a place near one of the 10 x 18' windows, which has its benefits and downsides. Toilet provision is rudimentary, with Ian emptying the tins out the window through the iron bars. Some of the men 'have the runs'.

Food consists mainly of a small bread ration, a limited quantity of meat and occasional coffee. The men receive a cup of tea from the Red Cross on the platform at Niš and Belgrade. Drinking water is obtained using paper spools through the small window openings. The train passes through many places including Salonika, Dresden, and Gorlitz, eventually arriving at Lamsdorf.

As they travel up through Bulgaria and into Austria the weather gets colder. Like most other troops captured on Crete, Ian is wearing summer weight clothing and has no blanket or overcoat. He will never forget this long and tedious journey as long as he lives. To pass the time he records details of the buildings and agriculture.

Tired, cold, and miserable after nine days in unheated goods wagons, Ian and the other prisoners arrive at Stalag VIII-B on 2 September 1941, He will spend the next three years here.

Like the other prisoners, Ian is registered, photographed, fingerprinted, and given a POW number, in his case 23468. Their possessions are checked by the Germans. After the search Ian is allowed to keep his diary notebooks, they are stamped 'Stalag VIII-B *Geprüft*: 9/'.

The Geneva Convention of 1929 allows non-commissioned officers and other ranks to be required to work (supervisory duties only in the case of NCOs), though they must be paid. At Lamsdorf there are around 700 work parties, or *arbeitskommando,* spread around the district working in factories, tanneries, mines, civil engineering tasks and, in Ian's case, a sawmill.

Ian is assigned to Arbeitskommando E255 in a sawmill in Hartenau on 17 September 1941. Hartenau is around 50 kilometres south-east of Lamsdorf, known as Twardawa since 1945. There is accommodation at the sawmill. The work involves unloading railway wagons of wood, and processing timber.

On arrival at Stalag VIII-B, the prisoners are issued their first Red Cross parcel, shared between four men. Ian shares his with William O'Donnell, Hamilton Milligan, and William Heath Wingham. It seems likely they have met in Athens or on the train and decided to stick together as a foursome. Their POW numbers are very close to Ian's so they would have been close together in the registration queue. They all end up in E255 and inhabit the same hut in Hartenau.

Ian and his fellow prisoners from Crete arrive in Germany in autumn, still dressed in the warm weather Mediterranean climate clothing in which they had been captured. Soon after arrival in the camp there is an issue of Red Cross-provided British Army battledress, greatcoat and boots.

Accommodation is uninsulated wooden barrack huts with built-in bunks heated by a cast iron stove in each room. Fuel supplies are limited, and definitely at a premium in the bitter central European winter. Bedding includes palliasses (a large sack filled with straw) Red Cross blankets and the prisoner's greatcoat. For Christmas 1941 in Hartenau there are even cakes, buns and two glasses of good beer.

The arrival of 1942 sees a continuation of the established POW routine. Work at the Hartenau sawmill continues, hard physical labour in all weather. Winter means no escape from the cold, whether working outside or in the uninsulated barrack huts. Life as a prisoner of war is dull, repetitive, and uncomfortable. Ian refers to the guards as *postens,* which is a German word for post, employment, occupation, or guard. In this and other instances the POWs use German words as a form of slang. He thinks the Hartenau guards are 'good chaps'. These are probably older men, perhaps World War I veterans, who have some empathy for the prisoners.

Ian's records show he receives a fairly steady stream of mail, although it can take several months to arrive. He writes many letters to his wife, Laura, and his daughter, Merlyn, as well as the Houghton from Camberley, Annie Goudie from Glasgow and Cedric Eyre from Lytham St Annes, who send him much-needed tobacco parcels. Letters, although censored, contain war news which is important to the prisoners, some of which is contributed to *The Clarion* camp magazine. Rumours are rife and Ian makes notes from BBC and other radio news broadcasts.. Radios (known as a 'wireless' in 1940's) are strictly banned by the Germans, but most camps have illicit sets made by enterprising prisoners using stolen or bartered parts. Ian takes part in disseminating news from radios around the camp (Ian says in July 1944 there are around 16 illicit radios in Lamsdorf, and one of these ends up at Annaburg).

The Germans subject the POWs to a variety of propaganda to make them more malleable and dispirited, though most of the propaganda sheets end up as toilet paper. The Germans publish *The Camp* weekly propaganda newspaper, which includes a series of articles entitled *The German Point of View*. Until late 1942 these articles are triumphant in tone, but as the war turns against Germany from early 1943 the emphasis shifts to how the Germans and British should work together.

Ian and his hut-mates grow a vegetable garden at Hartenau, producing an impressive array of potatoes, lettuce, radishes, turnips, beetroot, spinach, peas, runner beans, cabbage, kale, leeks, marrows, and carrots. Despite the regular Red Cross parcels, at this time Ian notices the first signs of health problems. In 1942 he has back pain and receives treatment with some improvement. He also starts to become breathless on exertion and his ankles become swollen when walking any distance. But for now, he continues with work at the Hartenau sawmill.

On 20 January 1943, Ian leaves Hartenau to go to the hospital in the main camp, with the annotation '*Krank im lager*' (sick in camp). He has a severe attack of jaundice in 1943, where the skin and whites of the eyes turn yellow, normally indicating an underlying condition. His shortness of breath on exertion and swollen ankles continues.

By March 1943 Ian is deemed fit enough for work, and on 24 March he is transferred to Arbeitskommando E351 at the *Heinrischsthaler*

Papierfabrik, a paper mill 90 kilometres south-west of Lamsdorf. E351 numbers 104 British and Commonwealth prisoners. Ian seems to get on very well with the *Heinrichsthal Boys*, who present him with a photograph album, probably made from paper 'liberated' from the mill.

Ian's papers contain a clipping from *The Camp* propaganda newspaper, dated 30 May 1943, of a poem entitled *Death of a Comrade*, which has the handwritten annotation '*Heinrichsthal*'. The name of the prisoner is not mentioned. Prisoners grow sick and die of a range of ailments, brought on by hard physical work, a harsh climate, basic facilities, and a barely adequate diet.

On 1 September 1943 Ian is moved back to Stalag VIII-B/344. This is due to either the jaundice mentioned earlier, or his reduced ability to work due to lower leg swelling and breathlessness. On 6 December 1943 he is formally transferred from the Heinrichsthal Arbeitskommando E351 to Stalag 344, and he says, 'I'll do no more work in this country'.

By the beginning of 1944, Ian has been a POW for two and a half years. The hard physical work in the sawmill and paper mill, the barely adequate diet and austere living arrangements have taken their toll on his health. Having been brought back into the main camp in September 1943 for medical reasons, by March 1944 Ian is attending a series of medical appointments and spends time in the camp lazaret. He is given additional rations such as powdered eggs and pineapple crusts. A blood pressure reading showing he has high blood pressure, classified these days as Stage 2 hypertension. He is 'in Review' as the first step to going before a Mixed Medical Commission, which visits the POW camps assessing prisoners for repatriation.

The *Gemischten Ärztekommission* (Mixed Medical Commission) is appointed by the International Committee of the Red Cross under the terms of Article 69 of the Geneva Convention 1929. Its role is to visit POW camps twice per annum to assess prisoners for repatriation on medical grounds as part of reciprocal repatriations of prisoners arranged by Germany and Britain. The decision is based on whether or not the prisoner is fit for further military service. It usually comprises two neutral doctors, often Swiss, and one doctor from the Detaining Power, in this case Germany, all of whom are high-grade medical professionals. The process of confirmation of prisoners for repatriation is lengthy and, until later in 1944, requires diagnoses by British and Commonwealth medical staff to be verified by German doctors before they are considered by the Mixed Medical Commission.

Ian's condition is deemed to meet the repatriation criteria at his appearance before the Mixed Medical Commission on 25 April 1944, then he begins a long wait until the arrangements can be made. He notes the departure of a group of POWs bound for an earlier repatriation in May 1944 and awaits his own departure date. Each repatriation is the result of protracted negotiations about timing, how many prisoners would be exchanged, locations and logistic arrangements.

Ian notes the population increase in Lamsdorf, mainly due to the transfer of POWs from Italian camps after Italy's armistice with the Allies. This has two effects; firstly, the Germans start to move groups of POWs to other camps, including a non-working NCO camp with better facilities at Thorn; and. secondly, the Germans encourage the POWs to hold sporting and theatrical events to keep their minds off the overcrowding and poor facilities as much as possible. For the Germans, reasonably contented and busy prisoners are much easier to control than discontented ones. Not everyone was contented, but they were busy. On 18 May a group of prisoners had escaped through a tunnel at Block 3, with Ian noting; 'good job'.

Examples of these follow, a Whit Monday Carnival is held on Monday 29 May 1944. It includes the Camp's bands, and a range of displays entered into a competition. There is coffee for sale and a highly authentic-looking cow dispensing milk. A range of displays include farming methods and various side shows. Ian is hugely impressed by the effort and ingenuity put into the displays. He notes the Carnival raises 60000 cigarettes and 4,370RM (Reichsmarks in *Lagergeld* camp currency) for the Welfare Fund. That night Ian attended an excellent show, *Ghost Train,* produced by civilian internees from a different camp. Ian sees a POW production of *Journey's End* on 15 July 1944, the R.C Sherriff play about World War I. A tremendous amount of effort is put into these productions by the prisoners.

On 26 April 1944 Ian attends the funeral of fellow New Zealander, Lance Corporal Renata Matengaro Wanoa, 28th (Maori) Battalion, who died in the Stalag hospital four days earlier.

In August, Ian and the prisoners selected for repatriation are moved by train to Stalag IV-D/Z at Annaburg in preparation for repatriation. The camp at Annaburg is a *Heilag* (short for *Heimkehrerlager*), a camp for POWs awaiting repatriation. Opened in early 1944, it has much better facilities than other camps, including good showers with hot water, washing done by 'electrical machines' according to Ian, and a well-stocked canteen. Single beds are provided, many with spring mattresses. The time waiting is spent on card games, books in the well-stocked reading room, and games of cricket played between the different nationalities.

In early September 1944 Ian and the other members of the repatriation contingent travel to the ports of Settin and Sassnitz on the Baltic on hospital trains. There they set sail on the German ferry *Deutschland* and make the eight-hour journey to Trelleborg in Sweden, and onward to Gothenburg. After a few days in the care of the British Consul and Swedish Red Cross, the repatriating German POWs arrive from North Africa and Britain, and prisoner exchange is made on 9 September. The next day, the British and Commonwealth former POWs embark on the *Arundel Castle* for the journey to Britain.

With 2000 other former POWs, Ian arrives at the port of Liverpool on 15 September 1944. On disembarkation the 116 New Zealanders in the group are taken under the care of the New Zealand Reception Group, and they travel to Hartwell House, Buckinghamshire which is the temporary headquarters of the New Zealand Reception Group, until 3 October 1944.

After processing and initial medical assessment, the returning POWs are given 28 days leave and a rail warrant to anywhere in the UK. Throughout this period, Ian is accommodated with the other repatriated POWs in the Freyberg Wing, Old Park Barracks, Dover, which is the new headquarters of the New Zealand Reception Group. He makes some purchases for home during this period, including a tea cosy from a bombed out shop in Dover.

The NZ POWs are sent to Egypt on the hospital ship MS *Oranje,* pending onward travel to New Zealand. Having travelled from Dover to Glasgow by train, Ian departs Gourock on the Clyde on 16 November 1944 (where the 22nd Battalion had arrived over four years earlier), with a brief stop in Gibraltar on 19 November 1944. The *Oranje* arrives in Port Said on 23 November 1944. At the New Zealand hospital in Maadi Camp Ian is examined and a Preliminary Medical Report completed for a Medical Board to be conducted on return to New Zealand. After some six weeks in Egypt, where Ian makes his last entries, the ex-POWs embark on the TSS *Nea Hellas* (voyage KMF37) for Bombay, carrying British troops to India. The Suez Canal, closed for most of the war, has been opened a few months earlier. Ian boards the ship at Port Suez at the southern end of the Suez Canal, having travelled by road early that morning from Maadi Camp 100 miles to the west. The TSS *Nea Hellas* departs Port Suez on 30 December 1944, arriving at Aden on 3 January 1945. After 48 hours in port, the *Nea Hellas* departs Aden on 5 January 1945, arriving in Bombay on 11 January 1945.

On arrival in Bombay, Ian travels by lorry from the dockside to Worli Transit Camp with the other ex-POWs and British service personnel disembarking from the ship. During his approximately two weeks in Bombay, Ian spends some time visiting the sights, including the horse racing at Mahalakshmi, Chowpatty Beach, the Beach Kandy swimming pool, and the shops of 'Tin Town'. He would have been briefed that shopping in Bombay is expensive. Well-known entertainers George and Beryl Formby are in Bombay at this time.

Ian departs Bombay on 26-27 January 1945. This voyage takes around 23 days. After nearly five years away, Ian arrives in Auckland on 18 February 1945, and his Medical Board is held the same day.

He is hospitalised until April 1945 in Wellington and Lower Hutt and continues outpatient treatment for some months afterward.

Ian's daughter, Merlyn, remembers meeting him, and how his hair has gone from strawberry blond with curls in 1940, to grey hair with no curls. At his February 1945 Medical Board his disability is recorded as 'hyperpiesis' meaning abnormally elevated arterial blood pressure and probably permanent, with an initial disability of up to 20%.

After many months of hospital outpatient appointments, he is finally discharged from the New Zealand Army on 24 January 1946. His medical condition endures; he will be granted an 80% disability in a periodic pension review in 1964.

The official history of 22nd Battalion says '...the backbone of any battalion is no heroic figure, but the ordinary man, who quietly leaves his civilian life, quietly and steadily performs his army duties, and then, just as unostentatiously, disappears into civilian life again. He's the one who counts'.

RSM SIDNEY SHERRIFF

1 Battalion, Royal Welch Fusiliers

By Andy Sherriff

Author Andy Sherriff was born one year before the RSM died in 1954. He has a varied career: trawler skipper, mountaineering instructor, first aid instructor for 35 years. Andy Sherriff lives in northeast Wales.

The first part of my account shows what made this man, my grandfather Sydney, who he was: resilience and robustness in character. To his dying day he retained this formidable military presence.

Sydney was one of four children (three sons and a daughter) of a London baker. Before WW1, he became a silversmith. From then onwards, right until his death, he was with the Royal Welch Fusiliers. Ours was a very military family. All three brothers survived WW1, although in different regiments.

Sydney's second cousin, the author Robert Cedric Sherriff, also served in WW1, and went on to write his virtual biography, *Journey's End*. (He seems to have served in a very intellectual regiment, having esteemed poets in its ranks such as David Jones, Hedd Wynn, Robert Graves and Siegfried Sassoon).

During his WW1 days, whilst still in the U.K., Sydney rose rapidly from private, through to lance corporal and corporal, to lance sergeant, in 15 London Battalion.

In December 1915 he went to France as a lance sergeant, completing WW1 as a sergeant in Battalions 15 – 13 – 3rd. His regiment served at Loos, the Somme and Passchendaele.

Between the wars, Sydney was with 1 Battalion in India, in the Waziristan campaign.

Interestingly, his records show demotion whilst in India, stating, 'for inefficiency.' After a brief spell as colour sergeant and A/CQMS in 1927 he was back to sergeant until 1933, when he was promoted to warrant officer 3 / CSM. 1935.

Back in the U.K., he was RSM 5 & 1 Battalion Royal Welch Fusiliers. He had long associations with Kinmel Park Army Camp (*Bodelwyddan*) and Hightown Barracks in Wrexham.

The regimental diary shows that Sydney was part of the 1939 British Expeditionary Force that went to France and Belgium. After the initial gentle days during the so-called phoney war, concerts, football and St. David's Day celebrations, things got serious. Over a period of three to four days, the German advance entailed extreme hand to hand fighting, whilst being bombed and shelled.

For Sydney the fighting ended when he was taken prisoner at Saint Venant in France, recorded as Missing in Action on 14 May.

That intense conflict was part of the rear-guard action, incorporating the Scottish regiments, for the Dunkirk Evacuation (Operation Dynamo), enabling the evacuation of three of Sydney's sons (my father, Sidney Sherriff, and uncles Donald and Fred).

After capture, Sydney was taken to Stalag VIII-B, where he became (and remained throughout the internment) the overall camp leader / man of confidence of this large multinational POW Camp, until the Russian Army advanced and liberated the camp.

Sydney was not part of the Long March, as he remained at the camp until this liberation, being responsible for administration and care related to the POWs, whether these were in the main camp or satellite camps/working parties.

He learned German, and both the German *Wehrmacht* OCs and he had mutual respect. The German officer commanding (*oberbefehlshaber*) once told him that they knew the English POWs had a radio, that was okay, but please don't tell the German guards just how Germany was doing in the war!

A major part of Sydney's work there included reporting status and well-being of POWs to the International Red Cross in Geneva, especially during their site visits. He also reported on transgressions and murders by the German guards.

On occasion, the Germans tried to embed 'spies'. These were weeded out and disposed of appropriately.

At one time, the Germans refused to supply the Palestinian (Jewish) POWs with Red Cross Parcels. This ultimately resulted in solidarity amongst the POWs in refusing to accept their issues. This put the Germans in a very difficult situation, causing them to relent and eventually the Palestinians received their parcels too. They expressed their great gratitude by giving Sydney a carved, painted and dedicated wooden covered photo album, made, appropriately, from Red Cross boxes.

A little-known fact is that there were also civilians in the camp, notably Polish women and others deported from the Channel Islands. Copies of letters are now held in The Warsaw Rising Museum and respectively The Channel Islands Military Museum, Jersey.

The Polish contingent comprised 342 women officers, nurses and civilians – including children. Many of the women were pregnant. There was a total of 1032 Polish non-combatant POWs in the camp in 1939. The hand-written letter we have of Sydney, appeals to the RSM to help in securing a list of food and clothing essentials. I have no idea how the Germans responded to his requests.

We also have a letter of thanks from the Channel Islands Refugee Committee, thanking Sydney for his kindness and support to these POWs.

Another of Sydney's functions was as a financial trustee, ensuring that POWs 'wages' were transferred to bank accounts. An official German postcard shows a transfer of 230Rm 50 Ffgs for No. 16483 Greaves – bringing his account to 251Rm 38Ffgs.

With so many POWs in the camp, sub-camps and off-site working parties, discipline and maintaining mental well-being was just as important as food and health. To these ends, Sydney actively encouraged 'disobedience' and escape. When the library burnt down, he arranged for more books and donations from the UK. A college and learning facilities were established, enabling education, and also awarding of proper educational 'certificates'. Music and drama were developed, with many concerts and plays staged. There was a camp newspaper, *The Clarion*, which Sydney helped develop and wrote brief articles for. Pastoral care was so important.

Sydney wrote home to his wife on a regular basis. These were not ordinary letters, cryptic and coded comments were embedded, so all the letters were immediately handed over to the War Office.

After the war, Sydney provided vital evidence for the Nuremberg war trials, and received letters of thanks from the Canadian government, the Channel Island government (Civilian internees at 8b), and also an MBE for services whilst in the camp.

He finished the war as an RSM, finally being released from duties in November 1945. He joined the General Post Office Rhyl and remained RQMS RWF TA Rhyl until his death.

There is some irony that, after his long and combative career, his ultimate demise was due to lung cancer. His Funeral at St. Thomas' Church, Rhyl, was with full military honours, gun carriage, attended by Lord Lieutenant of Flintshire.

Sydney's awards included:

1914-15 Star

British War Medals 1914-18, and 1939-45

Victory Medals 1914-18 and 1939-45

General Service Medal

Indian General Service Medal 'Waziristan' 1919-21, 1921-24

MBE (Member of The Most Excellent Order of The British Empire)

I am proud he was my granddad, and to have met him, although just briefly as a toddler, whilst he was in his final hospital stay. A vivid, lasting memory.

FRED CRIPPS and TOM LEITH

By Jason Cripps

Born in Durban, South Africa, Jason Cripps now lives and works in Sale, near Manchester in the UK. Married to Carolyn, they have two sons, Charlie (13) and Will (11). Jason is very interested in history, having studied it at university. Since becoming a father, Jason has taken an interest in genealogy too.

Outside of work, he is a keen musician and also engages in a variety of shooting sports.

When his first son, Charlie, was born in 2007, he had an urge to do some family history research and this is how he uncovered the two stories of his grandfathers in WWII.

I was born in South Africa, as were my parents, but both my grandfathers were from UK heritage. My paternal grandfather Fred Cripps was

English and born in Buckinghamshire. My maternal grandfather, Tom Leith, was born in South African born, of Scottish descent.

All I had to go on when I did my research, were some family stories supplied by my parents and my grandmothers, and some basic personal information about my grandfathers.

Using the internet and contacting the South African Ministry of Defence and the International Red Cross, I started to piece their stories together.

Fred and Tom both volunteered for the Union Defence Force, the South African Army. They both fought at Tobruk, in North Africa, but six months apart. Fred was taken prisoner at the battle of Sidi Rezegh on 23 November 1941 and Tom was taken at Gazala on 16 June 1942. Both men ended up in the same POW camp, Stalag VIII-B/344 Lamsdorf, in southern Poland.

Even though their back gardens in Durban shared a border, they unfortunately never knew each other or of their shared experience. My mum and dad attended the same high school in Durban, started a relationship as teenagers and eventually I came along just as my father started his national service in the South African Army in 1969.

FRED 'SONNY' CRIPPS – SIGNALMAN

Fred was born on 2 July 1912, in Stoke Poges in Buckinghamshire, 30 miles from the village of Waddesdon where the Cripps family had lived for hundreds of years. In 1937 he set sail for South Africa. Family information on why he did this isn't clear. He was an accomplished musician who played in a band on a cruise ship and this seems to be the accepted reason why he went.

I grew up with a story from my grandmother; she always told me that I was named after a ship that my grandfather had been on in the war. Both of my parents, however, say they were unaware of this when choosing my name. My grandmother is no longer with us and so I'm still unsure of the truth, but Fred's story threw up a massive surprise once I started my research.

Fred volunteered for the Union Defence Force on 1 April 1940 at the age of 25. He was 5'10', weighed a little over 10 stone and had a 34' chest. He was posted to 1st Brigade, South African Corps of Signals. This unit became part of the 5th South African Infantry Brigade and the 1st South African Infantry Division in August 1940. The unit was posted to Marsabit in northern Kenya as part of the East African Campaign, fighting against the Italian Army and local tribal groups in Abyssinia and Ethiopia. In May 1941, the 5th South African Infantry Brigade was sent to Egypt to bolster the Allied forces against Rommel's push towards the border.

In Egypt, the brigade was assigned defensive duties at Mersa Matruh while the Allied forces prepared to lift the siege of Tobruk in Operation Crusader. The South Africans were assigned to protect the left flank of the 7th Armoured Division and were the most southerly of the Allied forces as they pushed forward when Operation Crusader got underway on 18 November 1941. The various moves and countermoves between the Allies and Rommel's forces culminated in a massive battle around Sidi Rezegh, an airfield south of Tobruk. Unfortunately for the 5th South African Infantry Brigade they were caught between both German and Italian armoured divisions as they attacked the British 7th Armoured Division.

An account of the battle on 23 November 1941 states: 'By 13:15 a major tank battle was underway between Axis forces and 7 Armoured Division. At 15:55 – 1st SA Division were passing a signal to 5 SA Brigade when the brigade interjected, "Wait ...". Those were the last words received from the 5th SA Infantry Brigade. Some units retained some form of unity and managed to escape east through the New Zealand and Indian fronts. Against the German tanks, the South African infantry had no real means of defence with limited anti-tank capabilities; they were compelled to use 25-pounders in a direct fire role. By the time the Panzers had broken into the rear of the brigade, the artillery had been subdued and all anti-tank capabilities had been destroyed. By nightfall, all that remained of 5 SA Brigade was "... little groups of disconsolate prisoners... between frequent flares and the light of burning ammunition." The 5th SA Brigade had been caught by an overwhelming force in the open desert, quite unprepared and without inflicting any negligible damage on its opponents.'

The battle had resulted in a victory for the Afrika Korps, but the 7th Armoured and 1st South African Divisions had not been annihilated and the loss of the 5th SA Brigade was not enough to set off the loss of almost 50% of the Afrika Korps tanks which went into battle. At 1 a.m. on 24 November, Brigadier Brink reported to XXX Corps that 5th SA Brigade had 'ceased to exist as a fighting formation.'

Fred was captured on that day as his unit was overwhelmed.

The heavy cost of the day's fighting to Rommel's forces earned it the nickname *Totensonntag*, 'Death Sunday'.

From Sidi Rezegh, Fred was transported across the desert to the port of Benghazi in Libya. On 8 December 1941 he was loaded, along with around 2000 Allied POWs, onto an Italian supply ship named the MV *Sebastiano Veniero*.

I have found photographs of this ship, and if you look closely you can see the words 'Jason - Holland' on the side of the ship. The ship was originally named the Jason before it was captured in Holland and renamed. This is the ship my grandmother told me I was named after.

The ship began its journey to Italy, but on the afternoon of 9 December 1941, in a storm, while sailing close to the south coast of Greece, it was torpedoed by the British submarine HMS *Porpoise*. There is speculation on whether or not the commander of the submarine knew there were Allied POWs on board, however, my view is that the ship would need to have been sunk regardless so as to prevent it taking vital supplies back to Rommel's forces. Around 300 POWs from South Africa, New Zealand, Australia, and the UK were killed when the torpedoes hit, but the ship did not sink. The Italian crew abandoned ship, however a German merchant seaman stayed and worked with the POWs and their officers to run the ship aground on the shore of Greece. The ship was run aground at Methoni, an ancient port on the southwestern coast of Greece.

Once the POWs had managed to get off the ship they were faced with a force of Italian and German troops and were swiftly recaptured. Fred then made his way to Pylos, Kalamata and eventually Patras, where the camp was called 'Dysentery Acre'. Many of the POWs suffered horribly with exposure to the winter weather and the illnesses they already had or contracted there.

Fred spent several months in Greece until transported to Italy in May 1942. During this time he was ill with rheumatic fever due to the exposed conditions in the Greek camps. However, he was well enough to take part in some sabotage of a factory he was working in and was fined 6000 lira by his Italian captors. In Italy, he spent time in Camps 85 Tuturano, 65 Bari, 70 Monte Urano and 75 Torre Tresca. While in these camps he was mainly put to work in farming and labouring. Then, with Italy's surrender imminent, the Germans moved Allied POWs out of Italian camps. Fred was moved to Stalag VIII-C Sagan in southern Poland in September 1943. This camp was adjacent to Stalag Luft III, the camp portrayed in the film *The Great Escape*.

From there Fred was moved to Stalag VIII-B/344 in Lamsdorf (Łambinowice, southern Poland) in October 1943.

While in Stalag VIII-B he was assigned to a number of work camps which were satellites to the main camp. The questionnaire he completed once he was repatriated via England in May 1945 refers to the following *arbeitskommados,* or work camps:

From October 1943 to April 1944 he worked as a labourer in a power station in a place called Beuthen (modern day Bytom) near Katowice, the main city in the region; April 1944 to January 1945 he worked in a coal mine at a place he calls *Schwarzes Meer*. I haven't been able to identify exactly where this is, but it is likely to be somewhere in the Katowice/Niwka/Dumbrowa industrial and mining area. The conditions in these mines were very dangerous and POWs were generally used as labourers to support the Polish miners. This means they did the worst and most physically demanding jobs.

Fred's time in Stalag VIII-B came to an end in January 1945. As with many other Allied POWs, he took part in the forced marches which were during the winter of 1944-45 when POWs were marched out of their camps and into Germany, to prevent liberation by Allied forces. He started marching from Lamsdorf in southern Poland on 22 January 1945. There were two marches from the camp. One went through southern Poland and into eastern Germany via Gorlitz and Dresden ending up south of Berlin. The other march took a route through northern Czechoslovakia into Bavaria to a camp near Nuremburg. I'm fairly sure that the route through Czechoslovakia was the one he took due to comments in his Liberation Questionnaire where he tells of a soldier who died on the march in central Czechoslovakia. These marches by thousands of POWs took place in the depths of a European winter, in dreadful conditions. Often they slept in the open, went without food and were subject to appalling treatment by their guards, including the execution of those who couldn't carry on. In his Liberation Questionnaire Fred detailed, 'The appalling conditions and treatment of men who marched from Poland to Germany from Jan until Apr 1945.' He also detailed the death of a man called Jack Letwin on the march through Czechoslovakia: 'There were many cases of both sick and exhausted prisoners who received no treatment whatever, but I am not able to give details as required. The above case was caused through neglect on the part of our MO on the march.'

Fred finally arrived home in Durban during the summer of 1945. He married my grandmother on 22 September 1945 and was discharged from the army on 27 November 1945.

I never knew my grandfather, unfortunately he died in 1958 when my father was ten years old. His untimely death also took a big toll on my grandmother, who burned all his belongings from the war as she firmly believed what he had gone through was responsible for his death.

As with my other grandfather, the journey of uncovering Fred's story has had a big impact on me. The times when he could easily have died were many, and I am grateful that he had the good fortune and the resilience to make it home when so many others didn't.

GUNNER THOMAS ARTHUR LEITH

Tom was born on 16 November 1915 in Durban, South Africa. He volunteered for the Union Defence Force on 21 June 1940 at the age of 24. According to his enlistment papers he was 5' 9', weighed just shy of 10 stone and had a 34' chest. His records show that he suffered ill health shortly after joining and was admitted to hospital during August and September, and then again in December 1940. He embarked aboard the SS *Llandaff Castle* on 30 November 1941 from Durban as part of the 2nd Natal Mounted Rifles, arriving in Suez on 18 December 1941. He was then transferred to the 1st South African Irish in January 1942 and then to the 1st South African Anti-Tank Regiment in May.

Rommel's offensive to take Tobruk in May/June of 1942 is often referred to as one of his great victories. For the South African military, the first battle in November 1941 is known as one of their worst defeats. Tom was part of reinforcements that arrived in Egypt to replace those lost in the battles around Tobruk in November 1941.

Tom was stationed at the northern edge of the Gazala line in spring 1942. Much of the initial action during May happened to the south of these positions as Rommel used his famous flanking manoeuvres to try and encircle key defensive boxes and avoid a costly frontal assault. This work was done mainly by the 15th and 21st Panzer Divisions while Italian infantry with some armoured support made attacks on the northern / central defensive positions to keep the troops there engaged and give the impression that this was where the main push would come.

The 15th and 21st Panzer divisions engaged in some furious battles to complete their flanking manoeuvre, most notably the Cauldron and the subsequent break out to the north, which left the Knightsbridge box surrounded and various British armour regiments seriously depleted. As Rommel gained momentum, he ordered the 15th Panzer Division to push north to try and reach the Via Balbia coastal road and cut off the troops in the northern positions where Tom was, so they couldn't retreat to Tobruk itself.

Tom was part of the rear guard for the South African 1st Division as it desperately tried to avoid being cut off in the retreat to Tobruk and then on to El Alamein. Various accounts tell of the order being given on 14 June to abandon the northern Gazala positions, the Gazala Gallop as it became known, and retreat. Tom was captured on 16 June, which coincides with an account in a regimental diary that states: 'This left the 50th British and 1st South Africa divisions stuck in boxes to the north of Knightsbridge, cut off by the Axis, who were swarming towards Tobruk. These divisions were ordered to break out east while the 15th and 21st Panzer tried to cut them off. Weary units of 7th Armoured managed to delay the German armour allowing most of the 50th Division to escape and the 1st South Africa Division, withdrawing along the coast road lost only its rear guard. By now most of the 8th Army was in retreat to the El Alamein line.'

After capture, Tom was listed as a POW in Italian hands. He made his way through various camps and hospitals in Italy. His records from the

International Red Cross mention transit camps from June 1942 to November 1942, then a hospital in Taranto for three months (December 1942 - March 1943), Camp PG 65 at Bari and Camp PG 52 at Chiavari. Eventually Tom arrived in Stalag VIII-B, Lamsdorf on 28 September 1943.

While in Stalag VIII-B he was assigned to a number of work camps which were satellites to the main camp. The questionnaire he completed once he was repatriated via England in May 1945 refers to the following *arbeitskommandos* or work camps: October 1943 to December 1943 he worked in a sugar factory at an unspecified location but which was in the upper Silesia region where the main camp was located; December 1943 to May 1944 he was engaged in building and excavation in Dabrowa, a mining and industrial area east of Katowice, the main city in the region and from June 1944 to January 1945 he was working in a coal mine in Niwka, one of Poland's oldest mining areas, also near Katowice. The conditions in these mines were very dangerous and POWs were generally used as labourers to support the Polish miners. This means they did the worst and most physically demanding jobs.

As many other Allied POWs, Tom took part in the Long Marches during the winter of 1944-45. POWs were marched out of their camps and into Germany to prevent liberation by Allied forces. He started marching from Lamsdorf on 22 January 1945. There were two marches from the camp. One went through southern Poland and into eastern Germany via Gorlitz and Dresden ending up south of Berlin. The other march took a route through northern Czechoslovakia into Bavaria to a camp near Nuremburg. It's unclear exactly which route he took, but from the work camps he was in, it seems the route through Czechoslovakia is the most likely. These marches were in sub-zero temperatures and heavy snow, often sleeping in the open and with little to no food. As a child, my grandmother would always tell me to eat what was on my plate and be glad of it because during the war Tom had to eat potato peelings out of bins to survive. Another family story says he was left for dead on this march and thrown on a pile of other POW bodies. The story goes that he was found by a priest who noticed that he was still alive and rescued him. I haven't been able to corroborate this part of his story.

71

I knew Tom briefly as a child, he passed away in hospital in Durban, South Africa when I was six years old. My memories are hazy but I'm glad I have them, especially the ones of visiting him in hospital. My parents say he rarely talked of the war, but on occasion, over a beer with my dad (who was in the South African Army at the time) he did let some things slip. He talked with respect of the devastating accuracy of German artillery and tank gunners; and also the cruelty and barbarism of their counterparts serving as prison camp guards.

Uncovering Tom's story has been a sobering experience. Never again will I feel sorry for myself when life gets difficult. What I face day to day will never come close to being left behind to slow enemy tanks while my friends retreat to fight another day. I am in awe when I think about the consequences of a tank shell, a bullet, an artillery fragment, hypothermia, and exhaustion. Any of these could have claimed his life, and if it had, I would not be here to write this.

HAROLD LATHAM

By Julie Gilpin

Julie Gilpin is 57, born in Blackpool, currently resident in Devon. One of eight grandchildren of Harold and Agnes, and custodian of Harold's original diaries and medals.
   She is passionate about keeping the history of her grandfather alive.

My granddad, Harold Latham, enlisted as a volunteer in the Royal Artillery and quickly (for reasons unknown) changed over on the 2 February 1939 to the Royal Engineers. According to the war diaries he was part of the Tunnelling company.
   From the war office records he was blowing up bridges, tunnelling and digging trenches around the Boulogne area of France.

Harold was shot twice in the arm and taken to a church in Lille where he was looked after before going to a French hospital in Boulogne. He was taken to a few prison camps before ending up at Lamsdorf in 1940.

This was a working camp and from a questionnaire on his return, he noted that he worked in the paper mill.

These are extracts from his diary (note that Agnes was his wife, June his daughter):

'All the time we are heading for Gorlitz, where there is a big English Lager, also a striking coincidence it was the first POW. camp I was at in October 1940. Whilst we were in Lauban we heard that Joe had broken through at another place and was making for Gorlitz, so we retracted on footsteps, but the time we were heading southwest of Gorlitz, for no one knew where, the Western front we hoped?'

'Up to press no hot water for a brew. Departed from Zittau on Tuesday 13th, 3 weeks on the trek arrived at a place called Strahwalde.

Stayed the night, this time in a barn.'

'Had only marched 8 kilometres, when we came into contact with a large colony of English, Russian and Lebanese, 1200 all told and roughly 300 Englishman.

20 kilometres the next day to Ottenhaim stayed the night and the following 2 days. It was hell on earth with the Russians and Serbs, it was like a menagerie, never heard such bad language and such bad habits.'

'I'm still in the same place, waiting for god alone knows what too darn cold outside to walk, nothing to do inside but sit in the straw with our feet wrapped up, too damn cold even to write these few words without gloves, nothing to do but wait, I hope and pray for more food, today we had 1/6 of a loaf, 7 or 8 spuds today and for a change a few grams of sugar.'

'Picked up a few more fellows from the local hospital, including several Yanks. One was only two months a prisoner said everything was ok in England, bags of command etc. war news also a red letter day for us. We received 1 spoonful of jam and 2/3 of a spoon of sugar per man. ½ of bread and a little soup made from Ox's head and spuds in their jackets., very little else for several days now it has been forbidden to peel spuds, that goes for the civilian population too anyone caught are severely punished. Yesterday we received a soap issue 3 tablets and 1 of shaving soap, never been known before, we can only surmise that Joe must be very real! If we received the same food everyday as today we could manage.'

'We are still in the cursed place, today I have heard that when we move, we shall march 3 to 4 weeks to Bavaria, Probably Munich or Luxemburg. Heard also that Gorlitz had already fallen, Dresden heavily bombed larger numbers of Galangers killed including English, that Joe was only 25 kilos from here, don't know if this is all true of course we hear many rumours but we can at least hear heavy gun firing continuously, we do know that the civilian have evacuated this place a few days ago, and now back again with nowhere to go. Had a little excitement in the night, a fellow fell from above and broke his right thigh, finishing his marching days, well anyway until after the war. Lucky blighter!! Many wished they were in his place. Yesterday another fellow was caught stealing a (commander's bread ration and was badly beaten up for his sins.'

'Today another fellow was caught stealing a loaf from a ration wagon, so the entire command ration for that day was given to the Russians.'

'Heard that Turkey had been in the war for eight days against Germany, heard that 5000 prisoners liberated by Joe, and had already reached home. No one seems to know when we are leaving this joint. Heard that they had stopped Joe again.'

'Heard that when we move it will be worse as regards food, as us prisoners were currently in the farming district.'

'Still no signs of moving had a smashing Sunday morning breakfast, dry bread with a pinch of salt for a luxury!!'

'Heard that it was all fluky about Joe sending the 5000 prisoners home that Egypt was now in the war against Germany. Our 11th day in this godforsaken hole and still no signs of moving off, by this time everyone is thoroughly cheesed off, bored of each other's company.'

'Yesterday two English lads broke into the jerry's food store but were very unlucky and were caught inside the place. Two commanders had their bread ration stopped; the culprits got three days in the bunker.'

'We had a little impromptu sing song yesterday evening. But it didn't go with much of a swing, they even called in the yanks for a song, but they were far too shy or weak maybe.'

'Still in the same place, as usual waiting for the bread to come.'

'Got in touch with the outside world last night, a commander comprised 70 men, but they had been out of prison for some time, we did manage to get 10 invalid parcels between approximately 400 men. And learnt that there was a Stalag lager 45 kilometres from here 10 kilometre from Dresden, have finished writing about things I hear it's a waste of time, pencil and paper it's worse here than it was in Lamsdorf in 1940.'

'Asked the German commandant if it was possible to find more hygiene quarters. He asked if we were afraid of lice. He amused us but what if Typhus should break out? he then asked if we were afraid to die, (Very helpful I don't think.)'

'1st March. Exactly a fortnight since we arrived at this dump. I still can't get to know why we are staying here.'

'Yesterday a Russian was shot and buried in less than ½ an hour for stealing spuds, admitting they had been stealing them continuously for days'

'Another Russian buried, he had eaten some beef or something with rat poison on it.'

'Heard the Russian advance had been stopped, but we were advancing in the west. And that Jerries were having another cut in their rations which made things look bleak for us.'

'Heard once again that we are going to a place called Duke in Bavaria and that we would definitely have transport, but not direct from this place, snowing again another cold spell set in.'

'Englishmen only moved from this god forsaken hole. We marched a few kilometres when we met a party of Russians. Our company turned us over to the new company.

The Russians went to our barn, and us to theirs. There were already 40 of our fellows there from Ottenhaim. We arrived at our billets in a similar farm to the other but not so much freedom and the rations were worse than the other place.

The German commander was a horrible person, that did just as he pleased and simply refused to hear complaints or anything. He considers himself a little (Tin God) (he was a perfect swine). I was very much afraid we had jumped out of the frying pan into the fire!!'

'Absolutely hopeless to escape, locked in at night surrounded at day in a small yard by guards armed with hand grenades.'

'Again nothing to do, this time we have very poor light. 26 of our boys escaped from the last place including my three mockers who were regular scallywags!'

'I prefer to be with my old comrades. Also I couldn't see the purpose of running away without some definite object in view. (They were simply browned off with me)

I was also having cravings for smokes, but I can honestly say this life has taught me to control my feelings. Nevertheless I think I would have gone, only for my thoughts of Agnes and the children. I seriously considered escaping but every time I thought of it I also thought of a letter from Agnes, asking me to be careful. This life is hellish, but ever since 1940, I have always said to myself "what another man can do so can I".'

'I am amused at what I have written about controlling my feelings, that is perfectly true but still I haven't learnt to control my temper.'

'This makes my third "To Do" as a prisoner with men big enough to eat me. Each time I have been the aggressor and each time I have come off second best. The last time I thought I had lost my front teeth. I really must remember my age and weight. I have come to the conclusion that I throw my weight about too much considering my size. I have always been in the right, I believe, but I really must learn to control my tongue when dealing with baby elephants. I have also lost a lot of weight. In Goberstdorf, and I must remember although I still appear so youthful, its years are rolling by and I must go easy.'

'9th. I have reason to believe it is Friday the 9th today but who cares what's a day to a 5 year old prisoner of war anyway.'

'Not feeling too bad at the moment having just consumed my Sunday dinner a bowl of watery soup. Had a huge stroke of fortune today I was its 1st man in for Bucketeers.'

'This morning we had a slight increase in the bread ration, 6 in a loaf instead of 7 and also received our first spread of honey.'

'There have been terrible cold winds recently but today the weather has let up and it was quite pleasant to stroll round the courtyard but still damn cold.'

'Quite a lot of the boys washed and shaved. Everything seemed much brighter. It must be the little bits of news we are getting. I believe we're having some Jam issues tomorrow.'

'I'm afraid mail, parcels and cigarettes are a thing of the past.'

'When we shall be able to have a bath and wash our clothing? we are all scared of becoming lousy again as we did in 1940.'

'I have had one clothing change in 7 weeks up to now and have slipped in all kinds of queer places.'

'I have realised that June is nine, today.'

'I saw the German Sanitator about a mysterious pain in my chest. He gave me the usual 3 large tablets and he would see how I felt when he came again.'

'(Information I found out that night from the Yank.)

America came into the war against Germany in November 8th 1942.

Pearl Harbour was declared 8th 1941.

The American proved to be a real nice intelligent fellow and was real interesting.

The yanks had also had a very rough time.'

'No news whatsoever, have just polished off soup inside the billet. Complete with a scarf and gloves things are a shade better now, we're getting a loaf between 6 men and in the last 3 days we've had honey, sugar and white cheese, a spoonful at least, but that's better than sweet fanny Adams! And the soup was a little thicker today. We are getting everything a little more organised gradually.'

'If only the weather would ease up a little, it would be a great help. I've contracted another damn cold, coughing, and sneezing to improve everything.'

'Managed to wangle a quick bath of lukewarm water and changed my underclothes feeling much better, apart from a continuing blasted pain in my chest. But why worry it must end sometime, WE would like to know when THAT'S ALL!!!'

'Still cold and wet today. Enjoyed my breakfast of white cheese 1/5 of a loaf, 1 spoonful of white cheese also had a stroke of good fortune. In the way of a little salt, must always remember if you "don't ask, don't want"'.

'It certainly pays to be brass necked. It's not easy when it's not your nature, but I have noticed that if you ask in a normal manner as if it's a natural thing to do you invariably get results.'

'It's nice to be independent, and keep your tongue and pride between your teeth, "you just go without", and that's another old proverb. I suppose if you want anything you must take a chance.'

'Feeling awful weak today, I don't know if it's on account of the pain in my chest the god damned cold is proving to be rather grim. I don't remember ever feeling so weak and hungry apart from when I lived a whole year in 1940 on similar rations, but that was some time ago and we mortals are easy to forget, which is frightfully jolly really anyway I've got the blues properly today.'

'Big issue today, spoonful of jam, and a pinch of salt, saw our boys over today, chased us all inside, heard they were evacuating Dresden on account of the intensifying bombing, very little news here we appear to be here to stay.'

'Wonders never cease! We had today 5 in a loaf, a little spreading sausage (lovely) "tell your mother"! hopes of parcel issue in the next few days - if only 4 in 1.'

'Had a bath in a small tub of hot water, felt champion afterwards did a little washing, yesterday the weather was lovely, today it's cold wet and miserable again. Can't see inside here, must pack in writing for now. The sausage issue was a one inch of nothing cut in half.'

'Weathers still terrible, wet and windy and cold-white snow again. Sunday of all days a roll call at 6 o'clock this morning because 20 men had been detailed for work, imagine that? working on their rations, you draw your 270 grams of bread and dessert spoonful of sour milk, known as cheese, or perhaps sugar and honey, which is consumed immediately and then at dinner time 1 pint of their watery soup, and then you've had it for that day.'

'They expect us to work on that, all day digging, probably soaked to the skin and the march back to the billet 5 miles to nothing, not even a hot drink. Fires and smoking are forbidden. We cannot even dry our wet clothing, it's a great life, keep smiling, keep your chin up, what they should say is, tighten your belt and hang your chin strap, show your teeth, bark and snarl like a dog to anybody and anybody.

But what use is that the very madness and hope springs ever eternal in the human (breast) our trustee has gone to a committee meeting somewhere in the vicinity of the barns, and it may mean a portion of Red Cross parcel in the near future at least. It would create a new atmosphere

79

amongst the boys immediately it simply horrid to be without food and smokes continually day after day, impossible to deal with one must experience it oneself to understand, Dante's Inferno cannot be compared with it.'

'Was compelled to work, but only for a few hours in the afternoon. had to march 5 kilometres, weak as a kitten positively staggered along at first, as usual was very fortunate and did my dig work.'

'Heard again 7 trucks of Red Cross parcels had been despatched from Geneva, 2 for our lads and that more to follow. In the surrounding barns some had already received a parcel and that we would be brought up to date as soon as possible. WE HOPE.'

'We saw an authentic list of rations we're entitled to.'

'German officer came and spoke to us in English today. What a phoney he was. He did let slip they had also been very short of food in the last few weeks and that it was as bad for him as us.'

'Rest Day today 1st of spring is still cold and wet and windy.'

'Today we had a little French coffee without milk or sugar of course, but it smelt and tasted real good.'

'Tomorrow I must work again. Worse luck.'

'Marched 8 kilometres. Dug a slit trench at the roadside, 2 meters long, ½ meter wide & one deep only just made and it finished at 11.30 a.m. I simply couldn't have worked all day. I was already Ill and then we had to march the 8 kilos back again.'

'Had a splendid view of the raid control one dived down firing in the road. (Did we dive for cover?) Not much!!'

'Met the Heimrich fellow that was in the lager as wartime broke.

One of the boys passed out this morning in the ranks on roll call from weakness.

Drew our bread ration for the day 7 men to a 1500 grams loaf and a dessert spoonful of jam.'

'Great improvement in the weather. 3 successive air raids today. All the guards are jittery today. They seem to be afraid of us hearing their radios almost sure they heard bad news today. They took 3 airmen away from us today. They took the sick men away to hospital early this morning and have also taken our place of birth and nationality, definitely some kind of organisation taking place. We hope it's Joe that's coming?'

'Today is Palm Sunday. We had our dry ration- bread crust 6 in a loaf. It was green mouldy with the crust broken from the top and all crumbly. I had the honour to divide some into 6 portions. and to improve matters we were given jolly old mint tea. it has always been the same since I have been a prison ration always seems to be worse for a holiday time. German sense of humour I believe, caught a glimpse of Jerries paper this morning I believe were advancing rapidly to the west.'

'NOTHING STARVING'

'Nothing new, 7 in a loaf.'

'9 weeks without food and still not getting any place only the eternal waiting can feel myself getting weaker every day. It actually requires a lot of effort to stand on my feet, no kidding to stand suddenly, means usually "Blacking Out"!'

'Took my American friend away sick, the temperature sky high.'

'Also the usual 6 in a loaf.'

'Nothing new.'

'7 in a loaf and another cubic inch of sausage and the long awaited parcels are here.

Well they've gone to fetch them anyway.'

'Life is sweet at last god is good. The parcels did arrive 1 between 2 and 10 cigarettes. We received only 10 cigs because the railway wagon had been tampered with. It was a real body blow after being without so long. It was marvellous to see what a little bit of grub and smoke made, not to mention the jolly old external BREW!! We even had a real old sing song Thursday evening. Never will I forget the Canadian biscuits they were like cream on my tongue and I shall never forget the greatest organisation the civilisation has ever known (THE RED CROSS).'

'We've only received half a parcel; we still have the same bread ration but it is amazing how much the atmosphere changes and cheerful the boys are already.'

'Conclusion!!We began our trek across Germany January 23, 1945, the gunfire from the heavies was already rattling our windowpanes.'

'When the order came to evacuate we all set to leave with our sledges, which we made at a moment's notice, we have already dumped all unnecessary kit.'

'The initial day we encountered deep snow; several sledges needed repairing. We stayed there but some went west. I could hardly lift my feet, and the time thought I'd have to pack in altogether but made it up to press.'

'Fed up of having a cranky stomach, cough and cold. Some of the fellows have already reached 1940 stage in a few weeks, selling everything they have including clothing and food for smokes and not bothering to wash and shave, can't blame them personally it's hellish to wash and shave under these conditions, you could die from exposure from wash under clothing, no means of drying it with also a 100 to 1 chance of losing them (or same).'

Agnes sent me a photograph from Ireland to be put in the back of a mirror together with 20 cigs, a week before we left Krapkowice. Joe broke through and we never came back, and my photograph went west after having kept safe through everything for 5 years, the one taken at Geoffrey bear lane when Agnes was 21.'

'3rd day of the trek lost my false teeth in the straw in a cow shed, kept them in my trousers pocket and a charming dairy maid came and moved my stuff and I came to the conclusion the cows had eaten my teeth.'

'Developed fluid under my left kneecap, I think from weakness caused by my old accident in the colliery that hadn't bothered me for 15 years. The right knee which has become the worst of the two, was I believe the cartilage and excruciating painful on the offside of the kneecap and then to make matters worse we stayed one night in a school room with central heating and dried my boots on a radiator making them stiff and hard, consequently developing foot trouble for the first time in my life. Fluid all around my ankles and a huge bandage upon each knee, what a life. And then 4 to 5 days with diarrhoea, but we are still smiling, at the moment weak for want of food and exercise, we've done nothing for 8 days but lay about in the straw trying to keep warm and waiting for the next issue.'

'I have had some great deals for food in the last few days but it takes the cake, 2 bones for a spoon some deals actually 1 fag for a bowl of soup 2 fags for bread ration couple of rolls for a lovely goatskin wallet.'

'1 loaf for a smashing pair of Brogue shoes. 2 rolls for 10 small apples and a few laid eggs.'

'I myself sold 2 plates for 2 rolls.'

'Another does shirt washing for souvenirs but they come by souvenirs there all come to my lady nicotine.'

'We started this trek with sledges but after a while we found they were clearing the snow in the streets in readiness for the German retreat, so we bought borrowed and stole, there was hand wagons by the roadside, our first covered wagon was not painted, the real old fashioned basket type, with high wheels. It consisted of 3,4 strangers and myself 3 escapees), it lasted exactly one day the good lady around us said it hadn't been used for 23 years it was their first child's so we were given a good little 4 wheeled wagon under cover of darkness, it was really amusing for me to stayed the night a few guards from where close by were we had lifted the wagon, and nationally the owner put 2 and 2 together and the next morning as we were all set to leave, he came inspecting our vehicle, but we made him believe that black was white, finally convinced him that it wasn't his wagon, but ours, the guard was highly suspicious. Then the day came to leave the hell hole, I discovered that someone had stolen my wagon, poetic justice, but who the hell cares.'

'April 1st, April fool's day also Easter Sunday. Reg and I and my new mucker a young lad from Birches head had our breakfast in bed, which consisted of bread, butter sardines marmalade with coffee, looks good it really was. 1 slice of bread and butter, 1 sardine 1 teaspoon of marmalade, and hot coffee (smelt of burnt barley) I received my Easter egg, ¾ of a loaf in exchange for my shoes, from a Ukrainian, pity the coffee was cold, and we went without a smoke.'

'Easter Monday. Weather looks very promising. Rations 1/6 of a loaf. Yesterday was ruined because we were not allowed to make fires. NO BREW hell when we have waited so long.'

'The *feldwebel* took the entire party out for a stroll 3 to 4 kilometres and we all had enough. I was looking forward to the walk and felt quite strong to begin with but soon petered out.'

'The yank known as "Californian Poppy" left us to go to hospital with yellow jaundice and bronchitis.

I don't know which was worse? said I must drop him a line about the old hunting trips.'

'We were going to have a real old chat this afternoon but the jerries crashed in on the arrangements as usual, the yanks were looking for a mate, he did manage it got his soup before he went, which was fairly thick for a change.

'We were really sorry to lose our yank, we had become quite attached to him, he was very interesting. The one bright spot in our daily miserable existence he was a real family man, I imagine him to be real good husband, who must have had real swell wife too from the way he talked of her.

I invited the yank up for a talk over a brew, after we had received our half parcel, but we were forbidden to make fires, so I said we couldn't allow jerry to mess us about too much, and gave the yank a slice of civvies bread, butter and marmalade and a mug of real thick klim milk, cold but still good. The yank was tickled to death, MUST drop a line about that and how eventually received his half Canadian parcel after hearing as many rumours and waiting to land ...'

'Another 200 men joined us heard that we all move together tomorrow.'

'Arrived in a new Stalag that was only half completed, saw once again many old and new faces. Received a drink of mint tea.'

'Today is the 9th of April on the journey here the countryside was marvellous, magnificent (Saxony) different entirely from above schlemiel, but the lager is deadly, unfinished, Reg has no blankets, neither of us have any bead boards. At the moment we were both sleeping on a little damp straw on the floor.'

'Again the rumours of parcels, but up to press have failed to materialise. They say we were fed by the civil contractors, the soups were not too bad, and we received 1/8 of a 2 kilo loaf 250 grams but have not yet received any bread.'

'We received a 1/10 of a loaf yesterday 200 grams the entire population here had another cut.'

'Received a whole Canadian parcel per man this morning I was qualified for work, went out without a wash, breakfast and not properly awake. Left a brew of tea on the stove. Heart rendering.'

'Reported sick this morning. The job yesterday didn't turn out so bad, we were on the side of the Elbe River. (The right side) the western. The weather was lovely, did nothing as usual, but stood about and chatted, saw the Sanitator, displaying my wounds, and was told to report the next day for work in the camp.

Tomorrow I move to a known working barracks.'

'I should have started work in the camp staff at 8 a.m. this morning. But I had an accident during the night. I fell in the receptacle of empty tins right at mealtime, cutting myself badly. To make matters worse my stomach is giving me grief today.'

'Heard that there is another cut in the rations, 150 grams this time, heard that more wagons had arrived carrying American, English and Canadian, no cigarettes but they are taking them out of the American parcels issuing 20 to every new man.'

'Caught a fellow stealing red arm issue from his muckers, beat him up, shaved his hair off and tied him to the barbed wire, threatened to give his rations to the man he robbed. He certainly looked pitiful hanging from the wire with blood streaming from his face. It may sound very stern justice but life in these circumstances requires drastic measures. Two more fellows were also beaten for selling tatty blouses to the froggies belonging to another fellow.'

'Heard that the jerries no longer! Heard news on the radio. Also heard Roosevelt was dead.'

'The mice again are at it they must not eat our spuds…'

'The new arrival received ½ parcels some of them were throwing up all night long.'

'The news was good indeed, we heard our troops were in Dresden, which is about 22 miles from here, we heard alarms from half the town.'

'Awoke to the sound of our planes scrapping in its near vicinity therefore causing a huge to-do.'

'News received the previous evening another 500 new fellows arrived today.'

'Beat a fellow up again for stealing another fellow's red issue …The same fellows they beat up a few days ago.'

'The 500 men left this morning; they consisted mostly of parachute airborne troops.'

'The working parties returned about 9 o'clock no work the civvies master had been called away.'

'Heard again that Dresden had fallen! Inclined to believe that it's true, as the new boys were chased out of Dresden.'

'They've moved me from the barracks into a hospital (revier), Reg and I moved in.

I had my first night's sleep, since arriving in the camp. It was terrible in those barracks. I was fast becoming mentally and physically exhausted. I just hope that we stay here until our boys take over, don't fancy going on march again. Wangled Reg into the revier along with me, he now possesses three blankets.'

'Wild rumours about our troop being 4 kilometres from Berlin, 15 from here, told of moving again, they have said if the yanks come for us we shall be turned over to them, but if it's the Russians come front we shall have to move, and they must protect us from the Russians.'

'Nothing definite life goes on very much the same its usual endless roll calls etc "The War without End"'

'Another 900 men down the road. No accommodation available here. I was in a stone building with no water.'

'A little excitement yesterday in the way of dog fights, one of few planes came down in bits and pieces.'

'None of the boys are going out to work as yet, but they called the froggies out to build roadblocks.'

'All quiet today up to press. Roll call once again, were hanging on for jolly old soup, which we have been informed is being specially made for us by "revier patients", there are spuds being peeled, but it may be a little thinner, but we hope not too thin good start won't be ready until about 3.30 or 4 o'clock.'

'The soup arrived it was clean, alright, but too thin, it's obvious that they were in on it and them officers, (no bugger sees) (what a racket again).'

'Must make a note of the rations up to press their much different since we've been on 200gram bread, 5 gram of sugar per day and extra items like white cheese twice a week. In this life anything's new immediately made a racket; it's for survival of the fittest with vengeance the weak go under all right here.'

'Had a wash in a cup full of water in a bowl after about seven other fellows. the water is terrible here.'

'Just thinking of brewing up the tea leaves for its last time everything else is grim. I think we've had it now, have heard that all communications have been cut off, a generous man managed to get us 4 cigs per man, but I think that is the last we shall ever see of the Red Cross issue, eats, clothing, smokes.'

86

'It's deadly here now news has not been good recently. I know everything so quick I think we are all impatient because we thought its end was so near. It now appears to have been another burst bubble, its positivity given here anyway.'

'Have just this minute heard that our troops are fighting in the west of Berlin the Russians on the coast of Berlin or so it goes on, it's uncertainty the eternal awaiting is enough to drive one dippy. A little more excitement, our boys are bombing again, we can see the bombs leaving its planes.'

'The soup was thinner today than yesterday I'm afraid we may retaliate tomorrow and demand our own soup tickets even if they sling us out of the revier.

It is more than flesh or blood can stand to be swindled out of our already too small rations.

Indecently Adolf Hitler's birthday 56 today Born 1889.'

'Saw a leaflet yesterday which read real well (if what read it was true) jerries have had it.'

'Very cold again today we had a drop of bucket soup last night with the same thin stuff. Reg and I have decided to hang on and see if the soup is any better today, there's not much point in remaining in here one way or another, but we skip roll calls etc and they may resume work and if there is a sudden move, they may provide the revier patients with transport so it's worth hanging on a while.'

'But we are most likely going to starve. The soup was thin again today but a little better.'

'Heard that the German newspaper admitted that the Russians were shelling Berlin, Bautzen and Gorlitz had fallen and Anglo American troops were only a matter of 15 or 20 kilometres from here. But we've heard as much baloney in the past that we cannot believe our troops are so near and that there's a possibility of us being liberated and being fed.'

'Although there is plenty of aerial activity, bombing and sounds of heavy gunfire continuously. We remain very dubious, put it all down to blasting in towns, or bridge blowing, even though no men out working everything's at a standstill indicating that the end is near after 5 years. It is very difficult to credit the news with any truth. But we shall see, they say everything as a beginning, has also got an end. Perhaps it's goddamned war will prove to have an end too.'

'Miserable cold day, I did intend to get up today and take a stroll around as I'm getting so weak as a kitten, limp in bed. The act of rising to go to the lavatory jiggers me up completely. I flop back in bed like an empty sack. I sure need these vitamin tablets we've had for the last day or two.'

'Heard that Berlin had surrendered. We have made a truce for 48 hrs whilst we hold the conference with the Germans (certainly hope it is a peace conference), we don't know much we can take.'

'All quiet! nothing to report, no signs of the Yanks or Russians, all the NCO's in camp held a meeting and decided to dig slit trenches for our own protection and that if Jerry's asked us to march again we must refuse and in the event of Jerry's buzzing off and leaving us to our own devices, it would be better to stay put for at least 36 hours. It would be foolish for any man to attempt to escape. That's ok for the big shots in this racket, but things are bad enough for us now, what are we going to live on for the next 36 hours?'

'The soup today was pure and simply water, the subject is more important in that all its war news hears today is Russians have already taken 1/3 of Berlin, Hitler had taken supreme command, but we've been hearing all kinds of tripe for 5 long years and Berlin is a long way from here and our stomachs are right on the job with the bucketeers. Was admitted into the revier on 15th April 1945 in the lager at Königstein.'

'Did receive a little treatment 3 vitamin tablets daily and a few cough tablets, on Monday 23rd April 8 or 9 patients in the revier on that date, 8 or 9 patients mentioned in despatch by its Polish MO by the way, on a little active diet for malnutrition including myself, Reg and Ted received 1/5 of a bar of Canadian chocolate, and 1 Canadian biscuit smothered with jam, Tuesday 24th April we also received 1/12 of a meatloaf , 1/8 of a tin of bully, ½ a dessert spoon of butter and a spoonful of jam, not forgetting on cup full of well brewed tea, with milk but without sugar, the little extras came as a bolt from the blue so we mustn't grumble, as it is there quite likely to opened discontent and jealousy all over the camp. As no one was informed of the arrival of the parcels they were smuggled quietly in and handed out has been left to the discretion of the orderlies which itself is enough to cause a riot.'

'We received a little extra today Wednesday, 1 cup of tea and milk without sugar, a second brew of well diluted 1/8 of bully. 1/12 of meatloaf, teaspoonful this time of butter and this time 1 teaspoon full of marmalade.'

'The whole camp had a huge surprise last night, the civvies in charge of the camp said he wanted 1500 men to go out working today. Its total strength of the camp is only 1239, so he said he must have a 1000. He was told that would be impossible, so he said he must have 700 today, and the MO should examine all the sick, not failing to produce 700 for work tomorrow the lieutenant said we couldn't have any extra rations today, but he would go make enquires today and they would more likely get extra soup on the job and rations on return to the camp.'

'The work was demolished at some place 15 kilometres from here, travelling by train today they went off before dawn at 4am. They departed at 5am most with empty stomach, reported to work all day clearing dead bodies off the railway station I believe, only drawing rations on return to the camp, probably because Jerry will not allow us to make the soup as the men in the camp, lit the fires, says they must wait until tonight, the usual Jerry punishment, tantalisation empty stomachs.'

'We in the revier have drained our soup, but it was worse than yesterday if that is possible, simply coloured water. I am at a loss as to which is the better of two evils to remain in the revier and starve on our special soup or go out to work on the ordinary rations. There maybe a little extra ration picked up outside but also a possibility of being bumped off by me own bombs, I suppose we must hang on as usual and hope and pray for the end.'

'The boys are already back, sent home in disgrace, told to bugger off at 1.15 pm (useless) but had to walk the whole distance back, 14 kilometres, I believe they only went as volunteers.'

'Heard the Germans had done a bunk to Sweden.'

'The splint was removed from my finger today. We received our extra diet again yesterday, ½ of bully, meat loaf ½ teaspoonful of jam teaspoon of butter and a cup of unsweetened tea.'

'Heard 18000 had been retaken including Lamsdorf, near Bavaria and transported home, the sick by plane and the rest by lorries.'

'The jerries in Berlin had used the tanks to convey the troop behind the Russians and the Russians had retaliated by using his artillery. Lots more news all good including its capitulation of Italy. Hopes of relief from the Red Cross for us is definitely out of the question.'

'Great change in the weather again, miserable cold wet day. Reg has to go to Königstein to the dentist. Ted gave him his orders to glue his eyes to the gutter for cigars butts and dog ends.'

'Yesterday we did a little cuisine. Ted, Reg and I flogged cake soap each, and netted together 2 cigs and 1 small cigar making for one the first and last time. I have never flogged soap before, that's me though, I appreciate the value of English soap highly for this kind of business, I'll get along without a smile.'

'The news was smashing last night, quite expected to see or hear something of our boys this morning.

Instead of the usual peaceful Sunday morning in the country, birds twittering and so forth, we heard that the war was over.

Heard Mussolini had been taken prisoner. The commander of the German Army close to Italy had capitulated near the border pass, our troops simply ploughed through "Brenner pass" and were nearing Bavaria, we heard that they disarmed the German troops in Italy given them tickets and told them to bugger off home, thousands of German troops were laying down their arms, donning civilian clothes and returning home.

Brenner was being frantically defended. Kettering was already in England. The yanks were in Dresden and last night sounds of heavy artillery were heard, but the morning it is quiet and peaceful as it is possible to be, it's enough to drive a man to drink but we can't find enough water to wash. A YMCA padre visited us this morning.'

'News Hermal had offered to capitulate to England and America but we refused saying the more they capitulate to all 3 powers including Russia. The MO said then our troops contacted us, the sick would be home in 24 hours. Jerry was expected to pack in any day now, we wanted unconditional surrender, had the American thrust not being diverted north towards Bavaria we should have been picked up before now.'

'Latest up to press (stop press news)

German troops ceased fire against British and American soldiers at 2pm today.

Was discharged from the revier but remained on the ration strength for the day, managed to wangle my little extras again, a teaspoon of butter and a little salmon. I think it was wangled out in the usual way by underhanded methods of RAME reminiscent of 1940. Agitating as usual. Today I moved into the same barracks as Reg, but the barracks appear to be fairly comfortable.'

'All quiet up to press! Met up with a Canadian I knew in Lamsdorf 1943 in the new barracks which is for permanent cranks by the way.'

'May day! Labour day and darn cold in the bargain have just heard on the BBC news read but can't be bothered to write it all down now I am no longer lying in bed in the revier.

'The news is smashing the hammer and sickle is flying over the Reichstag all Germany seems to be in Allied land except the particular spot where we are in. Just our Luck!!'

'2nd. Beastly day reminiscing of May 1941. Snowing and blowing and cold too. But not as cold as it was on May 9th, 1941, the day I came out of Lamsdorf to continue work for the first time in Germany.'

'Heard the BBC news again Adolf Hitler had died having a stroke. Berlin had (had it) Russian tanks were in possession, 300000 had been taken and repatriated home course our luck we look like being first in last out.'

'Heard more good news, can't be bothered to write about it. Anyway I'm hoping to be moving in about a week's time, I'm still a little optimistic even though I've been waiting 5 years on the 25th of this month.'

'Hope!! Is a wonderful thing, its springs eventually in the human breast. They'll certainly have to give in soon.'

'I'm too weak to stand right now, right now I'm even hoping to be home for my 5th anniversary, the day I was wounded 5 long years ago.'

'3rd. Heard last night 1000000 capitulated in Italy, that Churchill himself would personally announce the end of the war.

That the British and American Troops had taken a lot more places. Verified that Hitler was dead, Berlin was completely in Allied hands.

Socialist in German was finished, Germany now had a new leader, Admiral Von Donitz Me of Old!! Imperialistic type, he had immediately given Von Ludendorf the push.'

'Today and yesterday we received a treat from jerries in the way of a cup of fresh milk. It went down well, tonight we had another treat of 1 ½ Canadian cigarettes.'

'Berlin fell at 3 o'clock on May 3, 1945.'

Harold did not make it to London or his home in Leeds until he was medically discharged later in 1945. He was taken to Brighton Hospital suffering with malnutrition and other complications. When he did finally get home at the end of the year he lived the rest of his life to the full. Eventually they all moved to London where he worked printing coupons! They later moved to Stoke and from there to Blackpool, Stoke, Torquay and back to Blackpool in later years.

My mum has asked me to mention that Grandad always marched on Remembrance Sunday and throughout his life gave blood as regularly as possible, he was always thinking of others.

I feel honoured to have had the chance to bring him back to life and give him the chance to tell his story. It wasn't until I started reading his diary that I realised he had been on the forced march and that he and others suffered horrendous treatment, starvation and freezing cold weather conditions. I can't tell you how many times I have shed tears, felt sad and angry that anyone should have to suffer in this way. My granddad and all the other prisoners are true heroes, their stories deserve to be heard and read by future generations.

I am proud to say Harold Latham was my granddad and my hero.

HENRY DAWKINS

By John Dawkins

I am the only son of Henry Lawrence Dawkins. I have two sisters. I was born in 1949, and lived on Canvey Island, near Southend on Sea in the county of Essex. I trained as a graphic designer and had a career in the advertising business, becoming a senior manager, whilst spending much of my free time as a painter of marine and landscape subjects. I was married to my first wife Margery for 37 years before her death 11 years ago. I have 3 grown up sons and 3 grandchildren. I now live in Suffolk with my second wife Theresa and I'm still painting in my spare time.

My father, Henry Lawrence Dawkins, was born in 1919 to an Essex based family of traditional farm workers. He grew up in tough times and was placed in an orphanage with two of his brothers in the late 1920s, due to the ravages of The Great Depression having a devastating effect on the fortunes of ordinary rural families, such as his parents' family, including their ten children. Subsequently he left school at 14 and worked as a lift boy at Harrods in London for a time. At age 18 in 1938

93

he decided to join the army. He failed in his application to join his local unit, the Essex Regiment due to its being oversubscribed, but was successful in being accepted as trainee rifleman in The Kings Royal Rifle Corps. This regiment had an illustrious history and is now part of The Rifles Regiment.

THE RIFLEMAN

When WWII began Henry was fully trained. He was in B Company, 2nd Battalion, when this unit was included in the formation of 30 Brigade which in May 1940 was sent by sea to Calais in order to divert German units heading for the beaches of Dunkirk. The entire British force consisted of about 3000 men and with 1000 French troops was charged with holding Calais for as long as possible. Brigadier Claude Nicholson, 30 Brigade's commander, at once set about organising a perimeter defence of the town. My dad's Company was detailed enthe western approaches of Calais against the advancing German armoured division.

FACING THE ENEMY

My dad never explained to me how he felt about the possibility of coming face to face with the enemy, but anecdotally, there is an account by Airey Neave in his book, *The Flames of Calais*, which goes some way to explain the gravity of the situation facing B Company. Neave was detailed to check how they were faring and could sense the fear expressed by the Company CO, Major Jack Poole. His tone of voice ably demonstrated their desperate position. At this time, my dad remembers the feared command, 'Fix Bayonets' being given. As it was they engaged advancing German infantry across the fields with rifle fire. My dad was very reticent when I asked him, as a young lad 'Dad, did you kill any Germans?'.

Brigadier Nicholson's strategy was to progressively fall back, by stages, to the centre of Calais. They were only buying time, and many knew there would ultimately be no rescue. My dad recalls helping set up roadblocks on the bridges over the canals that go around the town. These road locks were bitterly defended, with much loss of life on both sides over a two day period. Later, the men of B Company were holed up, taking respite in a town house from the battering by artillery shells, mortar rounds, and bombs from Stuka's overhead.

CAPTAIN SCOTT

Dad recalled that a certain major Henry Scott, probably trying to give the men something to occupy their thoughts at this juncture, gave them the task of tidying the basement they were taking cover in. Scott opened a door onto the street to help dispose of the rubbish gathered, just as a mortar round landed very close. My dad said Scott was wounded severely in the chest and abdomen but was still conscious. An ambulance was summoned, but as it arrived, its red cross emblazoned on its side did not save it from a direct hit from another mortar round. It was soon decided to evacuate the basement by the back door.

It must have been judged there was little hope of saving major Scott and with his mortal wounds he could not be moved. My dad volunteered to stay with Scott until he died however long that might be. Scott was going in and out of consciousness and when able engaged in conversation with dad, pleading with dad to save himself. It's hard to picture this moment. This somewhat, from dad's account, father figure of an officer, in his mid-thirties, and the young 21-year-old rifleman, who was to become my father nine years later. Dad never conveyed how this traumatic moment must have felt, and only expressed the bald facts to me when I was about ten years old. After an hour Scott passed away and dad started to think what he should do. He looked out into the backyard, where his colleagues had gone, and wondered how he would get over the eight-foot perimeter wall of the yard. After some minutes, he heard a voice from the other side, and was relieved to find that two of his mates had come back to rescue him. They leaned over the wall and helped pull him over. It was soon after this the brigade made its last stand at the Calais Citadel and the garrison surrendered. Dad became a POW with approximately 3000 other valiant defenders of the town.

BURYING THE DEAD

They were detailed to bury the dead, including horses, of the French Army. My dad drily said that the hole is never big enough to bury a horse. Even when the hole looks impossibly large, at least one leg of the poor animal protrudes above the ground.

They were then marched east, toward Germany, sometimes taking verbal abuse and being pelted with rotten vegetables by German civilians on the route. I recall him saying that the last part of the journey to **Stalag VIII-B** may have been by train.

STALAG VIII-B

My dad only talked of his war experiences infrequently. This POW camp was very large with most nationalities represented. He said the Germans tended to treat Allied POWs differently. Russians, Poles *et cetera* were treated very badly. French, Dutch *et cetera* were treated better. The British, Canadians and Australians were relatively treated the best. Dad said many of the German guards were as fed up with the war as the prisoners were. Serviceable relationships were possible with some of these guards usually in terms of trading Red Cross supplies *et cetera*. As a young lad I inevitably asked him if he hated the Germans. He said 'Just like us there are good Germans and bad Germans.' Then, of course, there were the SS.

THE SS

My dad had a brush with the SS on one of their periodical visits to the camp. He was standing at the edge of the roadway when a small, open SS staff car came speeding down the road towards him. He failed to get out of the way in time and his ankle was clipped by the car's tyre. The car came to a stop some yards down the road. Dad thought briefly this could be it. The four SS officers in the car turned their heads to look at him, but no pistols were drawn. They just laughed and sped away. Fortunately his ankle soon was on the mend after being bandaged in the camp hospital.

Another more serious medical trial was when he contracted rheumatic fever after a lung infection, no doubt made worse by the poor food, the cold, and the stress. It was so bad he was read the last rites, but he eventually came through. He never even told his wife of 33 years, my mother, this in his lifetime. We only found out years after he died when my mother, by chance met a woman whose husband had been in the same camp and remembered my dad's near death experience. This as a secret he had kept to himself. I think this may have contributed to his heart condition later in life. This illness could have been caused by the effects of another story Dad told me: Some bread was stolen in the

British compound and as punishment the Germans stood the whole camp out overnight in their ordinary day clothes – and this was midwinter.

BLECHHAMMER

Dad was in work party E3 at the enormous Blechhammer oil shale plant. He worked there as a labourer and the Germans spent years building this plant. As it was nearing completion in late 1944 my dad remembers the sound of a distant aircraft very high up in a clear sky. Aircraft, especially on their own, were a rare occurrence in these parts. In preparation for the grand opening of the plant, the Germans, following tradition, hoisted a Christmas tree to the highest tower in the plant, which is meant to bring good luck. It was announced that the plant would open soon. Two days before the plant opened the US Eighth Air Force came and obliterated the plant. Many of the prisoners, especially the former craftsmen like bricklayers and carpenters, wept when they saw their work being destroyed. People often react strangely, to our eyes, in these stressful environments. The lone aircraft had clearly been taking pictures, awaiting the plant's completion.

THE LONG MARCH

Early in 1945, rumours went round the camp that the Russians were getting close. It was announced that the camp would be evacuated to the west. Dad was in a group of around 2000 men marching west. Sleeping in barns, or fields on occasion, in what was a very cold winter. The supply of food was sporadic. Men who became ill or unable to keep up were left at the roadside or just 'disappeared'. Many German civilians would pass food to the prisoners, others would just throw abuse. The guards slowly deserted so eventually hundreds of men were only being guarded by a handful of Germans. Dad said they knew something was afoot and he and some of his mates began to think it would be easy to escape if they wanted to.

One morning they woke up and it seemed all the guards were gone! The POWs, as if automatons, just started marching again, evermore to the west. Later that same day a tank could be seen in the distance – an American tank. They were liberated. The US soldiers had brought new uniforms to replace the prisoner's rags. The prisoners were then taken in pairs to the local German town, where the residents were politely asked to feed the men and allow them to use their washing facilities and to stay until military transport could be provided.

My dad was very stoical about his experiences, as were so many of his generation. He was a quiet, gentle man, and showed no outward signs of trauma for the rest of his life. He died at the relatively young age of 61. My two sisters and I were completely unaware of the gravity of his experiences whilst we were growing up, but then again many dads in the 1950s had similar stories to tell: they are greatest generation.

JOHN GEOFF BRYDEN

By Bob Davison

Bob is Geoff's son in law. He is now retired after spending 40 years in the retail industry in a variety of roles, both in Scotland and internationally. Married to Shirley for 38 years they have a son Richard and a grandson called Max. They live in a little hamlet called Hollybush in the Doon valley of Ayrshire. Bob had always aspired to write and took his first tentative steps by penning a book of Geoff's experiences for his great grandkids. The book is titled Great Grandpa's War *and tells the story of Geoff's war from joining the TA in 1940.*

Geoff, as everyone called him, lived in a little town called Bonnybridge, near Falkirk, around 20 miles from Glasgow.

Heavy industry was still the main source of employment in the late 1930s and Geoff worked in an iron foundry as a moulder. Although this was steady work, he chose to study to be a draughtsman and spent two days a week at a college in Falkirk. He was 18. It was a ten-mile trip and he cycled there and back in the vagaries of the Scottish climate, never missing a day.

In April of 1939 he decided to enlist in the Territorial Army (TA). He recalled there being talk of war and the bravado of his young friends in response to the newspaper articles of events in Europe.

It seemed to Geoff that there was still a chance there could be peace as Prime Minister Chamberlain seemed keen to avoid having Britain dragged into a war with Germany.

The TA training camp in a small village called Callandar which was close to Falkirk and was named Camp Barry. Events moved fast that year and on 1 September 1939, Geoff and his TA colleagues were mobilised and moved by train to Aldershot.

On arrival they were issued with a standard British Army helmet, a Mark 3 Enfield rifle, 5 bullets and a pack which included a spade for digging trenches. Everyone in the camp was in high spirits and Geoff later recalled, 'They said we'd be home by Christmas. They just didn't say which one!'

At the end of January 1940, they were told to prepare to mobilise. They were heading to France. On a cold winter morning they boarded a ship at Southampton headed for Le Havre on the Normandy coast.

On the first night they were billeted in a warehouse and slept on the cold concrete floor. Early next morning they moved 97 kilometres southwest to the town of Cabourg.

Geoff recalled that the main concern for everyone at that time was keeping warm and they quickly figured that the best place was in the back of lorries retaining heat from one another.

He said it was a valuable lesson for what was to come.

One morning, they were awoken by someone banging on the side of their lorry.

Startled, the boys grabbed their rifles and opened the canvas to find an old Frenchman with a tray of hot coffee and sandwiches. Having thanked him in broken French they enjoyed the crusty loaf and laughed as to how close he had been to being shot!

Fairly soon they were on the move again, this time by train from Gare du Nord station at Dunkirk before arriving at a base near the town of Bethune.

Here the men were allocated to their respective companies.

Geoff was to be in the RAOC or Royal Army Ordnance Corp. There was much discussion about the various companies and their importance to the fight, but Geoff remembered thinking that recovering damaged tanks, lorries and artillery from a battlefield strewn with mines might not be the safest job in the army.

Nevertheless, spirits were still high and one day Geoff was driving a truck with men in the back when the steering went. The front wheels went left and the truck went right causing all the men in the back to exit with it.

Thankfully no one was hurt and everyone had a right good laugh at the scene.

Most of the boys were local lads and Geoff struck up a friendship with a lad from the town of Larbert, which is around three miles from Falkirk. His name was Tommy Dyer and his job was to ferry officers from the RAOC around in a motor bike and sidecar.

Geoff said Tommy would take stick for having a cushy number as he sat around smoking and waiting for orders for his next trip.

When Tommy was issued with his bike, there had been no crash helmets available and so when he was told to collect one from the supply barracks, he set off at once.

Sadly on his way, Tommy was in collision with another vehicle and died at the scene.

The irony of Tommy's death wasn't lost on Geoff and he and the rest of his company took some time to get over the loss of their friend who never even made it into battle.

As part of the British Expeditionary Force, Geoff and his company were moved close to the legendary Maginot line in the area of Alsace - Lorraine. They moved around the area freely and with no sign of any hostility in sight, the main priority was still to keep warm. Geoff and a group of friends heard that the mayor of the small town close to camp had gone to Paris and so they decided to borrow his house for a while to keep warm. It didn't take long till they were discovered but sitting in comfort in front of a roaring fire was great while it lasted.

'It was a strange time,' Geoff said. The Alsace Lorraine area had once been German and so the French people were used to having Germans as friends and neighbours.

It wasn't unusual to hear German being spoken on the same streets as French. There were tales of French soldiers crossing the Maginot Line to have drinks with their German counterparts and then the Germans doing the same the next week!

On 12 February 1940, the commander of the 51st Highland Division, Major General Fortune, ordered his men to a base 260 miles North near the town of St Pol. They were to support the French defences around the area of the Maginot line.

Of course everyone knew the line was impregnable such was the strength and ferocity of the artillery positions. Morale remained high with only reports of small skirmishes being passed between the men.

On 10 May, the atmosphere among the men changed as news of General Rommel's circumvention of the Maginot line through the Ardennes Forest filtered through, at first as rumours but then the shocking confirmation came.

Conversations of a reported French surrender abounded and there was concern as to what would happen next.

Ten days later Major General Fortune ordered the 51st to move to the town of Etain near the border with Luxembourg.

Unbeknown to the men, and despite Major General Fortune's displeasure, a deal had been struck to keep the French in the war and the men of the 51st were now under the command of the French General Besson.

The news of Belgium's surrender on 28 May further dented the morale of young men who by now knew they were in a deadly serious situation.

Fighting on a line of almost 30 miles from the Somme to the coast proved impossible and despite Major General Fortune mounting a brave counterattack on 4 June, the order was given to withdraw, retreat and evacuate around 23000 men at Le Havre.

Rommel quickly cut off that route of escape and Fortune was left with the only remaining option, a sea evacuation from the small fishing port of Saint-Valery-en-Caux.

By now the cold bitter Normandy winds had faded and Geoff remembered his first sight of Saint-Valery-en-Caux on a warm summer's morning. It was a pretty town flanked by high cliffs, with a harbour and an inlet which allowed smaller boats to berth deep in the town centre.

Talk of evacuation was still positive as news of Dunkirk filtered through the gossip and chat from the men. However by 10 June the Germans had surrounded the town and taken the cliffs overlooking the harbour and the sea.

Geoff vividly remembered resting in the summer sun in a little hamlet called Ville de Roses and watching French cavalrymen set off to fight Rommel's Panzer tanks. The Scots soldiers were amazed at their bravery.

When news passed that the Germans had broken through the British and French defences a mad dash into the town began. On arrival they watched French civilians evacuating their town. Lines of crestfallen women and children carrying anything they could, slowly made their way inland. Geoff remembered wondering where they would all go.

The remaining French soldiers were in really bad shape and the Scots shared what rations they had with the grateful men.

By now the town was in chaos and with the Germans shelling the town from the cliffs the only hope was the beach and rescue by ship. Stories of men tying their belts together to climb down the sheer 100 ft cliffs and falling to their deaths did little to raise hopes of them being saved.

As the town was pounded by heavy artillery shells, Geoff and some others were ordered to attack a chateau high on the outskirts of the town where German snipers were hiding. On arriving at the chateaux, they luckily found it unoccupied and after reporting what they had found, they were attached to a group tasked with destroying British Army vehicles to make them useless to the enemy. The irony of this and his role in the RAOC was not lost in the madness.

The last hope for the British was a withdrawal by sea under cover of darkness on 11 June. Sadly, heavy fog prevented the ships from getting close enough and though a few small ships recovered some men, the overall evacuation of the 51st proved impossible.

After days of shelling and bombing, the pretty seaside town was now a burning wreck and with British and French defences deteriorating the Germans entered the town with a force of 20000 men and 300 tanks.

The fighting was now street by street and with little ammunition Geoff and his mates holed up in an orchard waiting for the German infantry to arrive. Instead at 10a.m. on 12 June the message came that Major General Fortune had issued the order to surrender and that all men were to head for the town centre. On arrival, they were marched by the Germans towards the harbour where they saw Major General Fortune with General Rommel.

They noticed a young woman with the general and someone shouted, 'Who's the girl'? A voice quickly quipped, 'That's Miss Fortune,' which brought a laugh in the face of an unknown future. Geoff was just 20.

He called St Valery 'a disaster' and recounted later the humiliation felt by the soldiers captured that day. Unspoken feelings of letting down their country, missing family, fear of the unknown future and why they were in France quickly disappeared with the stark focus of simply staying alive. Geoff recalled that there was little talking amongst the men, just scattered glances and the odd word.

They were quickly organised into lines by the German infantry, five a breast, and were marched out of town, not one of them knowing their destination or destiny.

The optimists had expected to be saved by the navy while others believed they would all be killed. No one had considered surrender and capture

The famous 51st had been routed and captured far from home and the ignominy of that day would reverberate in British military and political history for years to come.

Any idea of early escape was quashed by the sight of heavily armed guards on either side of the column and machine gun trucks every 100 yards or so.

For reasons he always struggled to explain, Geoff dived behind a bush to hide only to have a bullet ping off the crown of his helmet which brought him back into the column sharpish.

The Germans seemed totally unprepared to take around 10000 men prisoner and as they marched in the warm French sun, food and water quickly became an issue. At every rest point, the men would jump into the fields to gather anything edible they could find.

Geoff managed at one point to rustle up some nettle soup which he said was absolutely horrible but even then he knew he had to consume whatever he could.

The first day was a 20 mile slog to the village of Yvetot, where they slept in open fields. The summer nights were cool but mainly dry, and talk was of home and family.

All were happy to be alive, but the conversation quickly moved to speculation about their fate and final destination.

Over the next few days, the column marched northeast through Abbeville, towards Amiens and Bethune through Lille, and finally into Tournai in Belgium. The men had not had a proper wash since their capture and they were pleased when taken to the local prison for a shower. The water was cold but it was welcome, nonetheless.

Hunger was becoming more of an issue and Geoff recalled French and Belgian people laying out bread and milk by the roadside, a generous gesture which he would never forget. Nor did he forget the sight of some German guards taking pot shots into the milk buckets for laughs.

The 'ration' from the Germans equated to half a loaf of stale bread every three days.

The weary men marched north through Belgium, passing through Aalst, Lokeren and Sint-Niklaas before finally crossing the border into Holland at Dordrecht, on the Thure River.

The Dutch people were as generous as the French and Belgians, passing out whatever they could and even trying to help one or two more intrepid men to escape.

For the most part though, it seemed most men were resigned to their fate and there was more talk of finding food than of escape.

At Dordrecht in early July, the men were loaded onto coal barges. Each barge had ten holds into which they squeezed approximately 100 men. It was a tight fit. Geoff said he remembered a huge vat of honey which was rationed at one spoonful a day. Of course there were no toilet facilities and with no stops, the men had to swing their backsides off the side of the barge to defecate. Always with a couple of mates at arm's length holding on!

Word got round that they were destined for Germany. A few quipped they were going to meet Hitler but the destination was the town of Wesel on the border of Holland and Germany.

As the barges travelled north up through the Rhine, they became a source of amusement for the passing cruise and pleasure boats filled with Germans enjoying a warm summer on the river.

Their laughs and scowls were met with similar retorts from the Jocks who were having to relieve themselves as they passed.

Geoff somehow managed to get hold of German language book and whiled away the hours learning as much German as he could, which he thought it would be useful in order to understand what the guards were saying. This spurred a voracious appetite for languages later in life as he picked up some Polish, Russian and latterly studied French at college.

On arrival at Wesel, they disembarked and Geoff vividly recalled the pretty, picturesque German villages which reminded him of trips to York in his childhood.

However in several villages, their welcome was pots of urine and faeces thrown from the windows as they passed. The people screamed, 'Englander!' and Geoff would quip that when the men responded that they were Scottish, that the pots were still being thrown!

Back on the march the men realised cattle barns were the warmest places to shelter at night. Unfortunately they weren't alone and pretty soon the column was infested with lice.

They were then herded onto trains. Once again, they were packed like sardines with nowhere to relieve themselves other than their helmets or a corner of the carriage. The heat, the smell and the itch from the lice quickly became unbearable and as the poor diet and lack of water kicked in, many men began to deteriorate.

After three long days, the train came to halt at Poznan in the north of Poland.

The men were delighted to breathe some fresh air at last but were quickly sobered at the first sight of the camp. The name on the gate was Stalag XX1-D, near the town of Warthelager (Biedrusko).

Pretty soon they were put to work filling in shell holes and they watched as Polish carpenters quickly built barrack huts.

Geoff and many of the men were then moved to their first POW camp in Szubin in the cold of north-east Poland. This camp was Stalag XX1-B. The Germans had commandeered a girls' school and turned it into a prison camp. The camp still retained its old look and feel with a main building of three floors painted white and surrounded by playing fields and vegetable gardens. The men remarked that it was quite pretty had it not been for the barbed wire fences and machine gun watchtowers on the perimeter!

They were told to gather in front of the main building and were greeted by the Camp Commandant. His name was *Oberstleutnant* von Bodecker.

He had lost a leg in battle in the first world war and wore a monocle. In a very stern voice to an exhausted and silent audience he announced, '*Fur dich ist der krieg vorbei*'. For you the war is over.

They were told to strip and line up to shower. They were completely shaved and de-loused. Geoff remembered the strange confliction of feeling dehumanised against the pleasure of being clean and free of lice.

They were all given new clothes and were photographed and fingerprinted. Each man was given their individual POW number. Geoff's was Stalag XXI-B/6666. At least that wouldn't be difficult to remember.

Each man was allocated a card to send home to say they were being treated well.

They were allocated barrack huts with 20 men to each hut. Small wooden slatted beds offered at least some comfort but as ever the priority was food. The general offering was soup made from old fish bits which initially the men described as inedible. Fairly soon they wolfed it down as quickly as it arrived.

It took some time for some level of organisation and routine to be established, but soon it was clear that enlisted men would be expected to work, while officers would not.

One of Geoff's first tasks was to pick sugar beet from the fields to supply the local syrup factory.

Sunday was not regarded as a day of rest and when some men objected to working on religious grounds, they were told they would be shot if they refused. None did.

The men smuggled anything they could to eat back to the barracks as the lack of nutritious food began to tell on their health. Most men had outbreaks of boils and cysts with risk of further infection a constant issue.

Once the beet harvest was picked, Geoff and his colleagues were set to work in the factory itself. As the summer sun disappeared, there was at least, some comfort in being indoors and the opportunity to swallow some syrup from the vast funnels and vats on the production line.

It was risky, and Geoff recalled an elaborate system of lookout duty, enabling men to take turns quickly sticking their mouths under the dripping funnels.

The factory was manned by some German guards and Polish administrators. One day there was an unusual commotion and Geoff was dragged away from his work with two other POWs up a steel staircase to the factory managers office. The two other men were dragged in first and Geoff could see two German officers, the factory manager, and a young woman in the room.

By the time it was his turn he could tell the young woman was being asked questions about the men, and he understood that the woman was being asked if he was the man who had tried to rape her.

As preposterous as this sounded, the girl nodded with shame and was indicating that it was indeed Geoff who had attacked her. He of course protested his innocence and was only released when he dropped his trousers to show a large cyst on the end of his manhood proving any sexual activity to be impossible.

The work details were at least varied and Geoff was happy to be away from the syrup factory. He and a few mates were ordered on a regular basis to clear the houses of local Polish people. In broken conversations with locals they became aware of the use of concentration camps for Polish Jews and their families.

He recalled that even in their own situation, most of the men clearing those homes felt a deep sadness when removing all traces of a family who had been there days before.

After some time the message came that they were to move to another camp. They travelled around 240 miles to the village of Lamsdorf, to the camp they would know as Stalag V111-B/344. On arrival they were given a spoon, a fork, a mess tin, two blankets and a thin straw mattress which Geoff said contained more fleas than straw!

Every morning and evening the men would be made to parade for *appell*, in order that the guards could do their count. The Germans regularly barked the word '*kriegsgefangener*', which means prisoner of war, and the men quickly nicknamed themselves 'kriegies' for short.

Initially rations were no better than the other camps, but thankfully after a few weeks, Red Cross parcels began to arrive. In the early stages, the parcels would arrive, and there was only enough for six men to share one parcel every two weeks. They were simple shoe boxes wrapped in brown paper, but the contents were like gold for the starving malnourished men. There was tea, sugar, dried milk, butter, corned beef, sardines, cheese jam and biscuits and a bar of Cadbury's chocolate.

All were meticulously measured to ensure everyone had their share, but as much as the food was important, the consignment of 50 cigarettes in the box was manna from heaven for most! Geoff was not a smoker but took his share anyway in order that he could barter for extra food with the men, and sometimes even the guards.

As time wore on, escape attempts were becoming a more regular occurrence and Geoff recalls some guards taking the Red Cross parcels and emptying the contents into buckets in order that it couldn't be kept as rations for escapees. This kind of petty nonsense really angered the men but they painstakingly worked through the mix to make use of every last bit.

In later life, the family would marvel at Geoff's determination that he would never throw anything away and would never ever leave a morsel on his plate at dinner.

Once again, the men were allocated to work details, some of which were well away from the main camp at Lamsdorf. The men became familiar with another German phrase, *arbeitskommando*, which meant working party.

The preferred choice in summer was on farms in the fresh air and where a little bit of extra food would sometimes become available. Geoff was therefore less than happy to be allocated to Arbeitskommando E30 Oppelyn outside the town of Opole, some 25 miles from Lamsdorf. The work was in the local cement factory and was physically exhausting manual labour from morning until late evening. Geoff didn't last very long at Opole as in his first week a large steel washer became detached from one of the machines and crushed the big toe of his left foot. He was quickly transferred back to Lamsdorf for treatment.

Letters from home began to arrive sometime late in 1941. *Kriegsgefangenenpost* must have been an enormous boost to the men's morale and the system seemed to work well as Geoff received letters right through each camp until they left Lamsdorf. All were meticulously censored and allowed to contain only news of friends and family, but even this must have been heart-warming, knowing they had not been forgotten back home. On occasion they would receive parcels of clothing from home but these came so irregularly that the men suspected the Germans of stealing them.

There was little respite and when Geoff was able to walk again, he was attached to a work detail in another syrup factory number E283 in the town of Ratibor with a group of nine other men. Eight of his fellow workers were Jews from Palestine captured in North Africa. The odd one out was a terrified young lad who was an Arab from Aden.

The lad was the butt of jokes and general abuse from the others and eventually Geoff decided enough was enough. He took the lead bully aside and warned him if they carried on, there would be repercussions from the British back at the camp.

For the remainder of their time at Ratibor, the young lad acted like an unofficial batman to Geoff fetching and carrying just about everything he could. This didn't sit well with Geoff who tried to explain that 'We are all Jock Tamson's bairns.' This is a well-known Scottish saying that held that all men are born equal. But it was to no avail. Geoff often wondered what became of his young Arab pal.

After a time, life in the camp developed a strange normality, with regular *appells*, daily work details, and the constant foraging for a bit of extra food. Spare time was filled with any number of activities that could be arranged under the confines of captivity.

Geoff was a keen cricketer and long summer days in Poland took his game to a level where he opened batting for Uddingston cricket club after the war.

In an attempt to have a break from the hard labour of the work parties, Geoff decided to take on the persona of an NCO and for a few memorable days, he supervised work details, played cricket, and took German classes. This fine little ruse ended abruptly when Staff sergeant Coward questioned him on how he became a corporal. Geoff said it had been a field promotion as his NCO had been killed in battle. Sadly, Sergeant Coward said the Germans didn't believe him and he was sent back to the quarters with the rest of the squaddies.

Generally, the mood in the camp was one of resignation and boredom. Occasionally however, there would be an incident to set the men off. Geoff remembered one sunny afternoon when he and a group of other POWs were leisurely picking beets in a field.

The sound of birdsong and a whistling breeze was shattered by the noise of an uncovered truck which was heading up the adjacent farm track.

As it approached the men in the back were laughing, jeering, and shouting insults in Italian at the boys in the field. The men retorted in good fashion and suddenly the truck came to a screeching halt. The Italians piled out of the truck and a melee ensued. Geoff said they took a real pasting from the British boys, and the German guards had to intervene by pointing their rifles. This raised morale and gave the men some laughs for the next few days.

The officers made sure that out with the work details there was plenty to keep the men busy. Football, boxing and even choir singing kept the men from the unknown future of life behind the wire so far from home. By now though, escape was something that became an interest for some and an obsession for others.

Senior officers had formed an escape committee to maintain some order to the plans and Geoff explained that through time everyone was made to understand that captured pilots would be the priority for escape.

Around September 1942, word got around that the committee was looking for volunteers. Geoff and a man called Phillips passed the word that they would be willing to help.

The plan was for Geoff and Phillips to swap identities with the two pilots who were to escape. They were told nothing of the plan other than the name of the two pilots. One was the famous fighter pilot, Douglas Bader. Apparently Bader had been captured minus his legs and out of respect the Germans had agreed to have a new set dropped by parachute into France where they would be transported to Lamsdorf.

Unfortunately they didn't arrive on schedule and it was decided that two Royal Canadian air force pilots would go instead.

The man with whom Geoff was to swap identities with was a Flight Sergeant Moran. They were told to learn name rank and serial number by heart in case they were asked any questions by 'the ferrets', German guards assigned to sniff out any sign of an escape plan and thwart it at source.

On the appointed day, the men swapped camps and working parties under the noses of the guards. Geoff took his place in the more comfortable surroundings of the officers' barracks but only the next day was unceremoniously dragged away by the guards. He was taken to a room and interrogated by a tall Ukrainian guard in the presence of a young male secretary who was taking notes. Geoff kept up the pretence of being Sergeant Moran well and it was only during his third interrogation that the secretary interrupted and asked Geoff to lift his shirt. It transpired that Sergeant Moran had an appendix scar which Geoff did not and the game was up.

His sentence was 14 days in the 'cooler'. The cooler cells were bunkers approximately eight feet high by eight feet wide. There were no windows and in the late summer of 1942 they certainly weren't cool.

Geoff's cell had marks scraped on the wall in five bar gates. The guard was a grim, angry character and the cooler rations were even worse than the fish soup in Camp One.

The walls were pockmarked, etched with names and dates, and the guard explained to him that a section with five bar gates was by a British pilot boasting of how many Germans planes he'd shot down.

With his now decent command of German, Geoff calmly explained that the marks were in fact the number of flies the inmate had killed, and not in fact the work of a pilot.

From there they began a short friendship in which the guard told Geoff that he was from Hamburg and had lost his wife and three children to the British and Allied bombing in January of that year. Even in his confinement, Geoff could understand how the devastation of war would have driven this man to hate all pilots.

As they chatted in German about their lives and family, the rations improved and soon Geoff was released from the bunker, never to see the guard again.

On return, he learned that although the two Canadian pilots had escaped the camp successfully, they had been stopped by a local town policeman for cycling up a one-way street and immediately returned to the camp!

In March of 1943, Geoff was moved to a new work party at the Arturgrube coal mine E565 near the town of Seirza-Wodna which was situated between Katowice and Krakow in the area of Poland known as Upper Silesia.

While working at the mine, Geoff made friends with a Polish man called Tadek Godyn, a foreman whose job was to organise the work parties. Tadek was 27 years old and lived in the village of Krystrynka, close to the camp where his mother ran a general store.

The local people held no love for the Germans and Tadek would regularly smuggle sandwiches, meat, and cheese into the mine via a hidden compartment in the sole of his large rubber boots. In return, Geoff would trade his unwanted cigarette ration for chocolate and would pass this to Tadek. The Germans would regularly conduct inspections and there would have been severe punishment for Tadek had he been caught.

Despite the hardships faced by the men, Geoff recalled many small acts of human kindness and wherever possible, Tadek would allow Geoff extra time in the bathing area than the Germans allowed.

By this time, Red Cross parcels were arriving more regularly and some POWs were trading tea for vodka with the Poles. The Poles then traded the tea for cigarettes with the Germans.

Later that year, a rumour spread around the camp that some men were being repatriated on medical grounds. Geoff recalled one clever 'kriegie' who feigned mental illness by making a cardboard dog from a Red Cross parcel and walking it around the compound twice a day. Bizarrely the Germans fell for it and he was sent home!

That winter was tough but with the combination of Red Cross parcels and extra food from Tadek, the time passed without any further drama. By now the ingenuity of the captured pilots meant that information on the war was coming through via homemade radios and thoughts were beginning to turn to how and when their captivity would end.

Positive news was balanced with stories of *Gestapo* and SS soldiers murdering groups of POWs and many thought that the Germans would invariably kill all remaining prisoners. Long nights were spent debating the possible last days.

By January 1945, Geoff and the men at the mine were aware of the Allied incursions in the west but more and more concerned by the Russian approach from the east.

One cold morning, the Germans rounded up the men and told them to collect all their belongings. They were on the move; they just didn't know where. The only indication was the distant sound of Russian artillery coming from the east and the German soldiers were in a real hurry.

With his knowledge of German, Geoff said the guards were sure they would be shot on sight by the Russians and were even more terrified at the prospect of being captured.

Either at the coal mine or back at Lamsdorf, Geoff and the men grabbed just about everything they could carry, stuffing food down their coats in the knowledge that they were soon likely to be back to basic rations.

Some men fashioned sledges out of wood, but still there was some food left behind from what had been reserved from the Red Cross parcels. Rather than leave it to waste, some men headed for the part of the camp which was reserved for Russians, and men of other nationalities not covered by the Geneva convention. The men there were in terrible shape, mere skeletons in rags. Geoff was told that when the extra food was launched over the wire, there was a horrible inhumane battle for any scraps that could be had such was the hunger.

The Germans then announced that any attempted escape from the column would result in summary execution.

They marched the men in columns of 1000 with guards every hundred yards or so on either side. Geoff's column started east towards Katowice while other groups trudged off in different directions. Most men had their greatcoats on and wore makeshift gloves and hats they had made during the long winters in captivity.

On the first day, Geoff's friend Tadek had decided there may be an opportunity to help him escape from the column. Unfortunately, one of the guards who supported Manchester United walked alongside Geoff because he could speak German and could talk about football back home!

On the first night they slept in barns. They were reasonably warm, packed together as they were with the animals and guards.

There was no time for *appell* in the morning so the German guards would stick bayonets into the hay to make sure no one was trying to escape. Occasionally, the Germans would set them on fire as their discipline began to break down.

At any time, groups of stragglers would join from paths adjacent to the main route and the column would swell almost on a daily basis. Most were totally ill-equipped to walk in the harsh Polish winter wearing only thin uniforms given by their captors.

For many the cold was too much and as the days wore on, more and more would be left by the side of the road to their fate.

Later when Tadek wrote to him and told him of his failed escape plan, Geoff learned of the fate of a friend from Lamsdorf, a New Zealand squaddie called Alan Carson. It transpired on that first night, Alan had decided to find a quiet spot in a pigsty adjacent to the main barn and snuggled up between the hogs and the sows for the night. Such was his comfort that when he awoke, the column had gone without him!

Tadek recalled a foul-smelling man arriving at his farm and asking for help. He sheltered him until later the Russians arrived when he was helped to return home.

The cold and hunger were not the only dangers on the march. The threat from the sky came from Russian planes who would see the convoy as retreating German columns rather than Allied prisoners. Geoff recalls everyone diving into ditches as the planes strafed the road.

The German guards were usually first and Geoff said you had to be careful not to land on an upturned bayonet when they dived for cover.

Thousands of Russian POWs and Jews were also marching west and Geoff recalled the terrible sight of hundreds of black specks in the snow where they had succumbed to the cold in the night. Some guards dropped to the back of the column and the men heard shots fired as the weak were dispatched. Some said it was murder, others that it was mercy.

The *hauptman* in charge of the column was a former WW1 POW and he sat in a horse-drawn carriage with his wife and daughter, unaware of the summary executions being carried out far behind him.

It seemed to the men that the Germans didn't know which route to take as they marched the column south of Katowice and into the Tatra mountains of Czechoslovakia.

Temperatures were dropping to -25 degrees Celsius in the strong winds and it now simply became a battle to survive. As they trudged towards the city of Ostrava, local farmers would pass out any spare food to the starving column of men. Geoff said the farmers would be mobbed as soon as they came into sight.

Most evenings the German officers would head for a local village and mark a barn with a white cross designating where they would sleep for the night. Any food was now shared equally between guards and prisoners alike.

Everyone was starving. Including the guards.

Usually they would walk 20-30 miles a day in what has since been described as one of the worst Eastern European winters in history. Despite this, men would regularly sneak away from the column to find food. On one occasion Geoff and a group of POWs were walking through a village when they were stopped by a German *feldwebel*, who took them to another farm where cooks were boiling potatoes for the next day's rations.

They ate their fill but noticed the cooks were having more than their share. After being taken to an adjacent barn and alerting the other POWs of what the greedy cooks were up to, they started a riot before slipping away to their own barn!

Geoff recalled he and five others stealthily leaving the barn one night to head for the local hamlet. Thankfully the villagers were welcoming and invited them into their home. They served the starving squaddies warm bread and soup and toasted the president of Czechoslovakia with a glass of the local drink called *Becherovka*, which is a mix of strongspirits infused with herbs. Being unusually teetotal, Geoff nevertheless joined in as a thanks for the hospitality.

On the way back to the barn, shots rang out and they all dived into a ditch near the river. Quietly, they headed along the riverbank where they were spotted by two Czech policemen who had been sent to look for them. Geoff's good pal, Jock Buchanan (a Royal Scots Guardsman), shouted to rush them to grab their guns but by now Geoff had another rifle in his ribs and told Jock to stand down. They were marched to the village police station and held for the night. On the way one of the policemen apologised for capturing them and said he had no choice or the Germans would have taken reprisals against him and his family.

The next morning German guards arrived to take them back to the column. They had discussed after being captured whether they would be shot. Thankfully the guards were now thinking about their own fate if captured by the Allies.

On leaving the prison, they saw the body of a man lying in the courtyard. Geoff recognised him as one of their party. He was a squaddie who had worked at the Savoy hotel in London before the war. He had been shot by the Czech police at the river.

It all seemed so pointless.

Jock and Geoff walked together most days. Geoff recalled one day the two of them slipping slowly to the back of their column with a sledge, to discover there were no guards around. While considering their best means of escape, they were spotted by four Czech policemen out for a stroll and returned to the column. He noted how smart they looked in their uniforms.

On another evening near Lidice, where the massacre of 500 civilians had taken place, Geoff and two others entered a house where villagers were playing cards. Geoff spoke to them in German asking for any spare food. The Czechs looked at them suspiciously and later explained that the *Gestapo* were visiting houses, pretending to be British POWs, to root out any collaborators.

Every day seemed endlessly cold and bleak. Geoff wrote, 'The situation is desperate. We are all starving to death, there's no food and the guards are in the same position.'

The *hauptman's* horse had become a bag of bones, collapsed, and died. What was left of it was consumed by the starving men.

One morning in the high mountain country of Czechoslovakia, they began another day slowly making their way through the heavy snow. Geoff was a Presbyterian man, and he remembered praying for relief from his ordeal that day. Fairly soon at the top of a steep mountain track, the clouds cleared and they were enveloped in the heat of brilliant sunshine. The view down the hill into the valley of Friedenthal was a beautiful sight.

One which improved even more when someone spotted Red Cross vans in the valley below. Geoff said it felt like someone had answered his prayers.

With some food in their bellies and a welcome rest from the freezing mountain range, the march continued through the Karlovy Vary region until the column reached Weiden on the German border.

Long after, Geoff would write his grateful thanks to the brave Czech people who fed them with anything they could on the march across the mountains.

Mercifully, the men were now boarded onto trains with open wagons heading west to the town of Regensburg. Men huddled together to keep warm against the wind and snow as the train tore through the wintry East German border country.

Again they were strafed by the RAF and Geoff remembers three guards being killed in one attack. He said no one celebrated this. It was only by chance they had survived.

At Regensburg they were made to work breaking up stones between the railway sleepers on half rations. Later during another air raid on the column, an old German guard clumsily pushed men into a barn to evade the fighters above them. He accidentally fired a shot in the air which ricocheted off the roof of the barn and hit his good friend, Jock Buchanan.

After all his time in the camp and through the worst of the march, he had been killed by a stray bullet. The guard was devastated at what had happened and was led away, inconsolable, by his colleagues. It all just seemed so desperately pointless and unfair.

Soon after, they were back on the march to a town north of Munich, called Landshut, which had been wrecked by bombing. It reminded Geoff of St Valery; such was the level of destruction. Train carriages were standing vertical where they had been bombed and there wasn't a building left untouched. That night Geoff met with some Canadian POWs who had Red Cross parcels. They ate their fill and drank so much coffee they couldn't sleep.

The next day they had just started a brew when another fighter appeared and peppered the ground with bullets. They all scattered and luckily no one was hurt. The Billie can was the only casualty. There was no tea that morning.

After that little encounter, the men took to painting red crosses on top of any buildings they used in order that they would avoid being killed by their own air force!

On 29 April 1945, their Long March was finally over and they were directed to an area to await the arrival of the US Army. While waiting for the Americans, they wandered the German countryside and farms finding food which they distributed among the hundreds of displaced people from the march.

118

They had walked for 99 days and covered 1200 kilometres in the worst winter of the century. Miraculously they had survived.

Geoff had been a prisoner of war for four years and 11 months.

The Americans moved the POWs to an airfield near Strauben. While they were waiting to be flown home, he watched the German soldiers being marched into captivity and said it was a marvellous sight. He nonetheless retained sympathy for their plight remembering the same emotions back in France, five long years ago.

While at the base the Americans told the men that there were still German soldiers hiding in the countryside around the base. The word was that for every German caught they could have 'K' ration. A 'K' ration was a box containing breakfast, dinner and supper and a bit of extra food was always welcome.

Pretty soon Geoff and a mate found two young Germans hiding in a forest. They were tired, dishevelled, and hungry. Geoff said they were no more than 15 years old.

Rather than take them into the camp. Geoff spoke to them in German and ordered them to remove their uniforms and join the line of refugees leaving the area. Even as young as 25, they could see the futility of taking two kids prisoner but laughed at the thought of being hungry later and regretting their decision.

Fairly soon Geoff was flown in a Dakota aircraft back to Tangmere air base in the South of England. Even then his luck had held as on arrival they were told the previous plane had crash-landed, killing all on board.

They were deloused again, given new clothes and any elation on being home was dashed when told that they had six months leave before being shipped off to Burma to fight the Japanese!

When I first met Geoff on marrying his daughter Shirley, he was a quiet man full of Presbyterian dignity and, it seemed, quite a stern disposition. He never discussed his experience in the war at any family gathering, but Shirley recalls him watching *The World at War* religiously after church on a Sunday. Of course, while in captivity, he had no idea how the war had been fought and won, and only later in the camp would the odd rumour reach the men.

Gradually, in his eighties, I spent more time with him and my interest seemed to spark him into telling his story. Initially, it came in bits and pieces but thankfully he would later give more detail in his interview for the British War Museum.

In his nineties, his status as a local celebrity was enhanced by stories in the press around Remembrance Day, and his piece in Craig McAlpine's documentary, *Dunkirk: The Forgotten Heroes*.

We would see his monthly magazine from the brilliant 'Not Forgotten Society' and through their auspices, I was proud to take him on a trip to Buckingham Palace to meet Her Majesty the Queen. In an amazing coincidence, the Queen explained that her cousin John Rhodes had also been captured at the battle of St Valery, and the two had quite a chat to the consternation of the Equerry in charge!

Never once in all my many conversations with Geoff was he critical of the enemy.

He maintained that there were good and bad Germans as there were good and bad Scotsmen and even when in my naivety I would rail against the French, he would quickly rebuke me and put me right.

To the end, in his heart, he was a soldier. I think in his later years he was prouder than ever and never missed a Remembrance Day parade with us, and even a week before dying of sepsis, he insisted in going on his last parade in a wheelchair, as guest of honour.

Like them all he was a truly remarkable man.

LT COLONEL DR BOGDAN STOJIĆ

By Irina Dimitric

Born and bred in former Yugoslavia, Irina Dimitric migrated to Australia with her family in 1964. In 2014, she published a book of poetry, Dreams on My Pillow, *reflecting her love for both Australia and her home country. In 2018, she published the first edition of* Full Circle: My Dad, a volunteer in World War I, *followed by the second edition in 2020.*

My dad's life story is a story of the 20th century Europe with all its upheavals and human suffering as well as human triumph over that suffering.

I was six years old when my father disappeared from my young life in 1941. He would be absent for four years. That evening when he came to my bedroom to kiss me good-bye, he was wearing his army uniform. It was the first time I saw him in uniform. With a smiling face he said he would soon be back, but I cried myself to sleep, clutching my white teddy bear. I was old enough to understand that a man in army uniform meant there was trouble in the wings. I was scared. Would I ever see him again?

After the war, my mother claimed she was convinced that he would come back. How could she have been so sure? I am tempted to think that she deliberately chose optimism to remain sane. Dad, too, never gave in to despair in the POW camp. He was called up on 2 April and left Zagreb on 6 April 1941, the day Hitler bombed Belgrade. On 10 April, the Nazis occupied Zagreb, our hometown, and The Independent State of Croatia was proclaimed. Luckily, my dad was already far away in Bosnia.

On 2 April 1941, Bogdan was mobilised into the Yugoslav Army and as a medical lieutenant-colonel in reserve appointed commander of the 44th Division Field Hospital. He was captured by the Germans at Doboj in Bosnia on 15 April and sent in cattle trucks to a POW camp in Lamsdorf for three months. There he got his doggie tag Stalag VIII-B/ Number 19522 and lost 10 kg on a very meagre prisoners' diet.

How lucky for Dad to have been captured by the Germans! Had the new Croatian government got hold of him, I would have lost my father. As a Serb and a volunteer in the Serbian Army in WWI, he was the enemy of the new Croatian state, along with Jews, Gypsies and Croatian communists. He would have been executed on the spot or transported to one of the concentration camps, possibly tortured first and then shot, thrown into the Sava to join hundreds of corpses on their journey out of the bloodstained home.

Dad was born to Serb parents in 1893, in Delnice, a small town in Croatia, a province of the Austro-Hungarian Empire. He finished high school in Novi Sad where he was imbued with Serb patriotism, thus interrupting his medical studies at Graz University twice to volunteer in two Balkan wars (1912-13). When WWI broke out, he was conscripted into the Austro-Hungarian Army and sent to the front. But, unwilling to fight against his own people, he took a risk and crossed the frontline to join the Serbian Army in October 1914 during the Battle of Drina. He was sent to serve with the 5th Red Cross Hospital in Niš.

Although the Serbian Army pushed back the Austro-Hungarians in three battles in 1914, the Serbs were not able to withstand the fierce attacks by the combined Austrian and German Armies in 1915. The Serbian Army was forced into retreat across the Albanian rugged mountains in the harsh winter of November and December, when thousands of Serbs died from exhaustion, disease and malnutrition, and thousands more at Corfu. That was his first long march. He was 22 years old.

Bogdan came through safe and sound and instead of accepting the French Government's offer of repatriation to continue his medical studies, he chose to serve in the Russian Imperial Army.

For his bravery to care for the wounded under fire, in Riga in July 1916, he was awarded the St George Cross twice. He continued his medical studies at Moscow University whenever on leave. During the Bolshevik revolution he was arrested for wearing the Imperial uniform but released on producing his Serbian passport. He left Russia in March 1918 on an epic journey via Siberia, Vladivostok, Shanghai and Port Said back to the Salonika front, after an anxious six-day crossing from Port Said across the submarine-infested Mediterranean. He worked there at the Prince Alexander Hospital until the end of the war when the Kingdom of Serbs, Croats and Slovenes came into being.

His medical studies were continued at the Universities of Rome, Bern and Vienna from where he graduated on 11 May 1922. His aim was to become a surgeon, and to this end he first worked as assistant for 4 years to Professor Saltykov, a Russian, at the Institute of Pathological Anatomy in Zagreb. In 1927 he trained as a surgeon in the Zagreb State Hospital. In 1928 he met my mother, his wife Maruša, of Ljubljana, and they were married in 1932. I was born in 1935, their only child.

Eager to increase his surgical skills, Bogdan worked with surgeons in Vienna, Paris, Berlin and most notably with the world-renowned Professor René Leriche of Strassburg, who had a profound influence on his medical career, introducing him to Neural Therapy, a treatment using local anaesthetic as an alternative to surgery for many complaints.

I discovered much later in life, when he was already in Australia, the full story of his wartime life in both World wars.

From September 1941 to September 1942, he was in Teschen Stalag VIII-D. Very soon after his arrival in Teschen the Germans offered him a post of chief surgeon in one of their military hospitals with approval to conduct private practice and a promise to get his family, his wife and his young daughter, to join him. He declined their offer telling them that the prisoners needed him and that, anyway, this war would end the same way as did the first! This kind of cheekiness wouldn't go down well with the Gestapo.

In the camp hospital he did his best to sabotage by keeping healthy men in hospital under false diagnoses. This is how he describes it: 'In my surgical ward 90% of patients were healthy men. The German chief surgeon, a major from Breslau, was very kind to the prisoners. He not only turned a blind eye to my machinations but actively prompted me to help him repatriate French prisoners on the grounds of my fabricated diagnoses. The prisoners came to my room in groups of ten and noted down the symptoms of their respective illnesses which they had to learn by heart. The kind *Oberarzt* then examined them in my presence quite superficially and recommended 250 Frenchmen for repatriation.'

While these lucky men went home to France, one of the Frenchmen from Teschen wrote to his mates in another *arbeitskomando* to feign illness, to come to Teschen where a Serb doctor would help them get repatriated. The *Gestapo* intercepted that letter, the kind *oberartzt* was immediately dismissed and Dr Stojic put in prison on 4 July 1942, accused of trying to stage an insurrection in the camp and being an open enemy of *Grossdeutschland*. After a month in prison, he was brought before a judge of the Division Court from Katowice, by the name of Jelinek, a peace time lawyer from Vienna.

Before Judge Jelinek appeared, he was taken into the room by a captain, a high-school teacher who was not a Hitler sympathiser, now a judge in the army. A very fine gentleman, Dad remembers with gratitude. As soon as Dad entered the room, he saw a young woman sitting at a table with a typewriter. She was crying and shaking. The kind captain took her out of the room, and when he returned, he gave Dad the document in which the *Gestapo* charged him with a grave offence against the Third Reich. Article 104.

Execution by shooting. That was what the young woman saw. She was so distressed that she wasn't able to type.

Judge Jelinek then said he would take notes himself. During questioning he found out that he had studied in Vienna with the daughter of the accused's father's friend, became quite friendly and immediately ordered that the accused be released. The *Gestapo* was not at all pleased and requested that Stojic be punished by sending him to the Russian camp in Hammersdorf, near Sagan, where daily 50 prisoners were dying from dysentery, and 50 new patients were being admitted. They were probably hoping the open enemy of *Grossdeutschland* would contract the disease and perish. But my father was made of stern stuff.

After six months, due to his knowledge of foreign languages, he was transferred to a hospital in Cosel, the Abyssinian Lager, in Upper Silesia, to take charge of 300 sick Russians, 100 Frenchmen, 100 British prisoners and about 10 Serbs. The hospital was under the command of *Oberstabsarzt* Preyss and run by Captain Dr R. Kaye-Webster. Bogdan recalls:

'The hospital was very well equipped so that we were able to perform stomach resection, craniotomies, and so on. When the German surgeon in their army hospital was not up to the task, he would call me to operate on seriously injured Germans. Each time I went there, I'd get from the nuns, in secrecy, all kind of medical supplies and medicines that I'd bring back for our patients. The operations I performed were very complicated aneurysms, but they were all successful.'

Dr R. Kaye-Webster writes: 'His surgical skills brought him much kudos, for in 1944 even the Nazi SS sought his services… In a German officer shot in the buttocks, the German surgeon made an incision thinking it was an abscess. It was an aneurysm of the gluteal vessel…Stojic was brought in a hurry to find the source of bleeding. He plugged the wound, turned the patient on his back, opened the abdomen, tied the internal iliac artery, and gave him 700 ml blood transfusion. The patient, who was pulseless and had stopped breathing, recovered. His most poignant moment was when the patient's German wife visited with her daughter and pointed to Stojic saying, 'There is the enemy doctor who saved your father's life.'

Dad mentions in his notes that Lazaret Cosel was a hospital for show to impress the International Red Cross in Geneva whose representatives

125

visited them every three months. A Russian prisoner who was a living skeleton put on 30 kg in two months. They were even allowed to play soccer twice a week. And they had two fox-terriers named Whisky and Soda. In one of his letters Dad promised to bring one of them home for me.

The Long March – Stalag VIII-B/344 – January-April 1945

(Southern Route: from Stalag VIII-B (formerly Stalag VIII-D) at Teschen (not far from Auschwitz) which led through Czechoslovakia, towards Stalag XIII-D at Nuremberg and then onto Stalag VII-A at Moosburg in Bavaria. Wikipedia.)

Lt Colonel Dr Bogdan Stojić, was in the group with Captain Dr Norman Rose (Australian), Captain Dr Roland Kaye-Webster (British), Captain Dr T. Atkins (Australian), Lieutenant Dr Jacques Rigal (French) and Private Frank Hebbard (Australian), medical orderly.

Bogdan writes in his notes: 'On 21 January 1945, about 10 a.m., we received this order: 'All patients who can walk and all doctors should get ready to start marching in 2 hours.' Our medical orderlies, Frank Hebbard from Australia among them, went to the German hospital, already abandoned, and they brought back a large cart onto which we loaded all the Red Cross parcels we had in storage. On a small sledge, manufactured in a hurry, we put our personal belongings and pulled the sledge all the way. The Germans were forcing us to walk 197 kilometres through Sudetenland to Braunau. We stayed in Braunau two weeks. Every day I visited a factory where the Russian POWs worked. They were all sick. Poor people, I saw them cook soup in discarded tins; soup made from rabbit hide they found in rubbish bins. Dr Norman Rose and I asked the German doctor to let us stay with the Russians to look after them – in fact, what we counted on was that the Russian Army would liberate us in a few days – lucky for us, he didn't let us stay.

'In Braunau we were lodging in a Methodist church. From Braunau the Germans sent us by train, in cattle trucks, to Nuremberg via Prague. As I spoke Russian, I was appointed chief surgeon at the Russian POW camp, where they had 14 doctors but no surgeon. I stayed at the International Hospital but went every day to the Russians to work.'

'On 17 April, American tanks entered the camp, liberating us.

126

'Two days after liberation, an American doctor came to see me, asking me to help them eradicate the epidemic typhus that plagued the Russians; there were about 500 cases. In the American Army there were no epidemic typhus cases because all American soldiers had been vaccinated. The Germans suffered the most - they were infected by the Russians. The Americans offered me to join their army. I would get a salary and they would recognise my rank of lieutenant-colonel and would immediately promote me to colonel, and after two or three years I would become a general in the American Army. I worked with them until the day I decided to go back home to Yugoslavia; I worried about my wife and my daughter as I'd had no news from them for a long time. On 22 June 1945, I set off in the Mercedes-Benz I received as a gift from the Americans. On 4 July, I crossed the border at Jesenice and arrived in Zagreb the following day, sent the Mercedes to the Ministry of Defence as a gift, but to my great surprise I was arrested by the Secret Police to be executed! The Communists didn't trust me because of my connections with the Americans and the British - I was wearing a British uniform. My release came on Friday 13 July at the intervention of a colleague who was a Communist.'

In 1948, when Tito broke relations with Stalin, Bogdan was again harassed, this time suspected of being a Soviet spy! Yet, all he was interested in was medicine. In the Zagreb hospital he was known as the surgeon with 'golden hands' and soon became known as the doctor with 'golden needles', offering Neural Therapy injections for various complaints and sclerosant injections for varicose veins, both in the hospital and his private practice. Always very generous, his idea of a holiday was to take his instruments along and treat the locals for free.

He came to Sydney with my mother in 1965 to join my family, became an Australian citizen in 1971 and lived to a ripe age of almost 102, still seeing patients aged 100. Unfortunately, Dr Norman Rose, Superintendent of Sydney Hospital, 20 years his junior, with whom he shared a room for two years at Cosel, and who helped him get medical registration in NSW, died suddenly of a heart attack in 1967. Dr Kaye-Webster, who moved to Sydney and became Superintendent of Prince of Wales Hospital, died in 1970. This was a great loss to Dad. He made many friends in Australia, but friendships made in the POW camp were very special. He was lucky, though, to have been able to continue one of these friendships, that of Frank Hebbard, a 20-year-old volunteer in 1940, who worked in the medical laboratory at Cosel, and marched with him in the Long March to freedom. Neither of them liked to remember the horrors of being forced marched in deep snow. They were both members of the Returned Servicemen League and the Anzac Memorial Club and regularly marched in the Anzac March on 25 April, cheered on by a grateful crowd.

I include four of several extracts from Dr Kaye-Webster's Letters to his wife regarding my father and kindly shared with me by Marion Farmer (UK), his niece:

19.4.44 - Old Bog is as usual in grand form. He really is a magnificent man, and all love him. He has a sense of humor, just like ours, and you need it to live in our 'mess', I can tell you. He can pull our leg just as much as we do his, even more.

6.9.44 - I am giving old Bog a hat as you suggested, as his own was getting rather passé, so he now has a khaki one, and looks very funny till we get used to him. He really is a very fine fellow, always in a good mood, and happy although at times he could easily have been so miserable, it has been chaps like him that have been an example to us.

17.9.44 - We are still very busy and have little time to think of anything but work, which is a good thing and passes the time. Norman Rose is still in fine form, as well as Tommy, Bog, and Smithy. Old Bog had a rib cracked at football but has now quite recovered and will be playing again this week...

5.11.44 -Old Bog was very pleased to receive another packet of 200 cigarettes this week; he is so pleased with Mrs Mary and says that you are very kind to him. He's a great old lad and is our mascot. I don't know what we would do without him and his benevolent nature. He is the happiest man that I have met for a long time.

--- Lest we forget ---

CAPTAIN PETER TATTERSALL

By Michael Tattersall

Michael was born in England in 1947 and grew up in Northern Ireland where his parents had moved to in 1950. He studied Mechanical Engineering at Queen's University, Belfast and, after graduation, worked in England, Germany, and Canada. In 2012 he retired from his position as director of Physical Plant at King's University College, London, Ontario. Together with his wife Carol he continues to live in London, Ontario.

The account below s primarily based on the diaries, written at the time, by Major T. McLardy, Captain W. Clare and Captain P. Tattersall. Secondary sources are published post-war accounts and correspondence with the families of those involved. In 2001 a group of

Peter Tattersall's family members followed the route that he had marched in 1945, by car.

THE ROAD TO LAMSDORF

On Tuesday, 23 January 1945, 1824 British Prisoners of War marched out of Stalag 344 Lamsdorf, Silesia. They were split into three groups, each group accompanied by a doctor: Captain Wesley Clare was with the lead group; Major Turner McLardy was next; and Captain Peter Tattersall with the last group. The three doctors had arrived at Lamsdorf by very different routes, and the military actions in which they were each captured represented major setbacks for the Allies during the early war years.

Tattersall had graduated from Leeds University and joined the Royal Army Medical Corps in January 1940. In March, he was sent to France with the 51st Highland Division commanded by Major General Fortune. On 12th June 1940 the Division was surrounded at St. Valery-en-Caux and surrendered to German forces under General Rommel. Tattersall was transferred to several POW camps before arriving at Lamsdorf in late 1944.

McLardy had graduated from Glasgow University in 1939 and, after working at the Maudsley Hospital in London, joined the Royal Army Medical Corps at the outbreak of war. He was sent to the Middle East and, on 20 June 1942, was evacuated by sea from Tobruk, as it was being overrun by General Rommel's Afrika Korps. He was on board the HMSAS *Parktown*, the last ship to leave the port. They were captured by a German E-boat just off the coast. After being held at various POW camps in Italy and Germany, he was sent to Lamsdorf in 1944.

Clare graduated from Queens University Kingston, Canada in June 1940 and immediately enlisted in a basic training course for Medical Officers. In March 1942 he was assigned to the Royal Hamilton Light Infantry and, on 19 August, was captured during the Dieppe raid. He was then transferred by cattle truck to Lamsdorf. At that time, Elfriede Hannak was working as a secretary to the German Administration at Lamsdorf and witnessed the arrival of the Dieppe POWs. In her wartime memoires she describes the scene: 'The prisoners were brought in wagon convoys and deposited at the side of the camp on Lamsdorf

Heath. It was a glorious day, warm sunshine, and a clear blue sky. The more prisoners that arrived the bleaker the heath seemed to become. The first squad marched in, then the second and the third…They marched past the guardhouse up to the barrier which, for the only time, would be raised for them. I thought I was not seeing properly, but it was true. The majority of them were marching into the camp wearing only their shirts, white undershirts with nothing else on top. On their heads they had flat steel helmets, many were limping and some were being supported. It was a really desolate sight that met my eyes. Somehow I felt ashamed to witness this spectacle, the arrival of the almost naked Dieppers in German captivity. Some comfort usually remains in every day, at least that was the case in our office, but on this day there was no sense of satisfaction.'

LAMSDORF TO GÖRLITZ

As the columns marched out of Lamsdorf on 23 January the roads were snow-covered and the temperature was minus 20°C. In the distance they could hear the sounds of tank-fire from the north-east, where the Red Army was attacking Oppeln, 40 kilometres away on the other side of the Oder River. The POWs had been notified the day before to be ready to leave, but many were ill-prepared for the conditions ahead, with inadequate clothing and footwear. At the gate they were each given a Red Cross food parcel (which included cigarettes) but had no idea how long it would have to last. Tattersall had made a sledge from scrap wood and loaded this with his kit including spare clothing, blanket, sleeping bag, toilet articles and mess kit. He also had a haversack of medical supplies including morphine, sulphaguanidine to treat dysentery, plasters, bandages, suppositories, aspirin, opium-based Dovers, and antimicrobial sulphonamide. The medical orderlies who were supposed to be with each group did not show up at the camp gate, so the doctors were short of the medical supplies that they were to bring with them.

The going was rough through the deep snow, and many of the men started abandoning surfeit kit, which was eagerly scavenged by local children. Tattersall was able to attach his sledge to a horse drawn wagon and, at dusk the exhausted groups arrived at draughty, crowded barns, where they were to spend the night trying to sleep on the straw. About 50 men had to sleep outside in the snow. It had taken them over eight hours to cover the 23 kilometres. There was no choice but to try to sleep fully clothed, and anyone who took off his boots found them frozen solid in the morning. McLardy's water bottle had frozen in the night and he woke to find icicles on his trousers and greatcoat. Most of the men were suffering from cold and exhaustion, and many had diarrhoea. The Germans did not issue any food to the POWs, so they had to use food from their Red Cross parcels. In a nearby barn they found another British medical officer, Captain Davidson, and 40 members of his party who had left Lamsdorf the day before. They were unable to continue any further due to sickness. An additional 150 sick from Tattersall's party were left with Davidson's party.

Thus began a 14 day routine of marching 20 to 30 kilometres per day in bitter weather, with few rest stops, little food, increasing sickness and exhaustion and poor shelter in rat infested barns or no shelter at all. Their destination was Stalag VIII-A at Görlitz, over 200 kilometres to the north-west. *Hauptmann* Max Baumgardt was the German officer in charge of the guards. He was a veteran of World War I and was generally sympathetic to the POWs in his charge, perhaps because his own son was a submariner in the German Navy and, after being captured by the British, was a POW in Wales. Between the wars Baumgardt had worked in the legal profession and had friends in the Lamsdorf area and on the third day of the march used his connections to provide vegetable soup from a local factory for the POWs.

The Germans had made advance plans for the evacuation of Lamsdorf, heading north on foot and then West to Gorlitz. These plans had been issued by the Chief of Staff to General Rudolf Koch-Erpach on 17 January from his headquarters at 36 Salzstraße in Breslau, under the operational name 'Krebs'. The plans covered the evacuation of all POWs from Silesia on foot. The rapid advance of the Red Army to the line of the Oder River, however, forced the march to keep further west than originally planned.

Every morning before the start of the day's march the doctors held sick parade. In addition to the inevitable hunger, many of the men were suffering from blisters, chills, frostbite, diarrhoea, vomiting, flu, *et cetera*. One of the worst cases involved the Roman Catholic priest, Father Bernard Desnoyers. He was from Farnham, Quebec, and had joined the priesthood in 1934. In March 1941 he and 16 other priests departed from New York to Cape Town, *en route* to work as missionaries in Basutoland. They were on board the Egyptian flagged *Zam-Zam*, and on 17 April, in mid-Atlantic, they were attacked by the German surface raider *Atlantis*.

All the passengers and crew were rescued by the Germans and eventually taken to France. American nationals (America was still neutral) were eventually returned home, but Canadian women were held in custody in Berlin and the Canadian men, including the priests, were treated as prisoners of war. Thus a Canadian civilian priest found himself marching through Silesia in January 1945. Desnoyers gets specific mention in the doctors' diaries because his feet were in such terrible condition. Throughout his life Desnoyers continued to have problems with his feet and even his obituary from 1993 describes how he had to use a razor to remove the puss from his foot during the march.

By Day 6, on 28 January, the marchers had already covered 121 kilometres with the weather still remaining below freezing. Just after leaving Neudorf the column was forced to the side of the road to allow a German staff car to pass. The officer in the back seat was obviously of very high rank; presumably *Generaloberst* Ferdinand Schörner, the German commander of Army Group Centre and a dedicated Nazi. Since on 21 January he had met with Albert Speer (Hitler's Armaments Minister) in Oppeln, and then travelled to the Divisional Command Post at Vorderheide, which he reached on 31 January, his route would have taken him past Tattersall's column. In spite of the German retreat in the east, Hitler promoted Schörner to Field Marshall on 4 April 1945. After the German surrender Schörner flew to Austria and gave himself up to the Americans who then turned him over to the Russians. He was held as a POW in Russia until 1955, and on his return to Germany he was tried for ordering the execution of German deserters and was imprisoned until 1960.

The next couple of days were in blizzard conditions with daily bread rations from the Germans being one loaf of bread among four to ten prisoners. On Day 7, they had reached Bohrhof, and the doctors were billeted in a crowded stable with the German guards and the sick. Day 8, 30 January, was a 'rest day' and at the sick parade the doctors dealt with blistered feet, frostbite, fevers, diarrhoea and vomiting, hernia and one case of hysterical blindness. The Germans issued thin hot soup in the afternoon. As the doctors settled in for another uncomfortable night, they were treated to a radio broadcast of Hitler addressing the German people. This was the anniversary of Hitler's becoming Chancellor of Germany on 30 January 1933 and was to be his last public address. He talked about the betrayal of Versailles, the dire state of the economy when he came to power and the restoration of German military power by 1939. He ranted about Jewish Asiatic Bolshevism and exhorted old comrades, soldiers, able-bodied, sick, weak, city dwellers, women, and girls to resist, to struggle and, to sacrifice. By contrast his first broadcast as Chancellor, 12 years earlier, had promised an awakening that would usher in a time of greatness for Germany. Ironically, the desperate tone of Hitler's speech might have afforded some cold comfort to the POWs that the war was, at last, moving to its end.

The next day it was still snowing but with slightly milder temperatures as they left their billets. In a somewhat surreal episode the marchers caught up with a travelling circus, leading their horse drawn wagons slowly down a hill. A private named Trickner, from the Royal West Kent Regiment, tried to assist them and, for his trouble, was dragged and kicked by one of the horses, and had to be treated for a contusion on his leg. Like most POWs, Trickner never discussed his wartime experiences, but did complain about a bad knee for the rest of his life. He survived the march, returned to England, was a lifelong Arsenal supported and lived to age 91.

The circus was probably the travelling troupe of the Sarrasani Circus, returning to their permanent home in Dresden. Two weeks later in Dresden the circus was in the middle of a performance when the air raid sirens sounded and the audience evacuated to bomb shelters. During the raid and subsequent firestorm, the magnificent circus building was destroyed and many of the animals killed. It is estimated that 25 000 people were killed in the Dresden bombings of 13 to 15 February.

After the encounter with the circus, the columns reached Seichau, close to the ancestral home of *Freiherr* Manfred von Richthofen, the Red Baron flying ace from World War I. Baumgardt told McLardy that some of the Vlasov Russians (defectors now fighting for the Germans) had molested *Gräfin* von Richthofen (probably the widow of the Red Baron's brother) and that the Russians had been court-marshalled and shot.

Day 10 on 1 February, saw temperatures above freezing and snow melting off the road, which meant that pulling sledges was no longer feasible, and many were abandoned by the wayside. The columns were now marching west, and the sounds of battle diminished as they moved further away from the frontlines. In addition to treating the POWs, the doctors were also treating local civilian families, many of whom had not seen a doctor in years. When they reached Pilgramsdorf on 2 February, the doctors were billeted in a kindergarten and were able to barter with their hostess: 40 cigarettes for milk, salt and bread; a bar of soap, 20 cigarettes and 8 squares of chocolate for an electric heater, 8lbs of potatoes and some wood. McLardy talked to the 24-year-old local teacher, *Fräulein* Brüschke. Even though her fiancé, a pilot, had been killed in action, she was a staunch Nazi and did not think the Russians would get across the Oder or capture Breslau, where her father was the station master. In fact, Breslau which had been declared a 'fortress city' by Hitler, did hold out until 6 May - only two days before the complete German surrender.

As the march continued so did the suffering. Rain had turned the roads to mud, food was still limited with most men only receiving one or two potatoes a day. Many of the marchers were suffering from blistered feet, and cases of diphtheria were increasing. On Day 13 they reached Schloß Heidersdorf, home of *Graf* and *Gräfin* Sponeck. The marchers were given thin barley soup and were billeted in barns. The doctors and *padres* were accommodated in the castle sleeping four to a bed. Their hosts received them graciously and the countess, who spoke some English, gave the doctors and *padres* a tour of the castle. Count Maximilian von Sponeck was born in 1877 and had served as a major in World War I during which he was gassed leaving him in poor health.

Three months after the POWs had left, due to his continuing frail condition and the dangerous situation in their area, the countess sent him, accompanied by a maid, to stay with friends further west. He was with a group of refugees south of Dresden, when they were attacked by the Red Army and in the final days of the war he was left, abandoned, at the side of the road. He was taken to hospital and died of a heart attack on 19 May 1945.

Countess Maria-Sylvia Sponeck and her two sons fled to the west, ahead of the advancing Russians. Their castle was requisitioned by the Russians at the end of the war and was destroyed by fire in the 1970's.

On 5 February, after marching 280 kilometres in 14 days, the column finally reached Stalag VIII-A at Görlitz-Moys. 1824 POWs had left Lamsdorf on 23 January and they picked up 15 stragglers en route. But only 1240 people reached Görlitz. The discrepancy of 599 (one third of the marchers) represents those who became sick or injured on the march and were unable to proceed on foot. Approximately 80 of them were transported to Görlitz by wagon while the rest were left in the care of the local authorities or at a hospital.

Even though the marchers had now reached a POW camp, things did not improve. The camp was overcrowded and muddy and food was in short supply with no Red Cross parcels available to supplement the meagre German rations. Conditions were far worse than the camp they had left at Lamsdorf. In addition to 5 000 British there were 2000 Americans, 1000 French, 1 500 Italians and some Serbians and Slovakians. There were also Russian POWs held in a separate area. The Red Army had now reached the Oder River just over 100 kilometres to the East. In the west the British, Canadians and Americans had only just reached the borders of the Reich.

From this point Tattersall's story diverges from that of his two colleagues.

McLardy had only a five-day respite. On 10 February he marched out of Görlitz in charge of 3 000 POWs. They went west, reaching Stalag IX-A Ziegenhain on 12 March. On 28 March McLardy left Ziegenhain with 1 700 British and American POWs, marching east to Diedorf, which he reached on 2 April. He was freed by the Americans on 6 April. These subsequent marches covered a further 850 kilometres.

Clare had developed dysentery, probably from drinking buttermilk on the march. He left Görlitz by train on 17 February accompanying 1 000 men, many of them bedridden. He reached Stalag XI-B Fallingbostel on 20 February and was liberated by the British on 17 April. He remained in the camp for a further ten days treating the liberated POWs.

GÖRLITZ TO DÜDERSTADT

After ten days of 'rest' in the uncomfortable conditions at Stalag VIII-A, Tattersall left Görlitz marching west with 2500 British POWs plus 250 French and 250 Slovakians. There were no pack wagons, so he carried his own rucksack and haversack. Going was slow due to constant alarms, and hundreds of American bombers passed overhead as the air raids on Dresden continued. Billets were in barns and, on the first night there was further hardship, as the guards refused to issue water to the POWs because a loaf of bread had been stolen.

By the third day the marchers had reached Bautzen and, on the road, they encountered a column of Jewish refugees with SS guards. 'The Jews were all emaciated and wearing striped pyjama style concentration camp clothing; their heads were bare, with hair cropped close in a two-inch band from forehead to nape. 36 of them were hitched by ropes to a German wagon which they were straining pitifully to pull up a hill. They failed. They were then unhitched from the wagon, lined up beside the road and shot by the guards. Another 36 were hitched to the waggon and, while being whipped by the guards, succeeded, somehow, in getting the wagon up the hill.'

By 20 February the POWs had marched 102 kilometres from Görlitz, rations were typically thin soup and bread, supplemented occasionally by potatoes, tinned meat or cheese; billets were barns, sheep stalls, stables and an army barracks cinema. But the weather was improving and, as they reached Radeburg they passed over an impressively wide four lane road. This was, of course, a stretch of the *Reichsautobahn*. Although there had been some autobahn construction before 1933 the Nazis took credit for their expansion and by 1941, when construction was halted, due to the need to divert resources to the war effort, had built over 3000 kilometres of limited access, dual-carriageway roads.

It was now 23 February, 33 days since Tattersall had left Lamsdorf and, as the column left Meißen, he was feeling ill. His temperature was 102°F, he had puss on his left tonsil and in addition to feeling lousy, he was quite literally infested with lice. He self-medicated with M&B 693 but felt even worse. M&B 693 was an antibacterial sulphanilamide and had famously been administered to Winston Churchill in December 1943 while he was at the Teheran conference with Stalin and Roosevelt. As Churchill convalesced he gave up cigars but drank whiskey and soda; he is quoted as saying 'Dear Nurse, pray remember that man cannot live by M&B alone.' Unfortunately, Tattersall did not have the extra medicinal benefit of whiskey.

Later that day a car pulled up to the column and the driver called out, 'Good morning Captain Tattersall.' The driver was M. Gabrielle Naville, a Swiss diplomat. M. Naville had been born in Geneva in February 1892 and, after a career in banking, he joined the Swiss Diplomatic Corps in January 1942, stationed in Berlin. As Switzerland was the Protecting Power for British interests in Germany, their diplomats were responsible for checking on the well-being of the POWs. Due to his weakened state Tattersall was happy to accept a ride for part of the day's journey.

Luxury was short-lived as that night he slept on the bare floor of a sawmill with nothing to eat or drink, except thin barley soup.

For Tattersall, the next ten days passed in a blur as his temperature remained above 100°F. During that time he covered 200 kilometres, held sick parades daily and like the other POWs survived on soup, tea and bread. By now it was 5 March and he had reached Mellingen, close to Stalag IX-C at Bad Sulza. He was billeted in a farm kitchen and, in nearby billets were 960 sick Americans and British left behind by previous march groups. These included Father Desnoyers, *Padre* McIntyre and RSM Muir who had been with him on the earlier march from Lamsdorf. Thanks to complaints from Major McLardy, who was with a group up ahead, several German doctors were dispatched to assist Tattersall and 120 of the worst cases were transferred to hospital.

By 7 March Tattersall was somewhat recovered and met with *Hauptman* Baumgardt who made arrangements for him to go by train from nearby Weimar to Stalag IX-C at Bad Sulza, to obtain food and medical supplies. The camp there was crowded with sick and dying from previous marches and had no British medical officers. The camp *kommandant* promised to send 400 Red Cross parcels to meet Tattersall's group at Linderbach.

Tattersall obtained 10 parcels of invalid comforts for the sick under his care and, after catching the train back had to walk the seven kilometres to his billet through a snowstorm, only to find no accommodation had been arranged and his kit was missing. He had to sleep on a couch in *Padre* McIntyre's room.

During the following week the march covered the 130 kilometres to Worbis, a village just outside Düderstadt, where the men were billeted in a barn. The promised parcels from Stalag IX-C had arrived, which eased the food situation. However, there were still many cases of severe illness and arrangements were made with *Hauptman* Baumgardt for 156 of the severest sick cases to be left behind. Due to the fast pace, many of the marchers were dropping 'like flies'. As well as exhaustion they were suffering from haemoptysis, diarrhoea, diphtheria, dysentery, pneumonia, pleurisy, jaundice, gastritis, and lice infestation. Hunger forced many of the POWs to scrounge for food wherever and whenever they could. For instance, Private Jack Poolton, with the Royal Regiment of Canada, had been captured at Dieppe and after three years in Lamsdorf was now on the march. Growing up in Kapuskasing where his father was the milkman, he was familiar with milking cows, and took the opportunity to fill his cup from a farmer's cow at a barn on the outskirts of Düderstadt. He was chased by the farmer wielding a pitchfork and managed to elude the guards with their rifles. Tattersall noted that it was 'lucky no one was shot'.

The eight days spent in Worbis allowed Tattersall to treat the sick, and for the POWs to rest, even though the conditions were grim. On 20 March Tattersall was called on at 7 a.m. by a German *feldwebel* with a request to treat American POWs in the next village.

After a 45-minute walk he found one American dead and two wounded; they had been shot while stealing food. Another three had been shot and killed while trying to escape.

On 22 March Tattersall moved the 13 kilometres to Düderstadt, where conditions among the thousands of POWs were dire. He treated a group billeted in a factory with 'shit everywhere'. He was baffled by the number of Americans with dysentery and exhaustion who would collapse, lapse into unconsciousness, and die within 12 hours, and was further frustrated by the lack of facilities, adequate diet *et cetera*. For the 11 days that Tattersall remained in Düderstadt he held daily sick parades and did his best to treat the sick and dying. The only high point came on Easter Sunday, 1 April, when the prisoners were issued a special meal in honour of the holy day. The best German food in five years of captivity: macaroni soup, veal, mixed vegetables, potatoes, ice cream, iced sponge cake and coffee. Easter Monday featured more good food, but, unfortunately, this was not to last as artillery fire was close at hand, and preparations were hastily being made to march out again.

DÜDERSTADT TO FREEDOM

The American Army had now crossed the Rhine River and reached Kassel, only 80 kilometres to the west. The Red Army had crossed the Oder River heading to Berlin and were still over 300 kilometres east. So, after months of marching west and north, the column went east and could hear artillery fire behind them. The pattern was the same: little food, increased sickness, and exhaustion, 20 kilometres or more marched per day, intermittent rest days, makeshift accommodation. Even though the weather was turning warmer and they were walking through the Harz Mountains, an area of outstanding natural beauty, the gnawing hunger and intermittent rain limited what little respite they might have had. Many bombers passed noisily overhead and, to the south, they could see Nordhausen in flames. After a day with no food, the column received a delivery of flour and the next day was a rest day to bake bread. They were close to a naval POW work camp at Thale and were able to obtain 120 Red Cross parcels, six invalid comforts, 60 pairs of boots and four sacks of clothing, soap and medical kit. In spite of this improvement in their conditions the deaths and sickness continued.

On the night of 10 April Tattersall was kept awake by artillery fire and was summoned to stitch a head wound of a local woman who had fallen downstairs. The next morning they moved on to Ditfurt and, that evening, the German officers, *Hauptman* Baumgardt and Lieutenant Mandel, invited Tattersall and Bill Chesters, his American medical orderly, to share two bottles of champagne. Baumgardt knew that liberation for his prisoners was imminent and said he would rather they drink it together than have the Americans drink it. At 7.30 a.m. on 12 April the Americans liberated Ditfurt. The German guards surrendered their weapons and now became POWs themselves.

Baumgardt handed over his binoculars, compass, *Wehrmacht* maps and Luger pistol to Tattersall. Tattersall kept these items but, during the Troubles in Northern Ireland, had to turn in the pistol to the police. That night Tattersall and Chesters invited Baumgardt and Mandel to a farewell dinner cooked by the farmer's wife in their billet at 15 Hauptstraße. The meal was interrupted by the arrival of American troops

140

and due to non-fraternization regulations, the meal was only allowed to continue after Tattersall gave his personal assurance that he would deliver the German officers to the prisoners' cage the next morning.

Prior to the war Tattersall had been dating Helen Kilburn who worked in the Leeds University Library. During Tattersall's time as a POW they were able to keep up a sporadic correspondence. By 1945 Helen was working as a Red Cross ambulance driver transporting sick and wounded soldiers (including returning POWs) to hospital from an airfield in Gloucestershire. From the POWs she received snippets of information about her boyfriend. These she noted in her diary: 'Patient who actually knew Peter says he was left behind', 'Found three men from 344 who had marched with Peter and said he was quite fit, but they had left him behind with some wounded. They saw him on March 10th', '2 ex-patients of Peter's. They said he was marvellous on the march and had a wheelbarrow of medicine! He also gave them cigarettes and had frostbitten ears', 'Spoke to a medical orderly who had been with Peter and says he is at Dudesberg'.

Finally on 17 April she wrote, 'Peter is definitely liberated and is apparently *burgermaster* of a town and is in charge of everyone!!'

Following liberation Tattersall was responsible for the care and treatment of the POWs and 'organised food supplies including five sheep, butter, milk, eggs.' On 18 April 1945 Tattersall and the other liberated POWs were moved to Halberstadt and flown back to England. At the time he swore that he would never return to Germany again. As a measure of how things change, within a generation Tattersall's first two grandchildren were both born in Germany, the second, a girl, on 18 April 1975 – the 30th anniversary of his departure. Naturally he visited Germany on both occasions.

Tattersall had been a POW for four years and ten months and, in 1945, had marched 850 kilometres from Lamsdorf to Ditfurt, over a period of 87 days. After the war he married Helen and moved to Omagh, Northern Ireland where he worked in the Tyrone County Hospital as a consultant physician. They had three children. Due to ill health from Parkinson's Disease, he took early retirement and died, at age 67, on 20 May 1982 while on holiday in France.

TIMOTHY E MAHONEY

By Katie Foster

London-born, Katie grew up happily in Westcliff-on-Sea from the age of 5. Graduated from Leeds University, then a rather peripatetic, serendipitous career including European tour managing, 20 years marketing the Ironbridge Gorge Museum followed by consultancy in marketing, tourism & heritage. Years of voluntary service, now for Alzheimer's Research UK, after dad's death from that cruel disease. Two brilliant married daughters born Shropshire, now in London.

Tim - aka 'Nin' - was born in Hull, near the fish docks, and nobody was sure whether it was 31 August or 1 Sept 1919, which as most people know, has a big impact on a life, as you're either the oldest or youngest in your school year.

He was the youngest and smallest. He had an older brother Henry and a sister, Kath, ten years older, who became a novice nun when she was about sixteen.

Tim was sent to nearby St Wilfrid's Primary School and taught by nuns. As a little lad, he was often at home alone, as his own dad - also called Tim - had died of WWI wounds when Tim was just four. His earliest memory was of being carried down the stairs on his dad's shoulders and also of being held high by a relative to view his dad lying in his coffin in the parlour, his head bandaged and everyone saying, 'Let the bairn see his dad'. It traumatised him.

His mum had to work hard to keep the family afloat and worked as a barmaid. When she went to work and he was alone in early evenings before his brother came home, he would stand on the doorstep whistling loudly, arms folded across his chest - pretending he was fine. There were plenty of widows around in the Zetland Street area who would mostly keep an eye on each other's kids. Nonetheless his brother and friends would often play tricks on him to scare him.

The family moved not far to St George's Road next to the railway line, where Tim made friends with 'Hooky', an injured WWI veteran who operated the railway signals with his hook. Imagine what HSE would make of that now - a young lad sitting in the signals box with Hooky.

His next school was Marist College - amalgamated with St Mary's Convent School for Girls in 1988, which his sister attended before the convent. It remains a mystery how the school fees were paid, perhaps related to what Tim told his daughter much later in life.

Leaving school at 14, he got a job with Reckitts, then a famous Hull company, and then a haulage company until the dark clouds were gathering over Europe. Tim and his friend Bob Larkin decided to join up, not to fight, but because they wanted to learn to drive in order to impress a couple of girls they fancied down their street.

Early in 1939, Tim joined the East Riding Yeomanry (ERY) - a Territorial Force outfit with a distinguished history. The ERY motto was 'Forr'ard' but, as Tim told his two young granddaughters years later, '... sadly we went backwards'... ruefully shaking his head.

Drill consisted of 'mucking about in the church hall with brooms on our shoulders, marching up and down', not a lot of use once they were dispatched to northern France in April 1940. Time spent at Catterick and Tidworth was not enough to prepare anyone for what was to come.

Tim was billeted for a while on a farm at Annet-sur-Marne near the present-day eastern outskirts of Paris. He was nineteen, and still with his mate Bob from Hull. It might have seemed pleasant to be in the countryside at the time and Tim never forgot the family at Annet and remained fond of the French for the rest of his life.

Everything changed once the war was on his doorstep ... driving his Bren Gun Carrier, feeling very afraid and recognising this was the reality of war and how unprepared he was. He found himself moving towards the front lines. He and his mates knew little about where and what their role was until the fateful day when their commanding officer, later described by Tim as a hapless minor aristocrat, announced that they 'had been given the honour of holding the line against German forces reaching Dunkirk'. Some honour.

Tim later reflected wryly, 'We knew then that was the end for us'.

Crashing his carrier through the dark, midnight streets of Lille, escaping German troops and tanks, he still felt bad to be damaging its ancient buildings.

His capture near Watou in the Battle of Cassel on 30 May 1940 was dramatic: realising he was outnumbered and outgunned by huge German tanks on the main road, he turned the carrier into a field and tried to get away. The track came off, he jumped out as he saw his mate in the ammunition tank blasted to smithereens by a Panzer and dived into a ditch where he lay terrified before realising there was no escape. Gradually he raised his, '*hände hoch*' and gingerly looked out to see they were surrounded by German tanks. And German officers waiting for him with guns cocked. By all accounts one of these officers really did say 'For you *ze* war is over', although in fact, surviving captivity was to be his own private war.

Imagine at that moment, not knowing if you would even survive. Not knowing where the horrendous journey east via Triers, on foot and by filthy, crammed cattle trucks would end. Then imagine, at last arriving at an unknown station, then marched up the road, then Chestnut Allee to the huts, the barbed wire, the watchtowers, and guards of Stalag VIII-B.

Tim, being a mere lance corporal, was made to work and in time ended up in E75, in coal mines in Knurow and at Mechtal, which he loathed. One winter evening, stoking the boiler, he saw two shadowy figures behind it. Looking closely he saw two frightened, shivering young girls. He put his finger to his lips and beckoned them closer to warm up. He never knew their nationality but kept them safe whenever they appeared.

A photo of two girls in national costume he kept may indicate they were Ukrainian rather than Russian.

Many times he refused to go down to the coalface and one day the guard pushed him really hard. Tim swung his lamp at him and the guard hit him round the head with his rifle butt: he thought he would be shot dead but instead he was put in 'solitary'. With no food, he felt pretty miserable. Then late one night a Polish (forced) guard brought him a black bread roll. It was his 21st birthday. He considered other ways to avoid going to the coalface, such as one of his fellow POWs had done by chopping off his thumb. The years dragged on, with ever greater privations and threats and an intense hatred of going down to the coalface.

His respect for the miners in the Thatcher years was matched only by his strongly stated belief that 'no man should have to go miles underground to scrape a living.'

Allied POWs were saved by the Red Cross parcels which started to arrive late 1942. Tim soon stopped smoking as he realised cigarettes were currency and food was more important. It didn't take long for agreed rates of bartering to be established.

Tim helped script some Christmas pantomimes which brought some respite to the POWs and much amusement when German officers bagged front seats and stood up for *Land of Hope and Glory*.

In another time Tim might have had a proper education and career and his love of words never left him. POW letters to and from home were bittersweet, with the censor's heavy hand obliterating any real information. Every letter he wrote that survived shows how much he worried about his 'Moth', how he always told her that he was well. Later in life it became clear that he felt guilt at being captured and hadn't done his duty, a feeling that persisted throughout his life.

Tim's eventual great camp friend was Bob Matthews who operated a radio hidden under the floor in their hut. This enabled many POWs to know more of what was happening in the war, via a complicated alert system in the huts, until it was discovered.

It was with Bob and 'Taffy' Morgan that Tim was eventually able to escape from the Long March trudging west in the freezing 1945 winter. Collapsing each night in freezing barns or village halls after walking miles every day, lousy, starving, and cold, scratching for mangels in fields, hearing unmilked cows bellowing in pain, they concluded they would most likely die anyway so might as well try to escape.

Around 23 April - Shakespeare's birthday and St George's Day - after overnight in a large barn near Plattling, southeast of Regensburg, with one bottle of water between them and two biscuits each, they hid in a narrow 14' wide partition while the rest of the POWs shuffled off. The guards themselves were fed up and tired and knew they were in retreat. The three men stayed silent, cramped, hungry and thirsty for five nights. Tim hung a stick with a rag out of the window to catch rain to suck, such was their thirst.

Eventually, after listening intently to the sounds outside, they dared to go outside as a cockerel squawked loudly, desperately hoping the voices they heard were American, not German. Emerging from the barn, these exhausted, bedraggled, dirty men were met by the cocked guns of the American 3rd Army, who relaxed once they were sure they were English POWs. Tim later recalled, with great distaste, how some gum-chewing GIs offered them guns to 'go get yourself some krauts,' even suggesting they might rape some local girls. His greatest delight, second only to washing, being deloused, and given a US Army uniform, was when one of the youngest GI's threw him a Hershey bar, amazed that Tim had never heard of them. Tim, Bob and Taffy were astonished at how much better equipped their opposite numbers were.

He was then quizzed by Lt Colonel Donald Sherman, who threw down an English 'threepenny bit' and asked him to identify it. Correctly identifying it was enough to earn Tim a small slither of tracing paper stating he was a genuine English POW, signed by Sherman. That slender, modest slip still survives, belying its huge significance.

Years later he told his family that the worst thing that happened to him was when the British Army personnel took away his American uniform and made him wear a British one.

They travelled with the US Army, then by train and then eventually in the bomb bay of a Lancaster bomber back to England, where Bob made his way to Aylesbury and Tim to Hull on around 6 May 1945, having been given rail warrants and sent telegrams to their families to expect them. Tim later wrote a short note explaining this when his granddaughters were studying WWII at school.

'I got off the train at Paragon Station where my mother was waiting for me. She said, 'Hello Son'. I said, 'Hello Moth'. Then we caught the bus and went home for a cup of tea. No brass bands playing and no flags.'

The aftermath was severe for Tim. Today he would, along with many others, have been diagnosed with PTSD. His life was defined by his POW experiences and, unlike most former POWs, he spoke about his experiences a lot to his family. He hadn't wanted to stay in Hull after the war, instead had a great desire to go to the USA and see the world. But his loyalty to his widowed 'Moth' stopped him.

Tim's opinion of the rehabilitation of POWs by one Walter Winterbourne of later football fame, is probably unprintable. He went AWOL one day from Tidworth, just running and running across Salisbury plain. 'Nobody understood what it had been like for us. They expected us just to go back to work as normal. As if nothing had happened'.

Tim never claimed his medals, though his daughter later did. He also apparently never knew that his own dad had been a POW in WWI, captured in 1915. But he told his daughter late in his life that he thought his father was not his biological father which is probably true looking at dates. He never added that his dad had exactly the same Christian names as him.

Tim's future mother-in-law was worried about her daughter marrying him after she met him, as she could perhaps see what others did not. Yet, on honeymoon in Paris in 1949, he was determined to revisit Annet-sur-Marne with his new wife Rita, where he had been billeted on the farm. Somehow he managed to find the family still on the farm and a young girl recognised him from afar shouting to her family, '*Vite, vite, c'est Tim, c'est Tim!*' She had been just a little girl but remembered him. The word spread and the whole village turned out and wine and food were rapidly consumed with many toasts to La France and Les Anglaise

Tim and Bob Matthews kept in touch for a few years immediately after the war but then lost touch when Tim, living in London and married with a child by then, had a nervous breakdown and moved to Leigh-on-Sea where the small family lived for a time at the in-laws.

It was not until June 2000, over 50 years later, after an article appeared in *The Times*, that they were reunited. Bob's sons had grown up hearing about his great pal in Stalag VIII-B, and Tim's daughter likewise had heard about Bob. Both had seen photos of their dads' mates. And thus within a short time of the paper being published that day, Bob's son Quentin had rung the journalist and within hours the two old soldiers were talking on the phone.

There was not a dry eye in the house that day.

It turned out that Bob had been trying to find Tim for years, even putting adverts in newspapers. And just a week later Bob and his wife drove up from Portsmouth to be reunited with Tim, sadly too late to meet his late wife, Rita. A wonderful day.

Tim was beginning to show signs of dementia, which Bob picked up. He rang Tim every week for the rest of his life - nothing was to divide them again. He told Tim's daughter, 'Your dad was the kindest man I ever met'. For Tim, Bob was nothing short of a hero.

In the last months of his life Tim, suffering from Alzheimer's disease, often had spells when he thought he was back in the POW camp. He lost his sight too, but never his sense of humour and love of puns and word play. He was never bitter and encouraged his daughter to visit her German penfriend in the mid-1960's saying that mutual understanding was the way to stop wars. Whenever Hitler appeared on a TV screen he would laugh and say, 'There's my old boss'.

Alzheimer's took Tim away long before he died in 2007, 10 years after Rita.

His daughter is now an Alzheimer's Research UK champion and fundraiser

HENRY TAYLOR ARNOLD

By Matt Arnold

Matt Arnold is a self-employed videographer, based in Adelaide, South Australia. He is also a keen musician, a loving father and doting husband who loves to cook and spend time with family and friends. Matt has maintained an interest in World War II history and escape stories since reading about his own grandfather's escapes as a child. It continues to be a bit of a passion and subject of interest to this day.

This is the story of my grandfather, Henry Taylor 'Slim' Arnold who was a private in the Australian Infantry 2/11 Battalion (later 19th Australian Infantry). The story below was originally written by a local reporter who interviewed 'Slim' in his hometown of Port Pirie, South Australia, before being discharged from the AIF at the end of the war. His story has fascinated me since I was a kid, when I used to ask my dad to read it to my older brothers and I every so often growing up. My grandfather's stories of escape and survival throughout the war were

149

especially intriguing because it sounded like something out of a movie, not something I could ever imagine him doing.

Slim passed away when I was still a boy but I got to know him reasonably well. He met my grandmother, Enid (a nurse) while in hospital recovering from frostbite. They removed a couple of his smaller toes in the hope that it would keep them from curling over but it didn't really help. It's possible Slim developed his frostbite on the Long March, upon his final escape, but I guess we will never know.

FOUR YEARS 'GUEST OF HITLER'

With his heavy military boots supporting 6 ft 3 ins. of fine Australian manhood, and putting on badly needed weight at a rate of nearly a stone a month, Pte. Henry Taylor (Slim) Arnold is home with his parents, Mr and Mrs H.T Arnold, Howe Street, Howetown, enjoying leave before his discharge from the AIF.

Three years and 10 months spent as a prisoner of war in German hands provided him with experiences which will remain in his memory for the remainder of his life. Twice he made his escape, only to fall into enemy hands again. He tells a story which is rich in incident, carrying much hardship, eternal hoping, and not a little humor, without which the Australian soldier could not exist.

Fifteen years ago Henry Arnold, a Port Pirie-born lad, went west to try his luck on the Golden Mile. He left with his parents at home a small brother, Dick, about whom we shall hear more later on. He enlisted in Western Australia in January 1940, and was placed in the 2/11 Battalion. In September 1940, he was in Port Pirie on his Embarkation leave, and one of the last things he heard when he departed was his 17-year-old brother saying; 'Gee Slim, I wish I were going with you!'

Henry sailed that month for overseas. He was in North Africa for some months, and was one of the famous 'Desert Rats' of Tobruk. Then came the transfer to Greece and later Crete. On 1 June 1941, came the British capitulation on that island, and Private Arnold was at the wrong end of the 'Speck' for the evacuation. Where he was situated, the Allies held 100 German prisoners, and the day following the capitulation positions were reversed, and he was one of a large group taken prisoner.

'All we had to defend ourselves with in the way of heavy stuff,' he said, 'were two Italian field guns from which the sights had been removed. The gunners had to sight along the barrels. I got mine just at the time of the capitulation and was in hospital with a bullet wound in a leg and a piece of grenade in my back, when the Germans took us over'.

With other wounded he was flown to Athens hospital in a German plane, and spent three weeks there. Then 700 prisoners of many nationalities were taken by train to Salonika.

'That was the hungriest trip I have ever undertaken', said the soldier. 'The Greeks did their best for us, giving us a few figs and bread. Salonika camp was the lousiest hole that ever men were placed in. Every man was covered with vermin and there were 10 000 assembled there in capacity. There were three latrines for all that mass of men, and five taps from which to obtain water. We had no soap. A loaf of bread was split up amongst nine of us daily, and each man had a bowl of weak soup. The Germans confiscated all horses in the district and if one died we might have got a little of its flesh. The existence was pretty bad'.

After nine weeks in Salonika camp, Private Arnold decided that it was time he did something about getting free, and made the attempt alone. Let him tell his story in his own words: 'I hid in an empty room from 8 a.m. until 11 p.m. by which time it had become dark. I had gained the room by pretending to do a little weeding in the compound. Then I made a break over the high stone wall, saw a house in the distance, and made for it. Peeping through the window I could see a Greek family and no sign of any Jerries. So I entered.

'You would have thought that Lord Duffield had arrived, so well did those Greeks receive me. The head of the household was one Ophisthen Ayias Parasgevis. The family took me in, bathed me and shaved me and cut my hair, I had not had a wash or shave for nine weeks. They gave me some clothing, and told me that henceforth I was to be named Stephanos Lambru. They said that, despite certainty of instant death if they were caught, they would help Aussies and New Zealanders.

'I was for two months in hiding among the Greeks. A richer family to which I had been taken took my photo, and gave me an identity card in the name of Stephanos Lambru. Then I linked up with some more Aussies at Moondany, near Salonika. The Greeks took up a collection and gave us 10000 *drachma* (about 160 pounds Australian), with which we purchased a 35-ton boat, complete with engine and sails.

'Our party by that time had grown to nearly 40. There were two Greek police, a R.A.F. officer, Greek Air Force personnel (eight or ten), two Englishmen, and 22 mixed Australians and New Zealanders. The previous owner of the little vessel stayed with us and at 5 o'clock one morning, we set sail for Turkey. We had on board only the two rifles of the Greeks, four revolvers, and a couple of home-made hand grenades.

'We were doing about eight or nine knots along the coast and had travelled 80 to 90 miles when we were spotted by a German seaplane, which shepherded us ashore. They must have wirelessed for a land patrol and it was there to greet us.

'I thought that the plane had been machine gunning us, and dived under a tree when it approached. When I looked up, I was gazing into the muzzle of a tommy gun in the hands of a dirty, big German.

'Six of us were picked up and the remainder broke clear. I heard of only two after that, one lived to lose an arm in the Pacific war, and I came across another in Germany later.

'Back to Salonika I went and spent two days in the cells. Then I was placed aboard a train bound for Germany. Twelve days and nights we travelled on cattle trucks, 10 in each, and in that time each man had to exist on two loaves of bread and two 6 oz tins of pork. At Dresden we were given a bowl of soup each.

'At Belgrade, the Red Cross people wanted to give us some comforts, but we were escapees, and they were not allowed to approach us. So we went hungry'.

UNAVAILING APPEAL TO GOOD NATURE

Private Arnold at that point related a little episode of the journey, which brought real humor into the narrative. When they were entrained, a German officer told them with fierce candor that for every man who escaped on the journey one would be taken out and shot. One night five men made a jump for it off the moving train, and in the morning when the count was taken their absence was discovered. Without more ado the officer pointed to five men: 'You and you and you'.

'There was a little Tommy cook lying in a corner, and he was one of those indicated. Turning swiftly to his next-door neighbour he said, plaintively: 'You go, Choom, I've got no boots or socks on'.

There was no response from the queue appealed to, the five were taken out but were not shot. They were placed somewhere else.

By means of his pay book, Private Arnold had promoted himself to the rank of corporal on Crete, and by the time the train had reached Lamsdorf prison camp, close to the Polish border, he had made himself a sergeant.

That meant that he did not have to do any menial tasks. Red Cross parcels started to arrive and Private. Arnold paused in his story to remark with conviction that had it not been for them, half the mass of prisoners would never have survived. There was no fuel in the camp, and the Pirie man found it expedient to do a little manual labour in order to keep warm.

'After the Dieppe raid by the Canadians,' he said, 'the German guards started to make reprisals. We had our hands bound every day with string from Red Cross parcels, and later they introduced handcuffs. The only man whom I met that had any connection with my home district was a chap named Percy, I never knew his surname. He was born in Solomon town and enlisted in Sydney.

'Our morale could not be lowered. We managed to smuggle in small wireless sets and knew all the progress of the war. While our own guards "kept nit" we would switch on and one of the chaps, a journalist would take down the news in shorthand, from the "whispering" speaker.

'Then at certain times of the day, with a strong guard posted, the news would be transcribed and read to the mob. Thus we knew more than the Germans about the true state of affairs.

'It was in January of this year, after having been through more than three years of prison life, that the hectic time really started. I was working with a party in a timber mill when we learned that the Russians were approaching from the banks of the Elbe River and the Yanks on the other side. When the Russians went to Niesse near Lamsdorf, the Germans marshalled us on a group on a march towards Czechoslovakia. The snow two feet deep. A part of it I feigned illness to get into a hospital. I was there one week and one night when the guard fell asleep and I made liberty.

'I was free for two weeks, and then was unfortunate enough to run into a German who could speak Polish. I had the big 'P' on my breast, and when it was found that I could not answer questions in Polish I was in it again. I had joined a little Palestinian, whom I advised to adopt the name of Freddy Johnson, an Australian, in case he was taken.

'He stuck to that name right through until he reached England. We were taken to Mühlburg, near the Elbe. Two hundred of us were sent each day to gather firewood, and then we learned that the Russians were almost on our heels. The Germans prepared to evacuate and my little pal and I made another run for it. We drifted toward Torgau, where the Russians and Americans eventually met. We were picked up by the Russians on 23 April, in our party were mostly French, Dutch, Poles and Czechs. We had had nothing to smoke for some time, and the Russians treated us well.

'I was amazed at the number of girls with the Russian forces. In every platoon there seemed to be five or six of them. They drove tanks and transport lorries, and were the acme of efficiency in everything they did. Talk about an efficient army.

'The Russians told us to take over any house we could find. We begged for and got some real bread and what with being able to kill geese and a steer or two we got by famously. There were plenty of vegetables to be had. We waited there for two weeks while they repaired the bridge over the Elbe. And then the Yankees arrived and joined forces. Those blokes sure had plenty of supplies - a wonderfully equipped army. They gave us plenty of everything.

'My Palestinian cobber and I were in a party which was taken by jeeps to Halle and from there by American plane to Brussels. Next morning, we were aboard a Lancaster bomber with an Aussie crew and were taken to Old England. We were taken to Eastbourne reception camp and given two days leave.'

It was while on that leave that Private Arnold got the shock of his life. He caught the train to Staffordshire to meet his uncle, whom he had never seen. The relative was Mr Wilfred Shaw, of Chapel Street, Cheadle. He arrived there at 6 p.m. and about 10 o'clock while the family was sitting round the fire there was another arrival, a young Canadian soldier.

To Private Arnold's amazement it was his brother Dick, whom he had left pining at home in 1940. There was a real Australian reunion, and the elder brother learned that Dick had joined a Swedish ship in their hometown of Port Pirie, South Australia, worked his passage to Canada and joined the Calgary tank regiment.

Three weeks ago Private Arnold set his eyes hungrily again on his homeland.

He said yesterday that nothing he had seen in his life looked so fascinating as Australia. Since April last, he has put on in weight three stone and is still building. He brought home with him a cruel looking knuckle-duster worn by a member of the German SS police. With loops for the four fingers and grip for the palm, the outside fittings consisted of four spikes quarter of an inch long, and sharp. Private Arnold said he had seen the 'duster' used on civilians mainly Jews, with terrible results. A blow square on the temple would kill the victim instantly and a favorite trick of the users was to twist the hand when making the blow on the cheek, thereby mutilating the face. He added vaguely that the German from whom he took it, was 'alive when I got it'.

He told of a remarkable escape made by 60 men from the hell-hole at Salonika. The prisoners discovered that in the centre of the compound was the entrance to a sewer pipe, which would take the body of a small man. Sixty men wriggled through it into the darkness and reached the outlet 800 yards away in a state of indescribable filth. They were whisked away by friendly Greeks and cleaned.

'I was one of the unfortunates again', he said 'for my body was too large to fit into the pipe. We had German guards all round us and could make the move only in the daylight before we were herded inside.

'The way the mob tricked the guards was most original. We formed the good old Australian two-up ring, and when the guards saw us gambling they were satisfied. All the big blokes formed the outside of the ring, and every time the pennies flew in the air another chap would slip into the hole and disappear. Sixty of them got out before the trick was discovered.

'Then the Jerries got hold of a little Cypriot and made a test with him. They belted him into the pipe and placed guards at the other end to time him. That was the end of our sewer chances for they filled it with barbed wire and padlocked the cover'.

A boon arrived one day in a little cart pulled by a donkey. 'No sooner had he disappeared round a corner than his donkey was rushed,' said Private Arnold. 'In less than five minutes its throat had been cut and

155

about 50 amateur butchers were round it. Blokes were seen running in all directions with bits of meat hacked from the carcass. We never waited to hear what the owner had to say. Anyway, we would not have been able to understand him. We had precious grilled donkey that day.'

On another occasion Private Arnold and a Tasmanian who had been a slaughterman in civilian life caught a cat. It was killed and dressed, and in the subsequent bartering an English officer offered 10 pounds in Egyptian money for the head and one leg. The Germans were in little better shape for food in the Lamsdorf camp. They never interfered with the Red Cross parcels, and generally treated the prisoners well, with the exception of Jews and Poles.

'I have on more than one occasion seen a hungry German guard pick from the rubbish cans a bully beef tin or margarine container and scrape out the fragments of fat we had left in them,' he said. 'For a little time we missed our Red Cross parcels, for our own bombers were blowing up everything round the country. They certainly did not miss much with their high explosives and gave the Germans a tough time.

'Once while working on a farm in Poland,' he said, 'I made a rash remark to the German guards. Blowing out my chest I told them that if Singapore ever fell I would contentedly work on that farm for the remainder of my life. I got a shock at 2 o'clock one morning when the guards entered and shouted. "Where's that Aussie?" They told me then that the Japs had taken Singapore. All the Germans seemed to have got drunk that night.'

Private Arnold is now in the sanctuary of his parents' home. He smokes in-numerable cigarettes and enjoys Port Pirie to the full. As a sort of afterthought he remarks that there is no beer in the world like that of South Australia and Port Pirie.'

Slim is survived by 6 children and 13 grandchildren.

--- Lest we forget ---

VICTOR EDWARD MARTIN

By Gwen Nelson

I am a retired mental health nurse/social worker. I switched between roles depending on which paid better. I have also been a riding instructor, bank clerk, lab technician and ran my own market stall. For a couple of years I was a stringer for a local newspaper and now volunteer teaching conversational English for different companies in Europe. I am a mad cat lady and, at one time had eight cats and five dogs, as well as various other assorted animals over the years, all rescues. I love playing bridge, genealogy and writing bad limericks. My degree is in Mediaeval History and I am passionate about social history as I believe the history of ordinary people is every bit as important as that of popes, princes, and politicians. I am a London girl but now live in Scotland with my partner and our very spoilt cat.

Dad was called up in 1940 although he had enlisted in the Territorial Army on 26 April 1939. It always rankled him that his name was incorrectly transcribed as Victor Edmund and the Army Records Centre refused to amend it. He and Mum married when he was on leave in November 1939 at St. Frances of Sales church, Stockwell.

Dad was sent to Woolwich Arsenal to join the 64th Medium Regiment, Royal Artillery and trained as a gunner. At one stage he was promoted to lance bombardier but demoted equally as quickly He was shipped out to the Middle East and fought in campaigns in Egypt and North Africa before being sent to Libya where he was badly wounded just outside Cyrenaica when the truck he was in ran over a landmine. I always believed Dad had been captured in Northern Greece as I remember him saying Salonika was his place of capture. It was only when I received his records from International Red Cross that I realised the error. Several of the others were killed but Dad was fortunate that he had curled up to go to sleep and thus protected vital organs. Nonetheless his injuries were bad enough, a fractured femur and both radius and ulna in his right arm. He said the German soldier who accepted his surrender uttered the cliché, 'For you, Tommy, the war is over'.

It was 24 June 1942 and my mother was informed that he was missing in action on 6 July although the Red Cross were informed of his capture on 28 June.

After being patched up and having his broken limbs reset at a field hospital, he was transferred to Caserta military hospital in the South of Italy on 3 August 1942. He always said he owed his life to the nursing sisters at the hospital as his leg wound became badly infected. There was a shortage of antibiotics so the nuns resorted to a traditional remedy of allowing the wound to become flyblown. The maggots ate away all the necrotic flesh leaving the wound clean and permitting normal healing.

Unfortunately, when the plaster cast was taken off Dad's arm it was discovered that the surgeon who had set it had made a mistake during the alignment. This, along with nerve damage, meant he was unable to perform actions that required fine movement or arm rotation so he taught himself to write left-handed. He also became a left-handed batsman.

Once his injuries had healed sufficiently, Dad was taken to Stalag VIII-A on 29 July 1943 and from there on to Stalag VIII-B Lamsdorf, Silesia, Germany, on 29 January 1944. Nowadays it is Łambinowice and in Poland. Dad always spoke very positively of his years as a POW and had the highest regard for the Camp Commandant and the guards. He said, more than once, that if he met any of them again he'd shake their hands and say, 'Fritz you were only doing your duty, the same as I was.' He commented that they were 'Damn fine soldiers'.

I don't know if Dad repressed negative memories or whether he genuinely had none but he only ever mentioned the positives. He spoke of how the local women would come to the camp in winter with big pots of soup made from turnips and someone from each hut would go to the wire and have it ladled into containers to take back for the men to have something warm to eat. They would also do mending for the men in exchange for Red Cross food. Dad was a non-smoker so always had useful currency in the cigarettes included in the Red Cross parcels.

The war also affected his vocabulary and I remember him frequently saying '*Jildi, jildi!*' if he wanted someone to hurry up or '*Raus, Raus!*'. Also '*Imshi iggri*' which I believe is Arabic when he wanted me to go away. He would refer to my mother as the '*Memsahib*' He'd also call someone a *bosthoon* if they did something silly but I don't know the origin of that word. Much of Dad's language was flavoured by his love of Dickens and Rudyard Kipling and he'd often quote Kipling when talking about Indian soldiers he had known. 'He's a poor benighted heathen but a first-class fighting man'.

Dad never got out of the habit of having been a soldier and would frequently bark at me, if he caught me slouching, 'Head up! Chin in! Chest out! Thumbs by the seams of your trousers!' If ever we went out anywhere it was never a gentle stroll but always the civilian equivalent of a route march. I owe my good posture and ability to 'step it out' at nearly 75, to this early training.

He mentioned many activities that were on offer for the men including the opportunity to attend educational classes, learn a musical instrument and other recreational skills. It was there he learnt to play bridge, although it was auction bridge rather than the modern-day contract bridge. It is a love he passed on to me.

There were many sports teams but, because of his injuries, Dad was unable to take part in these. He spoke also of the first-class entertainment that was on offer and how the guards would also come to watch the performances. Years later he recognised Denholm Elliot, by then a noted Shakespearian actor, as having been a fellow prisoner.

As a baptised Catholic, although not a particularly observant one, he received a diary/memorandum book at Christmas 1942 from Pope Pius XII. It has Christmas carols at the back of the book and, in it, he has written the names of other prisoners and their addresses. These include

159

Pat Sturrock and John McColligan, both from Dundee. As I now live near Dundee I have tried to find their descendants but without success so am hoping this might be seen by them. There is also Frank McBeth from Whangarei NZ; Thomas Thompson, Newcastle on Tyne; Johnnie Deane, Durham; Luc H. De Tissoles, Marseilles; Bert Hamilton, Northrand, Transvaal; Leopold Sinner (who Dad used to call *Peccatoribus,* which is Latin for 'to or for sinners') from Luxembourg; Maurice O'Sullivan; Lefty Catterall, Bath; Bob Botton, Sydney NSW; W. Wright, Leeds, Rowan Rozanski, South Benet, Indiana; Cyril Jackson, Camberwell; J. Shepherd, Forsberg (*sic*); C. Swan, Coliodenean (*sic*). He also carried with him throughout the war his Missal which had been given to him by the parish priest at St. Francis de Sales, so I must assume he found some comfort in the belief in a deity.

While he was in Lamsdorf, Dad met two New Zealand soldiers, Jim Bland and Ritchie Kelly, who were to become lifelong friends. Dad was repatriated in 1944 and, after the war had finished, Jim and Ritchie came to stay at Priory Grove with our family.

While there, Ritchie met and fell in love with Mum's younger sister Gwen, married her and took her to New Zealand as a war bride. Ritchie came from Kapuka, near Invercargill, and they went back to live there. Aunty Gwen suffered immense culture shock coming from London to what was, essentially, the outback. She wrote home many sad letters about how isolated and lonely she was but my grandmother's attitude was that she had made her bed and now she must lie in it. The marriage lasted until Ritchie's death sometime in the 1970s.

Jim Bland also returned to New Zealand but was killed when his tractor, to which he had forgotten to apply brakes, rolled down an incline and crushed him against the gate he was opening. Ironically his son, also Jim, was killed in the same way.

After the war came the reality of fitting into Civvy Street again. Dad was repatriated to the UK on 16 September 1944, discharged as being permanently unfit for military duty on 1 March 1945 and awarded a disability pension of £2 per week from 2 March, to be reviewed on 3 September that year. It wasn't a lot but Dad said, even if it was only a farthing, he'd fight to get it because, if he didn't fight for his entitlement, he'd be letting down some poor bastard (his words) who needed it more and was unable to fight for his rights. Surprisingly Dad refused to claim his war medals on the grounds that, because everyone was eligible for these, they were of no value, either monetarily or emotionally. Such things are only valuable if only a few possess them. Many would disagree but that was his attitude and one with which I concur.

I was born on 11 March 1946 and it was a joke between my parents that I was the result of repatriation. I was an only child. Mum used to say that they decided to only have one child as they could only achieve perfection once but I think the reality was that she wanted me to be her little girl all my life and not to have to be shared with anyone else. Although she couldn't prevent me interacting with Dad, she made sure it was limited and she was always seen as being the 'go-to' person if I wanted anything. Consequently, I never got to really know Dad as well as I now wish I had. His own mother had died when he was a young boy and he had to leave school at an early age because his father remarried to a widow with children much younger than him.

I have no doubt my parents' love was genuine but there was also a great deal of dependency on his part and manipulation on hers. I can remember her once saying to me, 'You're too blunt. You can always get what you want if you make the other person think it was their idea.' I was well into adulthood before I realised this is what she had done to both Dad and I all our lives.

After his discharge Dad, like so many others, was issued with his 'demob' suit. In his case it was a gingery Harris tweed which we always called his 'park keeper's' suit as the LCC park keepers used to wear ones of the same material.

His treatment for his injuries continued for several years after he returned home. I can remember, as a small child, accompanying him on trips to St Thomas' hospital. Although the injury to his arm had healed, he continued to get abscesses. The treatment seemed to be for him to sit with his forearm in a sink full of hot paraffin wax. This was a treatment that had been used for injuries since Roman times and was popular during WWI. It never seems to have occurred to the hospital to break and reset Dad's arm with the bones attached correctly or perhaps the damage was so severe that further intervention would have compounded his problems.

Before being called up Dad had worked for Sainsbury's before it became a supermarket chain, as a butcher, but with the damage to his hand, was no longer able to cut sides of meat so took whatever job he was offered. Thus followed a period of him working for a week or two in a job for which he was totally unsuited, chucking it in and coming home on a Friday with his pay packet which Mum would spend on clothes and toys for me. She would then say to Dad, 'Right we're broke again, you'd better find another job'.

Among the jobs he'd had were as a spray painter, making ladies' powder compacts at a factory in the East End and for a while had a window cleaning round but found it was too hard cycling and washing windows with a gammy leg and a fairly useless right hand. Eventually he confessed to my mother that his desire was to be his own boss and have a grocery store. With a loan from my grandparents, he secured the lease on a grocery store in Golborne Road, North Kensington, which had been run into the ground by the mismanagement of the previous owner. We moved there in 1952 and Dad made a roaring success of the business. His exploits there can be read in Roger Rogowski's excellent book, *The other side of Notting Hill, from Wartime to the Westway*. He made a great success of his business and by the mid-1960's, was taking over £500 per week, £100 of which was clear profit. We were living on the pig's back!

My parents would always attend the annual regimental reunion which was held at the Cock Tavern in Great Portland Street and Dad would reminisce with old comrades. The only exception to this was when the reunion was held at the Café Royal in 1960. It was the 21st anniversary of the regiment and the dinner menu included delights such as Coupe Otranto, Supreme de Volaille Alamein and Souffle Ardennes, each dish being named after a field of conflict where the regiment had fought.

The guest of honour at this reunion was Lt General the Right Honourable Lord Freyburg, who at the time was governor general of New Zealand. This was the first time I was allowed to go to a regimental dinner along with Mum and Dad, Nana and Aunty Mick and Uncle Frank. We were presented to Lord Freyburg because of Aunty Gwen being a war bride and living in New Zealand. I remember him as being a very upright, slim man, who appeared genuinely interested in talking to us and was happy to have his photo taken shaking hands with Dad. Alas, like so many things relating to our family history, this photo was thrown out when my parents emigrated to New Zealand and now remains only a memory.

1966 was a time of change for our family. It was the year my maternal grandmother died after she had disturbed a burglar in her home and suffered a heart attack as he pushed her out the way to escape. Mum became very depressed as she was the daughter most relied on, even though we had moved from Stockwell nearly. It was also the time when the Kensington and Chelsea Council was embarking on a great slum demolition and social cleansing project which directly impacted on their, by now, two shops in Golborne Road, one of which we lived above. We would have got compensation for either the business or the living space but not both, for some reason. The accommodation we would have been given would have only been a two bedroom flat in a high rise when we had lived in the three floors above the shop and also had the backyard to grow vegetables.

I had gone on holiday with my boyfriend, Keith, in August 1966 and it was while we were on holiday that he proposed to me and I accepted. I came home bursting to tell Mum and Dad my news but before I could, Mum said to me, 'Dad and I have decided to emigrate to New Zealand. You can come with us if you like or we'll leave enough money for you to support yourself for a year. By the way, Mick and Frank are also emigrating.'

I had also been accepted for the City and Guilds College of Art and was due to start that semester but, as a not very mature 20-year-old, panicked at the thought of being on my own without Mum and Dad and said I'd go with them. As it turned out, it was quite the worst decision I could have made and effectively ruined my life for many years. I later found out from one of my cousins that Mick and Frank had not, at that stage, made any plans to emigrate but were talked into it by my mother. Fortunately, Keith and I never totally lost touch and renewed our relationship in 2005 when I returned to the UK for a holiday after my marriage to a Kiwi had broken up.

We settled in Christchurch where Dad took on another shop, part of the Four Square chain, but found its rules too restrictive after the freedom of owning his own business. All shops in the chain had the same specials and shopkeepers were not allowed to buy goods from other warehouses or promote their own specials. Dad compensated for this by going to auctions and having part of the shop dedicated to curios and collectibles. Despite this he did little more than break even and eventually sold the shop and took a job as an accounts clerk with a local engineering firm for a couple of years until his retirement.

Dad died unexpectedly of a heart attack on 31 August 1976, just three weeks after he had retired. The *Last Post* was played at his funeral and *For the Fallen* recited as his coffin was lowered into the grave. He is buried at Ruru Lawn, Christchurch, New Zealand.

HORRIE WOODS

By Don Woods

Don Woods is the son of Horrie Woods and the co-author (with Ken Scott) of the book, Soldier, Prisoner, Hunter, Gatherer, *the incredible WWII story of Horrie Woods. The book was 34 years in the making, transcribed from Horrie's war diaries which Don found hidden away in the bottom drawer of his office desk.*

The book gives a detailed account of Horrie's early life and his basic training. It covers the fighting in Greece and Crete, his capture, his brutal journey to Lamsdorf, and his many attempts at escaping. For Don, the 80 000 words in the book capture raw emotion, and encapsulate the evilness of Man, but also the survival instinct of mankind.

Horrie arrived at Lamsdorf in April 1942, physically weak but mentally strong. His time in the boxing ring prior to the war gave him the mental strength to dig deep and find the will to finish the job when the body was hurting.

Much had happened during the previous twelve months. He had Stukas in his sights of his Bren Gun as they attacked Servia Pass in West Macedonia district of Greece in April 1941. Despite forcing the *Wehrmacht* to retreat at the pass, Allied forces retreated to Crete where they engaged the enemy once more, again heavily outnumbered. The odds were against them. He was in the front line at the legendry battle at 42nd Street in Chania, where once more, an elite regiment of Austrian troops retreated.

Outnumbered, outgunned and after days on the run with little sleep and proper food, Horrie was taken prisoner in June 1942. He was kept in a transit camp on Crete for 227 days. He described it as 227 days of hell, where hunger and disease robbed the last remaining strength from his body. He was transferred to a civilian hospital in Salonika. After two months in hospital, he was sent on to Lamsdorf after he was caught making plans to escape. The arduous train trip to Lamsdorf was not a pleasant journey in overcrowded cattle wagons, with the sick hanging on to life, some not making it, in bitterly cold and unpleasant conditions. Horrie's return to better health was undone by the train trip.

Horrie kept a diary from the time he was caught as a POW right up until the end of the war. He wrote home whenever he was able to, and this documentation provided insights as to what was happening in his life at the time.

Attached to Lamsdorf are various *arbeitskommandos* (work camps) and Horrie did not have much time to settle in before he was assigned to E312 Stramberg, a quarry in the Czech Republic. Filling wagons with stone in the cold conditions did not fit too well for Horrie and he escaped in March 1943 with an airman who assumed the name of a regular soldier. Pilots were kept in a separate compound as they were considered more valuable for the Allied war effort and when possible, swapped identities with regular soldiers.

Fourteen days later they were caught and handed over to the *Gestapo* where once more Horrie had to dig deep, this time after an interrogation.

166

He was sent back to Lamsdorf to spend some time in the cooler. Not a pleasant experience.

Lamsdorf was overcrowded and after Horrie's release from the cooler, he initially had to sleep on the floor, and waited a month before he received a regular Red Cross food parcel. Concerned for his health, his good friend Howard Holmes, who had previously secured a job in the tailor's shop, bribed a guard with cigarettes to secure Horrie a job as a tailor.

Tailors, for whatever reason, had access to better living conditions and Horrie soon moved in with them and attempted to learn the craft, but by his own admission was rather poor in comparison with the others, who consigned him to 'sewing buttons,' and not much else.

Horrie always had an active life and being locked up behind a wire did not sit comfortably with him. Boredom was something he had to deal with. When not busy at the tailor shop, he would walk the camp with friends, watching the odd boxing match, athletic event or games of cricket or rugby. He attended church on a regular basis and often sat in on lectures. One lecture was put on by an Australian journalist who had travelled to China and Russia prior to the war and another by a chap who had flown from England to Australia. Horrie, like all the other POWs, always looked forward to their regular Red Cross parcels that would usually come with fifty cigarettes and much needed supplementary food.

Horrie had enough and was once more working on a plan to escape. He arranged a transfer back to the *arbeitskommando* in Stramberg. Once back at the quarry, he had forgotten what hard work was like. He did not hit it off with the quarry boss and was soon sent off to the cooler after calling him names.

In his spare time, Horrie started making rings and pendants by remodelling toothbrushes' plastic handles. In one pendant he concealed a compass, which he would use in subsequent escape attempts.

After one failed attempt where the guards were alerted to the noise when a gust of wind caught a door, he finally got away in June 1944. After 24 days on the run with a pilot under an assumed name of a regular soldier, they ran into a patrolling guard at a border crossing and was soon back in the cooler at Lamsdorf.

Conditions at Lamsdorf had deteriorated even more since he was last there almost a year prior. Overcrowding and food shortages left him hungry. On one occasion the Germans searched all the barracks looking for a tunnel. Several escape tunnels had been dug by the prisoners over time and most were found, usually by driving heavy vehicles over them, causing a collapse.

Despite the hardships, Horrie kept a positive attitude by keeping busy and updating his diary. He attended farming lectures as he dreamt of having a dairy farm when he returned to New Zealand. A fellow prisoner, Brownie, who maintained his own garden, gave Horrie the odd fresh lettuce leaf which assisted with his recovery to better health.

Although work was harder in the *arbeitskommando* the food was better and after building his strength up, Horrie decided he would give escape another go. This time he was sent to E166 Saubsdorf.

His plan was to attempt escape again early in 1945. But with the war coming to an end, and advancing Russian and American armies, he had to endure a 350 kilometres death march away from the advancing Allied armies. They had to scavenge for food and endure appalling weather as they were forced to walk many kilometres on a daily basis. Once more the body was hurting and in Horrie's words, 'The going is incredibly tough, but we can take it'.

I hope I have given the readers of *Heroes of Lamsdorf* a very brief taste of what Horrie and many other prisoners endured. They should never be forgotten. I am proud to say that Horrie's full story, his legacy, will live on for many years to come.

As I once read, 'To live on in the hearts and minds of others, is truly not to die.'

The Escape & Evasion of Sergeants
PIOTR BAKALARSKI,
WITMOLD RAGINIS,
STANLEY JAMES VERSE PHILO and
Driver FREDERIC GEOFFREY WILLIAMSON

By Allan Hunn

Allan served in the Royal Air Force for 26 years as an engineer, his service on operational units includes 56(F) Squadron, 74(F) and 1435 Flt. He works in the aircraft design process as a Human Factors in Maintenance team manager. Allan's spare time is spent researching WWII escape and evasion journeys with a focus on replicating the mountainous elements of the routes, most notably the Pyrenees. Allan intends writing an escape and evasion walkers guidebook covering Europe.

This story describes the escape journeys of Sergeant Piotr Bakalarski, Sergeant Witmold Raginis, Driver Frederic Geoffrey Williamson from Stalag VIII-B Lamsdorf, as well as the evasion journey of Sergeant Stanley James Verse Philo during late 1943.

During the journey through the Pyrenees, Driver Williamson tragically died of exhaustion. Sergeant Raginis forged ahead in the interest of finding help for the group, he was incorrectly directed by a guide, became lost but eventually returned to the start of the Pyrenees journey to eventually make good his evasion at a later date.

Sergeants Bakalarski and Philo made good their escape in extremely difficult winter conditions.

SERGEANT PIOTR BAKALARSKI

Sergeant Bakalarski, a pilot of 300 Squadron (Polish) Bomber Command RAF was shot down on 27 July 1942 in a Wellington bomber by an Me 110. He crash-landed on beach near the Elbe estuary. All the crew members had been injured in the attack: Flying Officer Falinski, Pilot Officer Boguszweski, Sergeant Kobiela and Sergeant Olszeweski.

A group of 12 German soldiers from a nearby anti-aircraft battery tended to the crew and gave first aid, sadly Pilot Officer Boguszweski died during his extraction from the aircraft. Being uninjured, Sergeant Bakalarski was then separated from his crew and transported to Dulag Luft (Frankfurt-Am-Main), where he was interrogated. He was held in solitary confinement for four and half days, before being transported to Stalag VIII-B Lamsdorf.

Sergeant Bakalarski made two early escape attempts from Stalag VIII-B Lamsdorf. On the first occasion he appears to have been on the run from 7 Septeber 1942 into early November 1942 when he was recaptured. He was restrained with rope and then chains for about three months and was not allowed Red Cross parcels. On the second escape occasion he swapped identities with Private Moritz Leder, a Palestinian, and escaped from Jaworzno. During the attempted escape one of his helpers was killed but Sergeant Bakalarski managed to go on the run until he was recaptured by SS soldiers.

When working at Jaworzno he re-established communication with a Polish organization to arrange escape. On the 10 July 1943 he made his third and final successful escape from Jaworzno coal mine by simply walking away from his guards, disguised as a Polish workman. He met the helpers outside of the perimeter and rode to the house of one of them, four kilometres away from Jaworzno. He then moved on to Jelen, where, hiding in a hayloft, he heard of an impending German search, and was subsequently helped to hide close to Jaworzno.

Sergeant Bakalarski then moved onto Szczakowa, disguised as a railway worker, and started to travel onto Cracow when he stopped at Rudwa, where the area was surrounded by *Gestapo*. He managed to slip away and hide, but nevertheless witnessed the torture and murder of 27 men, one of a man being hung from a lintel by his feet and the shooting of his wife and child directly underneath his head. Before being murdered they had been made to dig their own graves.

Sergeant Bakalarski continued his journey and made it to Cracow where he eventually met up with his friend, Sergeant Raginis. He was incredibly pleased to see his friend again, in his MI9 report he indicates that Sergeant Raginis helped him greatly with his onward journey.

SERGEANT WITMOLD RAGINIS

Although Witmold Raginis was Polish, he had lived in France since the age of four. He left France for England to join the RAF in 1941. Sergeant Witmold Raginis became a Rear Gunner on 305 Squadron (Polish) Bomber Command RAF. He was shot down in a Wellington bomber near to Brest in August 1942 whilst on a mine laying mission. He and the crew were picked up by a French fishing boat and when the boat return to port the crew were arrested and questioned by Germans.

The crew were then transported to Paris where their interrogation continued. They were all transported to Dulag Luft (Frankfurt-Am-Main) where they were interrogated on four further occasions. During the interrogations Sergeant Raginis was reminded that he was a Pole in an attempt to gain information, however, the apparent threat does not seem to have gone any further.

Sergeant Raginis and the crew were then transported onto Stalag VIII-B. The journey took three days and nights. Their flying boots were taken and they were replaced with wooden clogs which were difficult to walk in. Sergeant Raginis talks of being at Lamsdorf for six months during which time he was held in chains part of the time. He then swapped identities with 10400 Private Lehem, who had been captured in Greece.

Sergeant Raginis began working at Tarnowitz railway station, loading and unloading coal. He worked here for three months looking for escape opportunities but none materialized as the railway station was under strict guard. He met Sergeant Bakalarski at Tarnowitz, who had also switched his identity and both men then volunteered for work at Jaworzno coal mine.

Sergeants Raginis and Bakalarski were put to work in the Jaworzno coal mine, where they made contact with a Polish organization that would assist their escape. They were notified that they were to be transferred to Beuthen and had to bring forward their escape plans. During a shift transfer they slipped out of their barracks and escaped through a hole they had cut in the perimeter fence. Sergeant Bakalarski was 15 minutes ahead of Raginis, however, the *Gestapo* were alerted and killed the guide waiting for Bakalarski. Although Bakalarski escaped, he was captured two days later.

Sergeant Raginis' escape continued via a farm at Dabrowa then onto Szczakowa where he stayed with a family before continuing to Cracow.

Sergeants Bakalarski and Raginis eventually met again whilst on the run in Cracow. Under false identifies both were conscripted as Polish civilian workers for work in Germany. They journeyed across Germany together, passing through Berlin, Saarbrucken and Sarrebourg. They were given assistance journeying through Hertzing, Foulcrey and eventually crossed the German frontier into France at Igney.

In Igney they were sheltered by a farmer and then advised to ask the *gendarmerie* for help at Lunéville. The *gendarmerie* confirmed their identities by contacting Sergeant Raginis' parents, who were living in Montlucon in France. They travelled on under the arrest of the *gendarmes* so as not to arouse the suspicions of the Germans and reached Nancy on 21 September 1943.

Once there they given false French identities and sent on to Lyon, they were handed over to the Marie Claire Line, and journeyed on to Ruffec, where they separated for a short time. Sergeant Raginis journeyed to Pamiers and Sergeant Bakalarski to Limoges. They met again at Luzenac for the crossing of the Pyrenees.

SERGEANT STANLEY JAMES VERSE PHILO

Sergeant Philo was in Lancaster III LM337 EA-V of 49 Squadron when it was shot down by flak fire returning from a bombing mission over Milan, 15/16 August 1943. He bailed out and landed uninjured near Verneuil-sur-Avre. He was directed by a peasant towards Senonches, where he was sheltered. He then cycled towards Champrond-en-Gâtine with a helper. After his helpers left, he walked south to Chassant, Dampierre, Unverre, Chattilon and then Lanneray where he sheltered in a hay loft on 23 August 1943.

On the 24 August he continued on to Cloyes, Lisle, Selommes, and north of Le Breuil he spent the night in a deserted shack at the side of a railway line. On 25 August he continued through Blois, La Chaussee St Victor, and Mont where he slept the night in new-mown hay.

On the 26 August he passed through Cour-Cheverny, Contres and St Aignan Forest of Brouard where he slept in a hayloft. On 27 August 1943 he continued onto Nouans, Villedomain, Chatillon and Azay where he was put in touch with an organization that eventually guided him to Luzenac.

Driver FREDERIC GEOFFREY WILLIAMSON

Driver Frederic Geoffrey Williamson of the Royal New Zealand Army Service Corps (RNZASC) was English, however, had lived in New Zealand for about 10 years. He joined the RNZASC and had been a driver but transferred to the intelligence corps for the interrogation of prisoners of war as he spoke German and Italian. At some point in his life he had lived in Germany.

He was using the name Geoffrey Marston; assuming to avoid being linked to the intelligence corps. He had been captured in Crete in 1941 and then held in Stalag VIII-B from which he had escaped on19 September 1943 with an as yet unidentified Australian flight lieutenant.

Very little is known about his journey from Lamsdorf to the Pyrenees, however, it must have been remarkable. Tragically, Driver Williamson was to die two days before his 39th birthday on 27 October 1943.

FROM LUZENAC OVER THE PYRENEES
What follows next is an attempt to retrace the route of the group and the point where Driver Williamson died, as accurately as possible. The description of the route that follows is made in good faith and utilizes the individual MI9 reports, Commonwealth War Grave Commission (CWGC) and discussions with the Peloton de Gendarmerie de Haute-Montagne de l'Ariege. The route is ultimately a hypothesis and is based on the group's starting point from their MI9 reports and the point where Driver Williamson's body was recovered, from the co-ordinates provided by the CWGC. The crossing into Andorra is again from MI9 reports.

The story of the escape and evasion of Sergeant Bakalarski, Sergeant Raginis, Sergeant Philo and Driver Williamson is now picked up from where they came together at Luzenac in the Pyrenees. It is worth noting that journeys across the Pyrenees were treacherous, escapers and evaders were often unfit due to long periods of inactivity, undernourished due to food shortages and poorly clothed for mountainous journeys due to having to blend in with local populations. Winter journeys were much worse due to the weather conditions, including the risks posed by avalanches. In the case of Driver Williamson, his older age may well have had an impact.

Mountain guides could be anything from idealists wanting to make a contribution to the war effort, to those who just wanted money to survive or for nothing other than greed. Many were *passeurs,* or smugglers, and many did not know the mountains as they would have escapers and evaders believe. There are many stories of guides being lost.

When the group arrived at Luzenac they were met by a helper, Jose Rodriguez, of the Marie Claire Line; they all walked to the hamlet of Urs where the group hid overnight in a cave.

At 6 a.m. on 25 October 1943 Jose Rodriguez handed over the group of three escapers and single evader to two French guides for the journey across the Pyrenees from France into Andorra. The group set off from Luzenac in the rain, but as they climbed the rain began to turn to snow which gradually increased in depth as their altitude increased.

It is believed that for the first part of the journey they were heading for the mountain plateau of Campalou at 2032m, they had walked 11 kilometres, ascended 1500m in six hours. From the survivors' MI9 reports it was clear that Driver Williamson was finding the first part of the journey very challenging; he was certainly very tired on the approach to Campalou. Before reaching the summit of Campalou they chose to rest for 45 minutes just before midday and lit a fire. The rest resulted in a slight recovery for Driver Williamson, which unfortunately did not last for long.

On reaching the Campalou, the group headed east descending quite steeply into Vallée de Savignac. Once in the valley, they headed south-southeast. The group was clearly concerned about Driver Williamson as his condition was continuing to deteriorate. They then turned south and ascended approximately 250m into a small hidden valley which contains the source of the Najar River. However, given the deep snow, Driver

Williamson was now rapidly declining and was receiving support from the group. Their pace was extremely slow.

At approximately 4 p.m. the group agreed that Guide Two and Sergeant Raginis should forge ahead to identify where to cross into the safety of Andorra and there find help for Driver Williamson. He was by this stage suffering greatly from the effects of a demanding winter journey and was being supported by Sergeants Bakalarski and Philo, neither of which considered themselves to be in the best physical condition. At approximately 6 p.m. Sergeants Bakalarski and Philo were unable to detect any life in Driver Williamson and they sadly placed his body in the shelter of rocks very close to the source of the Najar River. By now it is estimated the group had covered another nine kilometres, ascended 750m in eight hours.

Ahead of Sergeants Bakalarski and Philo, Sergeant Raginis and his guide had reached the Etangs de Fontagenta. The guide then incorrectly directed Sergeant Raginis to the north side of the lake rather than the east, and as a result Sergeant Raginis descended from the Etangs de Fontagenta, found a river and elected to follow the river downstream, thinking he was in Andorra. However, perhaps due to a sixth sense, he hid when he came across a hut and observed it for movement. He saw two German soldiers coming and going and realised he was still in France.

He then followed the river down a valley towards the town of Aston. He came across some French and Spanish workmen before Aston and stayed with them for three days to recover from frostbite. He was given some provisions and then walked closer to Aston where he hid on the outskirts for a week observing German soldier movements. Once it was clear he walked through Aston and stole a bicycle and head for Tarascon and then Urs to find Jose Rodriguez.

He was taken by Jose Rodriguez to Merens-les-Vals by train, from there he walked to the frontier via fields and hills on 3 or 4 November. He reached L'Hospitalet and then began a climb at night, and reached Andorra, eight kilometres southeast of Soldeu, after five hours. He then made his way to Escalda.

Sergeants Bakalarski and Philo, and the remaining French guide, continued west toward, but slightly above, the Col du Belh, following what is a shepherd track today. They continued southwest towards where

176

the Refuge du Rulhe is located today. The guide left Sergeants Bakalarski and Philo in this area and from here the two descended in the dark into the valley Rau de Estangnol, to the northern most Estangnol at 2099m. They carried a small, broken thumbnail compass; however, it may have assisted them avoid the route via Etang de Joclar which would have been extremely treacherous in snow with a high risk of avalanche.

From the valley floor Sergeants Bakalarski and Philo ascended towards Etangs de Fontagenta, on what was described as 'loose rock'. Sergeant Philo describes his shoes coming off in the 'loose rock', he sat down, fell asleep and was awoken by a pummelling from Sergeant Bakalarski.

Sergeant Bakalarski describes how Sergeant Philo fell asleep and that he noticed that he was carrying his shoes. Sergeant Bakalarski cut off Sergeant Philo's frozen socks and replaced them with a dry pair and then dressed Sergeant Philo's frostbitten hands and refitted his shoes. At this point Sergeant Bakalarski describes smacking Sergeant Philo all over the place to rouse him.

The awareness and presence of mind of Sergeant Bakalarski, in such a state of exhaustion, to care for his compatriot is incredible. He undoubtedly saved Sergeant Philo's life.

At this point Sergeant Bakalarski describes himself as being completely saturated and that it took four hours just to cover one kilometre of the rocky mountainside. From the area of 'loose rocks,' Sergeant Bakalarski forced Philo to continue in the dark toward the Etangs de Fontagenta. They lost Sergeant Raginis' tracks in this area and also became lost going three kilometres in the wrong direction, nevertheless they recovered the situation with the broken compass. Sergeant Bakalarski states that it took 12 hours to reach the Etangs de Fontagenta, a journey that would normally take between 30mins to an hour. It is extremely difficult to imagine how torturous this journey was.

From the Etangs de Fontagenta Sergeants Bakalarski and Philo were able to re-orientate themselves using Sergeant Philo's escape map and broken compass, and cross over the Col de Fontagenta into Andorra, descending to eventually reach a farm in Baladosa in the darkness, where they sheltered in a loft overnight. Sergeant Philo was then treated for frostbite for two days in an Andorran hospital.

Whilst Sergeant Philo was in hospital Sergeant Bakalarski was put in touch with a Spaniard working for the British Consulate in Barcelona, by a lady known as Miss Pla. After six days in Andorra, both men were taken by the Spaniard to Seo De Urgel in Spain. They had no problem crossing into Spain.

In Seo De Urgel they were handed over the Civil Guard and thence to the British Consulate in Barcelona, arriving on 3 November. They travelled to Madrid and arrived in Gibraltar on 8 November 1943.

Overall, their arduous journey over the Pyrenees was 28 kilometres with 2350m ascent and took approximately 37 hours, the vast majority of it in deep snow without rest, shelter or nourishment, an incredible achievement for Sergeants Bakalarski and Philo, and ultimately for Sergeant Raginis. What is astonishing is the determination to return to Allied territory to carry on with the war effort. They all underwent extreme hardship with Driver Williamson paying the ultimate price.

AFTERWARDS

After the war Sergeant Bakalarski settled in Blackpool, in the UK. He died on 18 November 1966. Sergeant Raginis resettled in Amilly in France and died on 3 January 1993.

Sergeant Philo became Warrant Officer Philo and was sadly killed in action 3 April 1945 serving with 96 Squadron.

Driver Williamson's body was eventually recovered and he is laid to rest at the Mazargues War Cemetery in Marseilles. He was the son of Brigadier-General Frederic Herbert Williamson, CB., CBE. and of Florence May Williamson (née Dawson), of Surrey and husband of Vida Vivienne Williamson of Parnell, New Zealand.

Staff Sergeant JAMES GORDON WINDRIDGE

11th Field Ambulance S.A.M.C.

1st South African Division

By Sheila Windridge

Sheila was born in England but grew up in Rhodesia (now Zimbabwe). She has three daughters and two grandsons. During her career she worked as an accountant and was financial director of several companies before her retirement.

In 2005 she founded the charity Edirisa UK which works in southwest Uganda in education, health and sanitation, clean water and sustainable enterprise.

A keen genealogist Sheila began researching the second world war experiences of her father-in-law in 2015 and has recently finished writing a book for the family: Gordon's War.

179

'The fact of being captured is so overwhelming a disaster that for a while one's mind fails to grasp its significance. It seems quite possible that one's command, one's freedom, one's right to think for oneself, have been taken away, and that henceforth one must obey the dictates of those representing all one hates most in the world ... but now I was caught!' *Brigadier James Hargest 5th NZ Infantry Brigade.*

Gordon Windridge was 'caught' on Sunday 23 November 1941 at Sidi Rezegh, Libya.

Gordon was my father in law. I first met him in 1976. At some point I was vaguely aware of his military involvement in World War II - that he had been captured in North Africa and held as a prisoner of war. However, it never really meant anything to me at the time. It was only much later, when I started tracing the family tree, that I started to realise what he must have endured. I decided to look more closely into his war time experiences and trace his time from enlisting to arriving home. It has taken me five years of on and off research to put all the pieces together. This is his story.

When Gordon arrived at Stalag VIII-B Lamsdorf on Wednesday 29 September 1943, after three awful days crammed into a cattle truck on a train from Italy, he had already been a prisoner for 675 days.

His journey to war, and thus to imprisonment, had started on the afternoon of 17 July 1940 when, together with the rest of the 11th Field Ambulance, he boarded the troopship HMT *Nevasa* and set sail from Durban harbour heading for Mombasa. With troops crowding the rails and thousands of civilians waving good-bye, the *Nevasa* headed out into the Indian Ocean. They endured a long, unescorted trip to Mombasa, almost via India, to avoid enemy submarines.

In Kenya the 11th Field Ambulance was assigned to the 5th SA Infantry Brigade, based in Marsabit. They saw action in the East African and Abyssinian campaign before setting off for North Africa on 24 April 1941.

They arrived in Port Suez on 4 May, then on 26 May arrived in Mersa Matruh where they were trained in desert warfare until early November.

The battle of Sidi Rezegh was part of 'Operation Crusader' – an effort to relieve the garrison besieged in Tobruk and reverse the threat of Rommel's troops blocking the route to Egypt and the crucial Suez Canal, Europe's supply link to the Middle East. The 5th SA Infantry Brigade and 11th Field Ambulance reached Sidi Rezegh on 21 November and were immediately confronted by the 15th and 21st Panzer Divisions. The battle raged for three days, culminating in a continuous three-hour saturation barrage on the afternoon of 23 November.

The battle of Sidi Rezegh was a disaster for the 5th SA Infantry Brigade. They had gone into action with 5800 men and under 2000 returned. 224 were killed in action, 379 wounded and about 3000 captured. It was South Africa's heaviest loss during the war, according to General Smuts. The 5th SA Infantry Brigade was destroyed and ceased to exist as a fighting formation.

Gordon was taken prisoner on the evening of 23 November 1941, despite the assumption that medical personnel would be protected by the Geneva Convention. Little did he know there were 42 months as a POW ahead of him. One cannot contemplate the state of mind of those captured, after three days of continuous fighting and the witness of so many friends killed and maimed. Gordon had seen his best friend die during the battle.

Most of those captured at Sidi Rezegh were marched to the prison camp at Benghazi in what became known as the 'Thirst Marches'. They were marched for three days in the fierce heat of the desert, sleeping in the open during the night when temperatures were freezing cold. Dehydration and hunger loomed over those poor prisoners, they were given very little water and only a biscuit or two for food. On the fourth day they were put on trucks and taken to the Italian POW camp in Benghazi. By 5 December 1941, the Benghazi camp (known as 'The Palms') held over 6000 British Commonwealth troops. The facilities were inadequate for such numbers and conditions were appalling. Dysentery was rife.

The prisoners themselves were ill-prepared for captivity. Although during training they were issued with instructions should they become prisoners of war, this guidance was wholly inadequate to prepare anyone for what to expect, especially in the desert of North Africa. In addition, at this early stage of captivity, no Red Cross delegates inspected any of the camps in North Africa and the POWs were left to fend for themselves in disorganized and very trying circumstances.

On 8 December Gordon's wife, Edna, received a letter saying that Gordon was reported missing.

It is uncertain exactly what date Gordon left Benghazi for Naples, but he did talk about having to wait some time for the boat he eventually boarded. The journeys from Benghazi to Tripoli, then Tripoli to Naples were horrific. Cargo spaces were packed to capacity. There was a severe lack of toilet facilities. I know the last ship that year left Benghazi for Tripoli on 21 December, arriving in Tripoli on 23 December, and staying there over Christmas, arriving in Naples on 1 January. These were the last of the prisoners from North Africa to pass through Naples; later prisoners were shipped through Brindisi.

Gordon was 'detained' in Caserta Military Hospital, according to a Red Cross list, dated 12 January 1942. The reason was not recorded, but it is likely to be connected to dysentery as he was not wounded in battle. It is also possible that he may have been working at the hospital.

After the hospital he spent a short time at PG66 Capua, a transit camp near the hospital, 40 kilometres north of Naples. He was moved further north to PG52 Chiavari in February 1942. His post war questionnaire states his arrival there as 4 February. This camp, although lacking in space for outdoor sporting activities, was regarded as one of the best camps in Italy. Charles Rollins wrote: 'The camp itself was superb after Capua. It was numbered PG52, was entirely of new wooden two storeyed huts, containing wooden slatted beds, one above the other, and had a brick-built washing trough with cold running water from a series of stand-pipes. Lavatories were of the usual type, a deep trench in the ground over which one squatted and tried to avoid falling in. The camp was situated in a fold in the hills with a steep ascent to one side and encompassed by a river on the other three sides which took up a "U" bend around the site.'

In June 1942 Gordon was moved, together with other medical personnel, to staff a new military hospital in Lucca; Ospedale Militare Territoriale Numero 4. He arrived there on 11 June. There were 106 of them transferred on that day, and one of the other men was Edwin N. Broomhead, author of *Barbed Wire in the Sunset*.

The hospital soon held 530 prisoner patients with 13 British doctors and 104 orderlies to look after them. The hospital was fairly well equipped with a good supply of medicines. Every ward had a sister from the Dominican Order in charge of ward equipment, bedding and the issue of food to the patients. It seems they were cheerful and solicitous towards both the patients and the POWs and made their lives a little more bearable.

In April 1943 hundreds of ill and disabled POWs were repatriated from Lucca, together with medical personnel to look after them on the journey. Edwin Broomhead describes what life was like at Lucca. How the hospital developed, how – as happened at most camps –, theatre groups and bands were formed, a choir got together, and a library was opened thanks to the Red Cross delivery of books. On leaving Broomhead states in his book: 'Those were our days at Lucca, when from so little so much evolved; when wounded men struggled up from valleys of pain to robust strength; when dull days became bright; when hunger left us and the parcels arrived; when strangers became friends, and when the quiet repression of a new prison hospital became a crowded round of concerts, games, rehearsals, songs, books and talk.'

Of the 106 who had been transferred from Chiavari only 18 remained in Lucca. Sadly, Gordon was one of those. Curiously he never mentioned this fact. We can only imagine what a terrible blow it must have been.

On 10 September 1943, the POWs at Lucca Hospital were all called on parade by the Italian officer. Italy had signed the Allies' terms of surrender two days previously. They would soon be free to join their own people. The officer asked the POWs to remain at the hospital until the Allied troops arrived. Everyone was jubilant. But the celebrations were short-lived. It seemed that the Germans were pouring into Italy to oppose the Allied advance, to take over the POW camps and ship as many POWs as possible back to labour camps in Germany.

On 26 September 1943, Gordon and his medical colleague prisoners, together with the patients, were crammed into cattle trucks and taken by train through northern Italy, across Austria and through Czechoslovakia. Private Terry Gorman remembers the train stopping at Innsbruck Station where they were allowed to get some water and a little food. Eventually, on 29 September, they arrived at Annahof Station, Silesia, on the border of Germany and Poland. It's hard to imagine what those men were feeling after three days crammed into cattle trucks – cold, hungry, tired, worried, confused, mentally exhausted. They were herded off the trains to be surrounded by masses of armed guards yelling 'Raus! Raus!

Schnell!' They then had to march around three kilometres to the camp along a country lane that was known as Chestnut Alley.

When the POWs turned the corner and first set eyes on Stalag VIII-B they probably couldn't believe their eyes. It was gigantic!

And so began seventeen months of life at Stalag VIII-B Lamsdorf.

When prisoners first reached the camp they queued for induction, delousing, fingerprinting and form completing. They were given a number and a dog tag, were issued with a spoon and a fork, a mess tin, two blankets, a straw-filled mattress and bed boards for the bunks.

Soon after induction they were photographed. The Germans gave them clean uniforms to wear, which had to be returned once the photograph had been taken and were given to the next group waiting. On a bench in front of a hut, the men sat in a long row, with a second row standing behind. Up to 18 men could be photographed in each group. Hundreds of men were photographed on that bench. The POWs sent the photographs home; this would show that they were still alive and were being treated correctly and in line with the Geneva Convention.

The size of the camp took some getting used to after the intimacy of the hospital at Lucca. Gordon described it as, 'like a small town'. The highest number of POWs recorded was in October 1943, after the arrival of the POWs from Italy. The Red Cross report mentions 31052 soldiers detained in the camp. Many of these moved on to the work camps, working in factories, mines and farms.

The camp was surrounded by double-banked, barbed-wire fences with twenty feet high sentry boxes on stilts. Sentries were armed with machine guns and searchlights and were about a hundred yards apart along the fences. The two fences were eight feet high, attached to thick pine posts six feet apart and with big rolls of barbed wire in-between them. There was a trip wire that ran about eight feet in front of the inner wire, fifteen inches high. Step over that at your peril! At night the fences were patrolled by guards and German Shepherd dogs.

POWs were assigned to compounds, each consisting of four barrack blocks and a common latrine. There were about 1000 men in a compound. Each barrack block was divided into two parts each accommodating about 130 men. The men slept in three-tiered H-bunks which stood along one wall and there were ten tables with wooden benches, where meals were eaten, on the other side.

Everything was very well-organised and one gradually got used to the daily routine.

Those recognised as medical personnel were given duties in the camp medical inspection rooms, camp hospitals or with working parties. Gordon was one of those. As a non-commissioned officer Gordon was not obliged to work; he stated in his post war questionnaire that he had never been in a work camp. Gordon told his daughter that he had assisted in the hospital, caring for patients, changing dressings, giving injections and at times assisting in the operating theatre.

All the medical orderlies worked on a three-month rota system, so that no one was exposed to infectious diseases for long periods of time. The hospital at Lamsdorf was called the lazaret. It had opened in October 1941 and was considered to be the best of all the POW hospitals in respect of facilities and equipment. It was about three hundred yards from the main camp, situated among the pine trees, fenced in and patrolled by guards.

In addition to the lazaret there was a camp infirmary situated in the main camp – the *revier*. A German officer-doctor supervised the lazaret and the *revier* but it was the British medical doctors who were responsible for the care of the POWs. Amongst the POWs there were medical doctors, surgeons, dentists and eye specialists.

The medical officers gave regular courses in nursing, anatomy and physiology. Gordon and the other orderlies would have definitely benefitted from working under such skilled doctors and surgeons.

One of the privileges of medical personnel was having the right of a walk outside the camp once a week, and during this time Gordon often collected wood for the fires. He said that the guard he usually went out with was older and was kind. He always helped him to carry the wood, often carrying it all for him and actually handing Gordon his gun to carry! Those walks outside the fenced camp were a small sense of freedom, walking through the gate, following the perimeter fence to a path that led off through the woods, being away from the noise and confinement of the camp. Gordon would stay out as long as he could. Sometimes, he and his guard sat down, leaned against a tree and smoked a cigarette, savouring the wonderful feeling of being outside the barbed wire, even if only for a short time.

By the time Gordon arrived in Lamsdorf the school system was well established. Courses were offered in a great variety of subjects targeting different levels of education. Some even offered university level courses with examinations. In October 1941, following an inspection of the International Committee of the Red Cross the school was officially registered in England as a College-University. The camp also had an extensive library with thousands of books. The books and teaching resources had been supplied by the Red Cross and various other organisations.

During his time there, Gordon chose to study mechanical engineering, which he did alongside his medical duties. He successfully completed the external examinations and at the end of his course received his certificate. Sitting a professional examination is challenging under any circumstances, but POWs who took the exams did so under circumstances much more difficult than the average candidate back home.

Food was an ongoing matter of concern and would have been far worse if not for the Red Cross parcels. As well as providing additional food for the POWs the contents soon became a form of trading currency between not only the POWs, but also the prison guards.

By the end of 1944 life in camp had become pretty routine. News filtered through about the progress of Allied troops. By January 1945 the Russian and western armies were racing towards each other across what was left of Hitler's Europe. The prisoners in camp heard the distant rumble of Russian guns, and Russian planes were seen flying overhead. The atmosphere in the camp was a mixture of tension and excitement as the POWs began to imagine an end to the war.

As the Russians approached the border between Poland and Germany, the German authorities dropped a bombshell – everybody able to march, around eight thousand men, would be leaving. They were given twenty-four hours' notice to pack up their belongings and be prepared to evacuate the camp. The previous week a Red Cross commission had repatriated 700 sick British POWs (they left on 15 January) but there were still many remaining who were ill and unable to march. They were left in the camp with doctors and medical staff.

The evacuation of all able-bodied men began on 22 January 1945. The prisoners were marched westward in groups of 200 to 300 men in the so-called 'Long March' or 'Death March'. The lucky ones got far enough to the west to be liberated by the American Army. The unlucky ones got 'liberated' by the Soviets who held them as virtual hostages for several more months. Many of them were finally repatriated towards the end of 1945 through the port of Odessa on the Black Sea. In total around 30000 Allied POWs from the camps were force-marched westward in appalling winter conditions from January to April 1945.

Gordon was one of those ordered to stay behind, at this time he was either at the lazaret or the *revier*. They all wondered, 'What next'? The main concern was a shortage of water, so they filled all the buckets and baths they could find. Some sick marchers limped back to Lamsdorf with bits of news. Russian guns continued firing. No one really knew what was happening. Then came news that a train was coming to move some of the patients.

A train left Annahof station with over 1000 extremely ill POWs on 21 February 1945, at around 3 p.m., under the care of Sergeant Major Noble and Captain John Borrie. They arrived in Hammelburg Stalag XIII-C nine days later on 2 March. Gordon remained at Lamsdorf.

A week later three more trains left, evacuating the rest of the patients and medical personnel.

I knew from Gordon's post war questionnaire that Gordon left Lamsdorf on 5 March, but it took several years before I discovered his actual route. My Eureka moment came when I read an excerpt from the diary of Cyril Howard Griffiths McGregor on the Lamsdorf POW Facebook page! He had been on the same train and recorded the train's route to Stalag XIII-D

Nurnberg Langwasser. Then, by chance, a few weeks later I discovered the diary of Sergeant Sydney Alfred Smith in the photo gallery on the website www.prisonersofwarmuseum.com. Both of these diaries showed the route from Lamsdorf, and an entry in Sydney Smith's diary on 4 April 1945 even mentioned Gordon Windridge by name. With his friend Arthur Riddle also being mentioned, both in Lamsdorf and Nurnberg, this was the confirmation I needed of Gordon's journey out of Lamsdorf to Moosburg.

Gordon had been working in the *revier* when they left Lamsdorf.

The men were drafted into groups of 42 and marched to the station at Annahof. They were hustled into cattle trucks after each receiving a loaf of bread and a small piece of margarine, according to Cyril McGregor and, 'trucks were dirty and it took some time to settle ourselves. The more thoughtful of the men had brought hammers and nails and soon most of the packs and heavy items were duly hung.'

The last train left on Monday, 5 March at 4 p.m., reaching Neisse at 6 p.m. and then travelling through the night.

Between 6 and 12 March the train took them through the following towns:

Pardubice, Kolin, Prague, Pilsen, Furth im Wald, Schwansdorf, Nurnberg-Maryfield, Bamberg, Schweinfurt, Thungen, Gemunden, Wachtersbach, Elm, Gemunden again, Wurzberg, Nurnberg-Maryfield again.

Sydney Smith's diary gives an insight into what the journey was like. They were allowed out for short periods most days, sometimes only five minutes, at other times twenty or thirty minutes. Twice they managed to get out for a wash. Some food was issued every day, usually bread, meat and soup. They also had a store of Red Cross parcels they had brought with them. There were signs of bomb destruction everywhere and they were often held up by air raids.

There was a roll call on 12 March at Nurnberg-Maryfield when it was discovered that 32 men were missing. It seems men had been jumping off the train along the way

The situation was chaotic; no camp would take them. The POWs in the camps wanted to get out, but the weary men from Lamsdorf desperately wanted to get in! There were so many POWs pouring in from the east and the Germans really didn't know what to do with all those men. They were losing the war and the POWs were not their first priority. The days in the trucks were cramped and tedious.

Eventually, on Tuesday, 13 March, they were disembarked and marched (very groggy from the long confinement) to Stalag XIII-D Nurnberg Langwasser.

Sydney Smith recalls: 'Mar 13th Tuesday: Up at 6 o'clock – packed – marched off at 7.30 a.m. to Stalag X111-D. It wasn't very far but with our kit it seemed miles. When we got inside the camp we lined up on a long road where we were counted and re-counted and then told we would be searched and excess food taken from us and put into store under our names and numbers. However only Bruce had his box of food taken and that was returned next day. Parties then went off for de-lousing and we washed and shaved while we waited. The flights are overhead and constantly going and bombing and anti-aircraft guns can be heard in the distance. It seems de-lousing is a very lengthy process because we did not get done today and had to spend the night on boards in tents. Quite comfy but very cold.'

Cyril McGregor noted: 'It was a large camp, plenty of barb wire. Were searched by civilians – *volksstrum* – and youngsters. Parties of 100 deloused every two hours. Met a lot of Russians picking up butt ends etc. in spite of bellowing guards. Soon the camp area looked like a huge fairground with music from gramophones and men eating in little groups near fires fed with wood torn from buildings etc. while guards and *unteroffern* looked helplessly on. We had arrived. Had taken possession of this camp and called it Home. The campfires blazed far into the night. A night of rumbles and explosions from raiding planes.'

Stalag XIII-D Nurnberg Langwasser was on the site of what had been the Nazi Party Rally Grounds. With the arrival of POWs evacuated from the camps in the east it was hugely overcrowded.

Conditions were deplorable, there was no room to exercise and few supplies. The rations consisted of 300 grams of bread, 250 grams of potatoes, some dehydrated vegetables and a little margarine. Fortunately, they received several issues of Red Cross parcels. Sanitation was lamentable. The camp was infested with lice, fleas and bed bugs.

With the approach of US forces the POWs were put on the road again in a forced march. These notes from the website of the US Air Force 392nd Bomber Group unit, many of whom had ended up at Stalag XIII-D, tells us more about this march:

'At 1700 hours on 3 April 1945, the Americans received notice that they were to evacuate the Nurnberg camp and march to Stalag VII-A Moosburg. At this point, the POWs took over the organization of the march. They submitted to the Germans Commander plans stipulating that in return for preserving order they were to have full control of the column and to march no more than 20 kilometres a day. The

Germans accepted. On April 4, with each POW in possession of a food parcel, 10000 Allied POWs began the march.'

'While the column was passing a freight marshalling yard near the highway, some P-47s dive-bombed the yard. Two Americans and one Briton were killed and three men seriously wounded. On the following day, the column laid out a large replica of an American Air Corps insignia on the road with an arrow pointing in the direction of the march. Thereafter the column was never strafed. It proceeded to Neumarkt, to Bersheim, where 4500 Red Cross parcels were delivered by truck; then to Mulhauser, where more parcels were delivered.'

'On April 9, the column reached the Danube, which Colonel D.H Alkire flatly refused to cross, since it meant exceeding the 20-kilometer a day limit. With his refusal, the Germans lost complete control of the march and POWs began to drop out of the column almost at will. The guards, intimidated by the rapid advance of the American Army, made no serious attempt to stop the disintegration. The main body of the column reached Stalag VII-A Moosburg on 20 April 1945.'

Sydney Smith's diary entry of 4 April actually mentions Gordon Windridge, and his friend Arthur Riddle, as having marched out on this day. The route taken was: Neumarkt, Berching, Buching, Josep Fuller – 1000-acre farm –, Fetanagger near Mindelstetten, Beilngries, Sweinbach, Holtzhauzen, Ober Munchen, Gammelsdorf, Moosburg – a total march of over 500 kilometres.

Gordon suffered from dysentery again during this march. Dysentery was very common. Sufferers had the indignity of soiling themselves whilst having to continue to march and being further weakened by the debilitating effects of the illness. Gordon said he had never felt so ill in all his life. He thought he was going to die. If it hadn't been for a fellow Australian POW, he may well have done. Gordon didn't think he could keep going, but the unknown Aussie picked him up every time he fell, constantly encouraging him to keep going and at times carrying him long distances. We don't know his name but will be forever grateful.

The main body of the column arrived in Stalag VII-A Moosburg on 20 April, and Gordon arrived on 23rd. The Germans had rounded up 100000 POWs and crowded them into the Moosburg camp. Conditions there were chaotic, with little food or water and no shelter. Many POWs slept on the ground. Fortunately, they didn't have long to wait—they would be liberated in under a week.

Eventually, the long awaited liberation came. On the morning of 29 April 1945, the 14th Armoured Division of Patton's 3rd Army attacked the SS troops guarding Stalag VII-A and, finally, the American task force broke through. The first tank entered, taking the barbed wire fence with it. The prisoners went wild. Climbing on the tanks, cheering and shouting. Pandemonium reigned. They were free!

Gordon was flown back to England on a Lancaster bomber, either via Rheims or Brussels. The exact route is uncertain, but he arrived in England on 10 May 1945, and was stationed in Brighton with his old friend from Durban, Arthur Riddle. They finally left for home from Southampton on 30 May arriving in Cape Town on 9 June 1945.

Gordon's daughter Jeanette recalls: 'While in Cape Town the soldiers were allowed to speak very briefly on the radio to their families. A friend of our family came to tell us that Dad would be on the air. Granny and I were in Kearsney but Mum had, unfortunately, on that day gone into Durban (approximately 2 hours' drive away) to buy a new outfit for Dad's return, so she missed the broadcast. Granny was completely deaf so she was unable to listen. But I did and I can remember so well what he said. "Hello, my darling Edna and Jeanette, I will see you soon."

'I don't know how soon after that it was that the soldiers left Cape Town, but I think the train journey took about five days. I remember so well the day Dad arrived. Mum drove into Durban with me in tow. Crowds of happy people on the station were pushing and shoving. As the train arrived the mob surged forward almost trampling me underfoot. A very kind gentleman then put me on his shoulders until the train stopped. A photographer from the newspaper took a photo of Dad and Mum together on the station, which was in the paper the next day. It was a lovely photograph, both looking happily tearful.'

Gordon actually arrived in Durban on 14 June 1945, his wife's birthday, almost five years since he had sailed out of Durban harbour. He had spent 1253 days in captivity.

BRIAN ERIC HURR
Photo taken 3 Aug 1939

Captured: 12 June 1940 : St Valery en Caux
Royal Norfolk Regiment : Army No. 5776061
POW No. 16992
Camps at and LAMSDORF 1940 - 1945
Dispatch Rider with 7th Battalion Norfolks
Born 11/07/1918 - Died: 18/11/1981

Brian : Ingoldisthorpe : 12 July 1973

BRIAN ERIC HURR

By Helen Lewis

Helen is the great-niece of Brian Hurr. She has a keen interest in understanding her family's experiences in World War II and the wider conflict. She is currently writing a book based on her great-grandmother's wartime diaries.

Brian Eric Hurr was born in King's Lynn in Norfolk on 11 July 1918. At the outbreak of the war he was a delivery man for a milk dairy. He put his love of motorbikes to use by becoming a motorcycle dispatch rider in the 7th Battalion, the Royal Norfolk Regiment. The 7th was a Territorial Battalion drawn from the towns and villages of North-West Norfolk, such as King's Lynn and Hunstanton. They were formed in 1939 and arrived in France in January 1940. The 7th was a Pioneer Battalion attached to the 51st Highland Division and spent their first few months in France making roads and constructing drains. They were originally deployed to the Maginot Line and when pressured by the German advance began a withdrawal to Abbeville.

192

The 51st Division was the only complete division left in France ordered to stay and fight with the French as Churchill was concerned about Allied unity. Facing relentless German Panzer divisions, the 51st withdrew on 10 June 1940 to Saint-Valery-en-Caux on the French

coast. Led by Major General Victor Fortune they fought on but in a chaotic situation and unable to defend their position or secure an evacuation by sea of sufficient scale, Fortune gave the order to surrender on 12 June 1940. 10 500 men were taken prisoner including Brian Hurr. Of the 7th Royal Norfolks who arrived in France six months earlier only 31 made it back to England.

In the chaos of war Brian was originally posted missing but several weeks later, reported as a prisoner of war. Brian and the others now faced a long journey to Lamsdorf where they would see out the war. They were marched for 220 miles until they reached the Scheldt River near Nijmegen where they were put aboard barges and sailed down the Rhine to Wessel, where cattle trucks on trains took them to Sowin in Poland.

They marched the rest of the way.

Brian arrived at Lamsdorf on 15 July 1940.

What we know of his time at Lamsdorf comes from his records and family diaries. He was part of the working parties at E67, an ammunition factory at Muna Niclasdorf, 50 kilometres from Lamsdorf, arriving there on 20 August 1940. According to other accounts conditions here were very hard with little food and heat. Brian was relocated in July 1941 to E35, a timber mill at Zwittau, 170 kilometres from Lamsdorf.

He was a keen boxer and we believe that he can be seen in a photograph of this activity in the Museum at Lamsdorf.

We also have some insight into what it was like for his family to know he was a POW, through entries in his mother's diaries. We only have 1941, 1942 and 1943 but they detail his mother, Mrs Beryl Hurr, writing to him every week, often more than once, knitting socks and gloves for him, buying other essential items including, pyjamas, chocolate and a kitbag and preparing Red Cross parcels. It also describes his family maintaining his motorbike ready for his return. There are some particularly poignant entries.

On 11 February 1941 an entry reads '… learned from the map in the mail where Bri's camp is'. On 12 June, entries for 1941 and 1942 respectively are, 'A year ago today my darling was captured' and 'Two years ago my darling'.

His mother sent several photos from home and in February 1942 she received a photo from him; sadly we do not have that now. They weren't entirely free to correspond as they wished as on 17 March 1943 she notes that, 'had beastly printed form of 'must nots' from Bri.'

The inside cover of the 1941 diary also lists his address and POW number:

Kriegsgefangenenpost
No 57961061 Pte B E Hurr
British Prisoner of War
No 16992
Stalag VIII-B
Germany

Brian's mother and father, Beryl and Samuel Hurr, had three sons all of whom were in the armed forces. Brian was a POW; Maurice was in the RAF and worked for Special Operations Executive in London and Mike was in the army in India. Samuel volunteered as a fire watchman and Beryl worked extremely hard supporting them all. It is very reassuring to know that Brian was able to be in regular contact with his family as Beryl recorded every letter and card that she received from him. In the three-year period we know of, Beryl sent Brian 173 letters, she received 92 letters and cards from him and sent him 12 parcels. We know that correspondence would have kept them all going.

We do not know which of the Long Marches Brian was on but on 18 May 1945 he came home to his family. This was such a special day that the family continued to celebrate the day for the rest of his life. After the war Brian married his pre-war girlfriend, Joan, in 1947 and they had two children, David and Barbara. Sadly the marriage didn't last but Brian remained very close to his mother and brothers. He never spoke of his time as a POW.

Brian died on 18th November 1981 at the age of just 63. It is hard not to believe that the privations of his POW experience had a bearing on his shortened life. He was a lovely man, always smiling, jolly and generous. He loved telling stories of his days at work as a delivery man and of his colleagues to whom he gave special nicknames. His special story was of the time he nearly knocked the Queen Mother over. He was making deliveries to Sandringham House (the Norfolk country home of the Royal Family) when he pushed a door open with his foot as his hands were full of parcels. Unbeknown to him the Queen Mother was on the other side. She appeared startled so he quickly made his apologies and carried on with his delivery.

In 2018 I visited the Museum at Lamsdorf in order to pay the family's respects to Brian and the other men who missed out on so much. I was able to see where Brian would have arrived in the railway carriages and the route that he would have been marched along into the camp. Finally, I was also able to see the Museum at Opole that bears witness to the POWs of Lamsdorf and does so much to keep their memories alive.

---Dedicated to the memory of Brian Eric Hurr 1918 - 1981. Gone but not forgotten. ---

ERNEST FREDERICK COLE

Sapper – Royal Engineers

By Wendy A Collens

Born in 1946 in Cheltenham, eldest daughter of Ernie Cole and Ivy Cole (née Wilkinson), Wendy lived in Cheltenham until 1973. She then moved to Sweden in 1986 where she lived for 4 years.

Wendy is a keen golfer and amateur photographer and she has produced nine coffee table books of her life 1946-2007 with the intent to carry on from 2008 to present day.

She is in the process of putting together a Family Roots book of the Cole/Wilkinson families and this will include her father's army service records.

My father enlisted at Bristol on 18 August 1939 with the Royal Engineers.

On 21 August 1939 he was posted to 'B' Company Training Unit with the rank of sapper. He passed his Plumber & Pipefitter exams group B, Class 3, in October 1939.

On 15 January 1940 he was transferred to 51st Division Engineers 237th Company. On the 29 January 1940, 237th embarked Port A, and disembarked BEF France on 30 January 1940.

He obviously continued training with the army in the UK and gained classification as Plumber and Pipefitter B1.

On 25 January 1941, my father married my mother, Ivy Wilkinson, at St Edmunds Church, Mansfield Woodhouse, Notts. They were married for 61 years when he died in 2003.

His war effort continued when, on 15 (or 18th) October 1942, 237th Field Company embarked for North Africa. Less than one month later, on 29 November 1942, he was reported missing believed to be a POW in North Africa.

On 29 January 1943 he was reported as POW in Italian hands, later confirmed as Camp no 70 Monturano (Parma), postal mark number 3300.

My father's army records show that on 20 August 1943, he was transferred to Stalag VIII-B (through Stalag IV-B), from Italy. A postcard from a friend to him shows his address as being in Working Party E711 Lamsdorf.

According to an article in the *Gloucestershire Echo*, 6 September 1943, Sapper Cole asked his relatives, in a letter announcing his arrival at a German POW camp, not to worry and added that the food was much better.

He also added that he had met two other Cheltenham men, Charles Cooper of 14 Leckhampton Road, and a son of Mr F.L. Otterburn of 11 Oakfield Street.

Dad was liberated, arriving back in the UK on 24 April 1945, when he was admitted to the 6th Battalion, Hampshire Regiment. He had a great love of motorbikes and he did some despatch riding during the war. I believe he was taken prisoner when he was a despatch rider, but I am not sure whether this was in North Africa, or previously in France. Apparently, he came across some Americans and they told him not to go any further, but Dad said he had to!

Dad never spoke about his time as a prisoner, although on occasion I would ask, and often Mum would tell me a few things, and Dad would put her right. He did mention that he and his fellow prisoners were so hungry that they tried to steal the guard dogs' food. He also attempted to escape and was shot in the ankle for doing so, we believe this was at Lamsdorf.

Dad had made friends with a Jewish man, and he used to write to his wife on his behalf, as apparently the Jews were not allowed to send letters home. One day the soldier was taken away and never returned. His fate we can all imagine.

Mum said life was a little difficult for Dad when he returned home and he suffered from nightmares. At his mother-in-law's home in Mansfield Woodhouse, Nottinghamshire, he couldn't bear to see her pet canaries in a cage and would regularly let them out, giving them their 'freedom.'

Dad and Mum lived at his parents' house in Cheltenham from the end of 1945 until they moved to rented accommodation in a prefab at Priors Farm in Cheltenham, and then they were able to put a deposit down on a house in Hatherley Road, Cheltenham in 1948, where they lived for the rest of their lives.

On his return to Cheltenham, Dad resumed his cricketing days playing for Hatherley and Reddings Cricket Club. Dad also played football for Burrows Football Club in those early days. Dad and his father Arthur, and brother Norman, were well-known local cricketers.

The earliest reference I have found that Dad played for the club was in a local newspaper from 1932, when Dad was 16 years old. Another reference to him was made in the 1980's, when he received a coveted award for 50 years' service. He continued to be connected to the club until he died.

Mum and Dad had just two children, myself being born in June 1946, and my sister Margaret, in October 1949.

When my parents visited me in Sweden one snowy January in the late 1980's, Dad said something to Mum, and there appeared to be a problem. I asked her what it was and she said the snow and the fir trees reminded Dad of the war and when they were forced to march. Regrettably, I was unable to get any other information from my dad. He never spoke about the events of those days.

Unbeknown to me, my dad kept a diary of his POW days and my mum told me he destroyed it just before he died in 2002, aged 86. I am not sure whether his diary would have been recorded by his unit on return from war.

Dad was a very hardworking man and would turn his hand to anything, and from his army service records, I quote the word, 'Exemplary'.

He was a great family man too.

I only wish I had asked Dad more about those days which were obviously most dreadful. I am making some attempts to find out more through the National Archives *et cetera*, but putting the pieces together is difficult and I dearly wish I could find the missing ones, although I expect the information would be emotionally distressing.

I am grateful that his name will live on through this book.

JOHN BURTON SHANKS

By Jeni Kingston

Born in 1958, I am the third of four children. We all had happy and privileged childhoods, enjoying life on the farm and embracing Mum and Dad's love of travel during our school holidays. I left home at 17 and went to Italy to au pair, ending up working on a ski resort for a season.

I eventually resumed my education and went to secretarial college in London, working in the city for several years before getting married and travelling to India, Sri Lanka, and eventually settling in Africa with my tobacco merchant husband. We lived in Tanzania for 18 years, then in Malawi where I was the country manager for IATA for six years, before redundancy brought us back to the UK in 2006.

During this time, we had two daughters. Our oldest, Jessica, was born 12 weeks early and had complex special needs. Sadly, she died in 2010, four days before her 23rd birthday.

I battled breast cancer in 2016 (from which my sister and mother both subsequently died) and needing a project to focus on, I was thrilled to be able to organise our surviving daughter's wedding for the following July.

In October of the same year, we found Dad's diaries when emptying his house to sell after Mum went into a care home. It was an incredible find - each book was tiny with almost illegible script that was only visible under a magnifying glass and strong light. We knew very little of Dad's wartime experiences and reading the diaries was a revelation. It was humbling and a testament to the resilience and true grit of that generation.

The transcription took me two years to complete and culminated in To Hell in a Handcart, *which was published in January 2021.*

I am now a very happy grandmother of George, born in Canada in September 2020, of our daughter Jo and her soldier husband, Kyle. I was not allowed to visit the family due to the pandemic but have made up for lost time since their return to the UK in December 2020 when they made us their 'support bubble'.

I live in Shropshire with my husband Tony, two dogs and two cats, and a lovely garden.

My father, John Burton Shanks, lied about his age to help the war effort when he was just 17. As a farmer's son he wasn't required to join up, but his desire to get into a cockpit, do his bit for King and country, and doubtless have a 'wizard adventure' was far too great.

As a consequence, he joined the RAF and, at the tender age of 20, was instructing other young hopefuls in the joys of flying his beloved Spitfire.

Dad wasn't overly happy to instruct, feeling that all the excitement was being had by those being sent into combat, so he was thrilled when he was eventually relocated to Biggin Hill to become part of 124 Squadron. Later in life he claimed this time with his squadron was the happiest period of his life.

He went on several sorties with his squadron, but it was on 19 August 1942, during the Battle of Dieppe or Operation Jubilee, that Dad's flying career came to an abrupt end after he was forced to crash-land in a field when his engine failed. He was 21 years old.

Dad spent the following two and a half years in Lamsdorf, where he wrote an almost daily account of his experience.

As an officer, Dad was not required to join the work parties and spent much of his time in the camp reading, playing bridge, attending lectures and concerts, and participating in, or watching, sport. These were especially important activities as despair and despondency constantly threatened the camp inhabitants. Even so, Dad mentions times when he was literally bored to the brink of tears and often felt very depressed at his frustrated attempts to escape.

He occasionally went 'through the wire' to find someone with whom he could 'swap-over'. He went on a coal party and was delighted to have the opportunity to 'do the Hun out of something', by filling his greatcoat pockets with coal, with more inside his blouse.

Parcels containing clothing, cigarettes, food and books, along with letters from home, were a tremendous highlight and every delivery was carefully recorded. Cigarettes were a form of currency in the camp, especially useful for those few who didn't smoke! Sadly, Dad had a 20-a-day habit (which continued until he was in his mid-70's.) Despite this, he regularly shared his hoard with his 'combine' and with friends in the camp who had been equally generous with previously received consignments.

Dad chronicled the punishments meted out in October 1942, where officers were tied up with string (and later chains which were much preferred, as they gave more room for movement) in retaliation for the treatment of POWs in England. They were also denied their Red Cross parcels – a literal life-saver for much of their time in prison – as well as all other privileges. They were denied access to their bunks during the day and some had stoves removed as it was assumed bed boards were being used to fuel them. Certainly, many men had to try and sleep on bunks with several boards missing for the duration of their stay at Lamsdorf.

Relying on German rations only was extremely hard for young men. The calorific value often fell below 2000 and, as a consequence, Dad's health suffered with constant colds, mouth ulcers, boils and weight loss. His oral hygiene was also very poor and he had to have all his teeth removed shortly after he was repatriated.

Dad starts almost every diary entry with a report on the weather conditions (something that continued throughout his working life as a farmer) and it is apparent that temperatures were extremely low in the winters, often reaching minus double figures. With only a thin blanket issued from the German authorities, Red Cross parcels containing extra blankets were extremely welcome and were supplied by many countries besides the UK, including Canada, United States, Australia and New Zealand.

Rumours were rife in the camp. Dad kept a tally of all the rumours he heard, crossing out the ones that eventually proved unfounded, often by newly captured prisoners. Radios were regularly discovered, often with harsh punishments meted out to their owners, but it was an unusual day which had no rumour recorded.

Despite the lack of nutritious food, Dad managed to maintain reasonable fitness by doing PT most days, much to the amusement of his fellow internees. It is likely, however, that this dedication to his personal fitness helped him to withstand the horrendous experience in January 1945, when, along with the majority of POWs across Europe, Dad was force-marched across Europe in January 1945, through deep snow and in the most appalling conditions.

His recollection of the march makes harrowing reading. He left the camp with one of the first groups and the organisation was very poor. Each day the men were driven up to 30 kilometres over snow and ice, often on side roads or across fields, and had to stand or sit around in the snow for several hours whilst a billet was being sought. This was often a barn or a stable if they were lucky, or a field if they were not. Their blankets were usually stiff with frost and their boots frozen solid by morning. Dad unadvisedly removed his boots early in the march and records trying to thaw them out the following morning. Later on, he says that his socks were soaked in blood and that everyone started to develop sores on their mouths. On several occasions they were given just water to drink and no rations at all, so they resorted to foraging for root crops which were often eaten raw and frozen.

Like many, Dad contracted dysentery and influenza on this trip, describing the agonies and indignities of the illness in his diary. In one instance, he had to make a hole in the straw at their night-time billet as

203

he was too exhausted to walk to the field to relieve himself. He thought he was going to die, as had happened to many of his fellow sufferers.

Along with 61 others he was finally deemed too ill to continue the march by the medical officer and, on 25 February, was taken to a hospital at Stadtroda for treatment. He had been on the road for four weeks, having trudged almost 600 kilometres, losing a total of 3½ stone in weight since his capture.

Dad was bitterly disappointed not to be in the UK on VE Day, but all returning aircraft seemed to be from the US and were commandeered for returning American soldiers. It took many failed attempts and an eventual camp-out on the air-strip to board a flight home. He was eventually repatriated on 14 May.

Dad desperately wanted to continue flying but, due to failing eyesight and lack of experience on multi-engined aircraft, he was unsuccessful in his endeavours to get back into a cockpit.

Dad eventually took over the farm from his father and was very successful, buying the farm from the Wrottesley Estate in the 1950's. He retired at the age of 82, and moved to a nearby village with my mother, where they lived for the next 11 years.

The card game bridge, learned in Lamsdorf, became a life-long hobby and a love he shared with my mother, Sheila. Along with Mum, he was a very keen and knowledgeable gardener, with a special interest in trees, and they often opened their beautiful garden to the public on behalf of local charities.

Dad rarely had a day's illness after returning home from Lamsdorf, although he was vulnerable to stomach upsets for the rest of his life.

He rarely spoke of his experiences as a prisoner of war.

Dad was an honest, fair, honourable man, who was incredibly hard-working. He had a wonderful sense of humour and was very generous with his time and knowledge. He was culturally aware and tolerant and held a fascination for the lives of those from different nations, religions and ethnicities. He and my mother continued to explore other countries until Dad was in his late 80's.

He died at the age of 93 in 2013, and the huge attendance at his funeral was testament to the love felt for him by family and friends alike.

ERIC WEST

By Dr John West

John West is the son of Eric West and is an NHS consultant cardiologist who trained in St Thomas's Hospital London, (the same as his father). He specialises and practices in cardiology as a consultant in Sheffield.

John is an amateur historian and the big gap in his father's wartime service stoked his curiosity enough to research what his father rarely talked about, namely, his artillery regiment, his time in captivity and the forced march home.

Comprehensive details can be found on John's excellent website dedicated to the men of 140 Regiment: http://140th-field-regiment-ra-1940.co.U.K.

John West is the co-author of the highly acclaimed book, The Psychiatrist, *published by Fortis Publishing in 2021.*

Eric Douglas West was born in 1919, the oldest of three boys. He grew up in Cheam, Surrey, on the border between London's suburban sprawl and open countryside where he and his childhood friend, John 'Jack' Portas, spent their leisure time on country walks and cycle rides. Despite the turbulence of the decade that they grew up in, it seems that the two friends had no concept of the disaster that was shortly to unfold and change their lives forever.

Many years later, after Eric's death in 1992, Jack Portas wrote to me from his home in Denmark, Western Australia and said: 'The natural world was a source of wonder to us and we collected plants, observed birds and I collected butterflies and moths. We had two walking holidays together in the Lake District in 1938 and another, climbing in North Wales, in 1939. How lucky we were not to suspect what was soon to come.'

With his letter, Jack enclosed a watercolour sketch of my father at the age of 17, entitled 'A Friend'.

After the false start of the Munich crisis of 1938, war was finally declared in September 1939. As a single man aged 20 years, Eric had already been recruited into the Territorial Army under the terms of the Military Training Act of April 1939, passed by Chamberlain's government, albeit reluctantly, in response to Hitler's increasing belligerence.

At the time Eric had left school and was a Clerical Assistant to the Public Health Department of Sutton Council.

On 20 October 1939, Eric West was enlisted into the Royal Artillery and given his army number, 947073. He was assigned to 367 Battery, 140 (5th London) Field Regiment, a Territorial Regiment based in Woolwich. His friend Jack Portas also joined the Royal Artillery at about the same time and was assigned the number 950300. Jack Portas survived the war and was mentioned in despatches for his bravery in North-Western Europe in 1945.

Eric and Jack kept in touch after the war but, sadly, Jack emigrated to Australia in the 1960's and they were never able to meet up in person after that.

Eric West joined his Regiment as a gunner. He was promoted to the rank of lance bombardier around the time of the final defence of the Dunkirk perimeter in May 1940. As part of 'D' Troop of 367 Battery,

Eric participated in the defence of Cassel, a vital strategic hilltop town that was heroically defended to the last round by Brigadier the Honourable Nigel Somerset's 145 Brigade.

Lance bombardier West was captured by German forces in Watou, Belgium on 31 May 1940, during the breakout from Cassel and as the men of 145 Brigade attempted to reach the Dunkirk beaches. Eric was first transferred, probably by forced marching, to Stalag VI-B, in the town of Versen, which is in the marshy flatlands of the Emsland area on the Dutch-German border.

Stalag VI-B was used as a transit camp for the thousands of prisoners of war captured during the conflicts in Poland, France, Belgium and the Netherlands. After another transfer across Germany, Eric arrived at Stalag VIII-B Lamsdorf, Silesia in the far southeast of Germany. The accounts of this journey suggest it was a combination of long forced marches with little food or water, followed by interminable train journeys, the whole process taking several weeks.

At Stalag VIII-B, Eric was assigned POW number 12965. In the autumn of 1940, along with many of the ordinary ranks, he was moved from the main camp at Lamsdorf to a work camp. In his case it was a coal mine complex at Beuthen, near Katowice (Arbeitskommando E72) where he was forced to work for the remainder of the war as a miner until the camp was evacuated in January 1945.

The German border town of Beuthen was in the heavily industrialised area of Upper Silesia, in the triad of coal-mining towns Geilwitz, Hindenburg and Beuthen. There were many POW work camps associated with Stalag VIII-B in the area, most were coal mining camps, but others included quarrying, railway and road construction, woodwork and farming.

E72, the Hohenzollern Coalmine, was just to the south of Beuthen. Two other POW working parties were associated with this mine, E411, which was a sawmill providing pit props, and E593, which was a Palestinian group based nearby in Schomberg. The E72 POW barracks were initially off-site at Schomberg at a disused beer garden, until 1942 when new huts were constructed on the campus of the mine itself.

The Hohenzollern mine was one of the most modern and efficient coalmines in Europe, daily extraction was up to 1400 tons of coal.

The winding tower was an iconic modernist tower, 57 metres high. It was made of brick and given the approximate shape of a mining hammer - a *pyrlik*.

A wider, concrete slab was placed on the narrower shaft, on which the upper part of the tower was erected. The windows form vertical lines. Inside, the first electric hoisting machines in Silesia, located on the head, operated. It is alleged that Adolf Hitler climbed to the vantage point at the top of the shaft tower just before the outbreak of World War II to observe Polish territory, shortly to be invaded, across the border. The plant was closed in 1997, and most of its infrastructure was dismantled in 2001. The winding tower remains standing to this day as a historic national monument, and an unofficial memorial to the POWs who worked and suffered there.

The E72 camp commandant, *Unterfeldwebel* Arthur Engelkircher was known to the inmates as 'John the Bastard'. Engelkircher was a committed Nazi and a notorious sadist. He shot dead at least four British POWs and was involved in several assaults. My father completed a war crime affidavit for MI6 after his liberation describing the death, at Engelkircher's hands, of Guardsman David Blythin on 23rd March 1943. Blythin was buried nearby and after the war re-interred to the Commonwealth War Cemetery at Krakow.

By 1944 Eric had become fluent in German and was appointed the camp interpreter, taking over the role from Norman Gibbs. This meant he no longer worked underground, but instead had to protect the men from the increasingly unpredictable violence of Engelkircher. He helped them feign sickness to get much needed rest and to avoid incriminating themselves by deft interpretation, always at risk of being overheard by guards who were able to understand English.

As the Red Army advanced westwards, the men were marched out of the E72 mine in Beuthen on 23 January 1945. They were given two days' notice to prepare, and no-one went to work. They were told to leave their blankets and collect three Red Cross parcels. They left in the evening and marched all night and throughout the next day.

Eric never spoke about his forced march, but his Liberation Questionnaire mentions an escape attempt on the first day of the march, 23 or 24 January 1945, at Gleiwitz, and his rearrest there by a German *feldwebel*. Eric remained on the Long March thereafter. He met the advancing American Army in Bavaria in April 1945, who greeted him by shooting in his direction. He completed a Liberation Questionnaire that was signed on 30 April 1945.

On his return to England in May 1945, at the age of 26 and weighing six stone, after five years in captivity, heavy labour in a German coal mine and the deprivations of the Long March, Eric West was transferred to 203 Field Regiment, Royal Artillery. His original 140 Field Regiment had been disbanded in 1944, having been decimated by the losses at Dunkirk.

In June 1945 Eric was told that, despite his ordeal, he was being prepared for combat in the Far East. V-J Day was not declared until August 1945, and a final land assault on Japanese territory was envisaged.

After V-J Day, Eric's skill as an interpreter was called on. On 7 September 1945, he was transferred to the RAOC (Royal Army Ordnance Corps) and based at POW Camp 167, Shady Lane, Stoughton, near Leicester, which held German POWs. The aim was to identify and risk-assess any hard line Nazis and prepare the remainder for rehabilitation prior to return to Germany. Because of the fairness shown by the British camp authorities and local people, some never returned and have settled in the area.

Staff sergeant Eric West was finally demobilised on 18 June 1946 and decided to embark on gaining the qualifications needed to enter Medical School. While studying at Kingston Polytechnic he met Joy Mills, whom he married in 1948. Joy pre-deceased him in 1979. They had three children.

While Eric West was in captivity, his younger brother Geoffrey had enlisted as an officer cadet in the Royal Engineers. There would have been a brief opportunity for the two brothers to reunite after Eric's captivity, but in July 1945 Geoff sailed with his Regiment to India. Between October 1945 and May 1946, Second lieutenant Geoff West completed his military training in the Queen Victoria's Own Madras Sappers & Miners, based in Bangalore. V-J Day was declared while he was in training in India.

In July 1946, Geoff was transferred to Roorkee in Northern India, where he suffered a decline in mental health. He had developed an illness that would now be recognised as severe clinical depression and on 19 August 1946 he was admitted to a Military Hospital in Delhi.

Although his POW experiences, and his brother's illness affected him badly, Eric was able to complete his studies and fulfilled his ambition to qualify as a doctor at St Thomas Hospital, London in 1955 with the support of his wife, Joy. He specialised in Psychiatry; his career choice possibly influenced by his wartime experiences as well as his brother's personal psychological trauma.

Dr Eric West became a fellow of the Royal College of Physicians and after his death in 1992, at the age of 73 years, his college obituary was written by Dr H.R Rollin. The part of the obituary relevant to his wartime service reads: 'Eric West's route to the top of his chosen profession was unconventional. The son of a manager of a pipe factory in South London, he was the oldest of three brothers. He was educated at local schools in the Surrey but before he could complete his studies to university entrance level he enlisted in the Royal Artillery. In 1940, aged 21, he was a member of the ill-fated British Expeditionary Force and in the retreat to Dunkirk he had the misfortune to be captured by the Germans.

'Typical of his intellectual prowess and his steely determination, West used his long years of captivity to the best possible advantage. With what available facilities there were he studied German to such good effect that he was able to act as camp interpreter. He made little mention of his POW experiences, but it was known among his colleagues that he had had a rough time, and that he had suffered physical maltreatment. It was perhaps his own suffering, and that of his fellow prisoners, that prompted his interest in medicine in general and in psychiatry in particular. He was liberated by the Americans in 1945.'

Shortly before he died, Dr Eric West was honoured by his colleagues by the *Eric West Guest Lecture,* presented in September 1992 at the training course for psychiatrists that he ran successfully for many years at the University of Surrey. The subject was *Mind, the Brain and the Law.*

Despite his deep understanding of the broken human mind, Eric never spoke about his wartime experiences, or of his brother's mental illness. He kept his thoughts to himself, although after his retirement in 1985 Eric felt he was ready to re-explore the battlefields near Dunkirk.

Perhaps it is only now, many years later, as we compare stories of the other heroes of Lamsdorf, that we gain some understanding of what he went through.

A more detailed account of my father's war time service and subsequent life afterwards, can be found in my book, *The Psychiatrist*. (The book is available at all good book shops, on Amazon worldwide, on Kindle and in e-book format.)

ERIC JOHNSON

Eric Johnson was born in South London on 11 October 1920. At the age of 19 years, he joined 367 Battery of the 140th Field Regiment, Royal Artillery, a Territorial Regiment based in Woolwich, close to his home. In this regiment he would have served alongside Eric West whose story is also told in this book.

Eric Johnson casually announced his recruitment to his family one day after his return from work. Gunner Johnson's military records confirm his involvement with all 367 Battery's battles, including the Battle of Cassel and the breakout towards Dunkirk on 29 May 1940. He was captured at the Belgian border town of Watou on 30 May 1940, as part of the breakout to Dunkirk. It is likely that his column was being led by Major Ronald Cartland MP, who was killed by tank machine gunfire alongside six members of Eric's 140 Regiment. After his capture,

Gunner Johnson was force-marched in sweltering summer heat, transported across Belgium, and was temporarily interned at Stalag VI-B on the German/Dutch border before travelling through Germany to Stalag VIII-B Lamsdorf.

Eric said that they walked all the way to the first camp, Stalag VI-B, and when he asked the guards how far it was to the camp he was told, 'just over the next hill', a phrase he used to say to his children whenever they went anywhere.

Eric's parents were informed by telegram that he was missing, presumed dead, after his capture and they received letters from friends saying how sorry they were to have heard this sad news. It wasn't until he started getting Red Cross parcels in the camp that he was able to get news back that he was alive. His grandparents received a telegram in December 1940 confirming his location so they were then able to send parcels and letters to him.

For part of his captivity he was assigned to the E72 Arbeitskommando coal mine complex at Beuthen, amongst various other work parties that included E543 Drmbrowa, E346 Lenschutz and E725 Konigshutte Bismarck.

Eric only told his family a few anecdotes about his captivity: he hid a radio they used to listen to the BBC to under the floor of his hut and he cut the floorboards with a razor blade; that he was going to try and escape one day, but the POW he was going to try to escape with was shot trying to get over the wire before they tried together.

One day his son asked him about his escape attempts while the family were watching the classic 1963 film, *The Great Escape,* on television. Although only a child at the time, his son now recalls how his father appeared visibly angered and distressed and his mother having to usher him out of the room. He knew not to ask the question again.

Eric Johnson participated in the Long March across Czechoslovakia and Southern Germany and was liberated by American forces in March 1945, weighing less than seven stone with his 6' 1' frame. He only spoke about the walk once, saying that his friend Bernard Clarke, who accompanied him on the walk, traded his watch for half a loaf of bread as they were starving. It was via Bernard that Eric was introduced to his future wife with whom he had two children.

Their route started in Katowice and went westwards through northern Czechoslovakia via: Raciborz–Nysa–Brzeg–Hradec Kralove–Kolin–Landshut–Munich–back to Landshut–Regensburg. It was at Regensburg that he was liberated by Allied forces and then taken by air or train to Reims.

One day, many years after the war, Eric shared a rough outline of his route on a school atlas with his children. Otherwise, he rarely spoke about his wartime experiences. On his return to the UK in May 1945, he was posted to 203 Field Regiment Royal Artillery which was preparing for the final onslaught of the Japanese mainland.

Eric Johnson died in 1997, aged 77.

DUNCAN CHARLES MCLACHLAN

By Janet McLachlan

Janet McLachlan Neatby is the only child of Duncan McLachlan. She has a Bachelor of Arts degree in Sociology and a Master of Education, both from the University of Western Ontario. She spent her career as an elementary school teacher, as well as an teacher of English as a Second Language, later in life.

Duncan, ('Bunny' to his family) was a first generation Canadian born to a Scottish father who was away serving in WWI at the time. Duncan grew up in the English community of Montreal, belonged to the YMCA, skied, played football and worked as an office boy at a very young age. He attended Montreal Tech, became a printer by trade, and was employed by Church Baines and Company.

At the age of 25 he joined the Black Watch Regiment of Montreal. He spent one year in England, awaiting orders to participate in Operation Jubilee. At 27 he was taken prisoner in France, on Blue Beach in a neighbourhood of Dieppe, called Puys. Five days later he turned 28, although he failed notice for several weeks.

His hands were chained and he was taken to Stalag VIII-B where he would remain for three years. His mother, Sophia, would receive two telegrams, three months apart. The first informed her that he was missing in action, and the second one telling her that he was a prisoner of war.

Duncan spoke often about the prison camp. He spoke of meagre rations and how each man would choose one card from a deck, receiving the piece of bread corresponding to his card. (The loaf was uneven, so the middle pieces were much larger than the ends). Duncan also told of how they would reminisce about the good meals they had at home, and missing even his sister Peggy's meatloaf, of which he was not fond. They received parcels from the Red Cross which would raise their spirits. When they were on work parties, they would delight in finding a vegetable for the taking. Card games were common pastimes, and Duncan learned to play and excel at bridge, favouring it for the remainder of his life.

In the camp there was constant hunger, constant fear of lice, and constant fear of being killed by Allied planes.

What many have since termed 'The Long March to Freedom', Duncan referred to as 'The Death March'. During that 1500 kilometres trek through horrific weather and inhumane conditions, he suffered an infected hand from trying to heat a potato with a lighter, resulting in osteomyelitis of the bone. His back was damaged from sleeping outside for months in the cold and damp. He even pulled out his own infected tooth to alleviate the pain. Later in life, when his granddaughter complained of the gruelling training she was enduring for the Nijmegen March, he told her of carrying another soldier who was too weak to walk, lest he be shot by a guard. (His granddaughter was rightly humbled).

At the end of the march, and the war, American tanks rumbled toward the marchers, and German guards began running. As the column of tanks rolled up and stopped beside the marchers, Duncan looked up at the turret of the one closest. The turret opened and an African American soldier appeared, looked down at Duncan and said, 'You're free, Soldier'.

Duncan weighed 87 pounds at the time. He spent time in a French hospital to build himself up before returning to his family in Montreal.

In 1945 he returned to his job as a printer but his eyes were too weak to continue so he returned to the Canadian Army and joined the Royal Canadian Ordinance Corps as a supply technician. His army career took him to Germany, and to Egypt with the United Nations Emergency Force (UNEF) in 1962, as well as postings to Montreal, Ottawa, and London, Ontario. After retiring in 1964, Staff sergeant McLachlan worked at the Canadian Embassy in Moscow, Russia, with the Department of External Affairs. On his return to Canada he worked at the University of Western Ontario's Engineering Science department.

Duncan married in 1945 and was married for 47 years. He was a loving father and grandfather and enjoyed travelling and fishing. In spite of his nightmares and compromised health he remained an optimist, but in his head, he said he still often felt like a prisoner.

HORACE 'JIM' GREASLEY

Selected chapter samples from the book *Do the Birds Still Sing in Hell?*
With kind permission of Bonnier Books

By Ken Scott

Ken Scott is an author and ghost-writer and has written or collaborated on nearly 50 books, including five books relating to Allied POWs. www.kenscottbooks.com

THE MARCH FROM CAMBRAI

The prisoners were a nuisance. Life was cheap; they were nobodies. Horace sensed this almost as soon as the column of prisoners left Cambrai. For the first four or five miles they marched along the main road out of the town. The line of Allied prisoners stretched as far as the eye could see along the road. At one point the road dipped and straightened and Horace could see the front of the march shimmering in the rising heat of the day. The road was lined by tall trees Napoleon

218

Bonaparte had planted to shade his marching troops from the sun. Horace gasped at the sheer numbers, the line of sorry souls stretched at least three miles.

German trucks and convoys passed every few minutes and the hordes of prisoners were herded with rifle butts into the ditches by the side of the road to allow them to pass. The convoys of German troops, tank operators and drivers jeered, goaded and spat at the poor helpless unfortunates. A shaven headed German thug hung from the roll bar of a truck with one hand for support. His trousers were at his ankles, his other hand on his penis as he sprayed a line of warm urine onto the prisoners below. His friends on the back of the truck bent double with laughter, pointing and gesticulating.

Later that day the line of tired, dejected and hungry men was moved from the road and made to march across the fields for no other reason than they were causing congestion on the roads, slowing up the masses of the Third Reich heading west. As night-time approached, the blue sky faded into a darker hue. A light wind brought a chill to the evening air and Horace felt a hunger like he'd never known. Surely the Germans had made provision to feed the march?

CATTLE TRAIN

The platform of the station was strewn with about twenty dead bodies - the Allied prisoners who'd been just a little slow in obeying the orders of their captors.

By the time the Germans bolted the door the men were packed in like sardines, perhaps three hundred to a wagon. Some men were panicking and screaming as claustrophobia kicked in. Horace couldn't even manage to lift his hands above his head. His feet ached and all he wanted to do was sit or lie down, but it was impossible.

An hour into the journey Horace had to take a shit. He was luckier than most, he could control the moment, unlike those with dysentery. 'I need a shit, Flapper,' he said in a whisper that only his pal could hear.

'Awwww... Jesus Christ, you don't, do you?'

''Fraid so, mate.'

Flapper decided to attract the attention of the men discreetly, spare some dignity for his friend. 'Make some space ... man here needs a shit,' he shouted.

A collective groan reverberated around the truck as men jostled and pushed Horace over into the far corner.

'Station approaching,' someone shouted, leaning from the open window of the truck, and suddenly Horace had an idea. He muscled his way over to where the man that had shouted stood. By this time the pain in his bowel was excruciating. He clutched at the cheeks of his arse.

'Any Germans on the platform?' he shouted up to the man leaning from the small opening.

'Dozens of the square headed bastards.'

'Then get out the way quickly, will you?'

As the rest of the truck looked on in amazement Horace dropped his trousers and emptied his bowels into the open flap of his Glengarry hat. The smell was overbearing but Horace managed to scramble up to the opening, taking care not to spill any of the shit from the hat. He studied the motion of the train. It wasn't slowing down, wasn't stopping as it trundled along at about twenty miles an hour. A wide grin spread across his face as he spied a line of six German soldiers a mere foot or two from the platform edge. He positioned the Glengarry so he could hold it with the two flaps in one hand. By now the rest of the train realised what he was up to and whooped and howled messages of encouragement.

He timed the action to perfection. With a flick of the wrist he released one of the flaps two or three feet from the line of Germans. The shit sailed through the air at face level like a flock of disoriented starlings, the momentum of the train propelling it onwards. The first German managed to turn his head away as he realised what was happening but his five friends were not as quick as the foul-smelling excrement exploded onto their heads and shoulders.

It was a direct hit and Horace's arm rose in triumph as the cheers of the carriage rang in his ears. He'd scored the winning goal in a cup final, the winning runs in a test match.

They threw shit at Darmstadt and Hammelburg and Kronach. Each time a soldier bared his arse and the smell of shit rose from the floor of the carriage muffled cheers rang out from the tightly packed masses.

But still men died.

BODY LICE

Every prisoner dreaded that first initial sign. The men would wake in the morning; minute dark brown specks of louse excreta would clearly be visible on the skin and then several days later the biting would start. There was no escape, no hot water to wash in, no soap, no earthly chance of keeping clean. The lice fed on human blood, and then after their feast would lay eggs on skin and in the creases of clothing. The body lice infection caused intense itching, demoralizing and degrading the men who could do little against it. They lived in the seams and folds of clothing, the dirtier the better.

The body lice were transmitted by contact with infected clothing and bedding as well as by direct contact with an infected person. The conditions inside the camp were a living lice paradise.

The itching and scratching were unavoidable, irritating beyond belief. Even when the skin had broken, still the poor men couldn't help themselves and huge sores grew into large ulcers as each day passed. And then the flies, part of nature's food chain, moved in. It was common for a man to awaken with hundreds of tiny maggots feeding on the exposed pink and yellow pus-infected mess.

The rat still gnawed away at his stomach lining and lice ran across his skin, torturing him each minute of every day. At times, even though he knew they were biting into his flesh, he let them. Let them have their fill of my blood, he said to himself, perhaps then they'll leave me alone.

And worse lay in store every couple of days when nature called and he was forced to defecate. The prisoners would put it off as long as they could but inevitably after two or three day's cabbage soup, their bowels would need to move.

ROSA RAUCHBACH

Rauchbach introduced his daughter Rosa and Horace drank in inch by glorious inch. She nodded her head shyly and blushed. Horace felt a nervous tremor well up inside him and realised just how long it must have been since he'd witnessed anything so appealing. There were no magazines or newspapers in the camps, no pictures or Pathé news footage. He didn't even possess a photograph of Eva. His memory of a pretty girl had been wiped clean ... until now.

Horace nodded and greeted her politely in German. Rosa smiled and looked to the ground. Eventually she looked up and spoke nervously. 'I speak English. Father wants me to translate. I need to practice more.'

Her voice was soft and delicate, and accentuated by her broken English, it was sensual and mysterious. This isn't healthy, Horace thought to himself.

Horace realised that for the first time in his life he had fallen in love. It was a forbidden love; one he should never have embarked on. He had never felt this way before about any girl. His heart ached. He felt nauseous, his mouth was dry.

Rosa had never felt this way before. This man had awoken emotions in her that she had never before experienced. She couldn't pinpoint what it was exactly. Was it the danger of being caught that had heightened her pleasure so much? Was it the fact that this man had been the first, or was it something deeper? ... Perhaps even love?

She had wanted to scream and shout; every muscle, every sinew of her body, every nerve ending seemed to explode at the same glorious precise moment. It was a crazy, stupid moment, one that if discovered would have ended up with them both facing the firing squad.

ESCAPE

Horace lay on his bunk studying the window two foot from the bottom of his bed. He began dismantling the architrave that surrounded the glass pane, housing six half inch iron bars that ran from top to bottom of the window.

'What are you doing?' Flapper asked as he looked up from the letter he'd received earlier that week.

'A little bit of joinery,' replied Horace, 'get back to your letter, you've only read it twenty seven times.'

'Speak to me, country boy. What's going through that turnip-filled head of yours?'

Horace pointed to the bottom of the bars. They ran to the length of the floor but were split in two and each one held together with a cotter pin. 'See here, Flapper.' He pointed at one of the pins. 'I reckon if we could get these pins out, the bars would separate and we could get out through the window.'

'And then what?' Flapper asked as he shrugged his shoulders. 'Then where do we go? Straight into the arms of the Bosch, that's where.' Flapper relayed the all too familiar statistics.

Horace whistled as he began to loosen the cotter pins. He leaned forward, spat directly at the pin securing the third bar and the moisture lubricated the pin just enough to remove it from its housing. He worked on another bar and figured that a man of his build could squeeze through quite easily. He turned around and faced his good friend with his arms outstretched. 'Hey presto, Sir Flapper! That's magic.'

Flapper Garwood let out a sigh, looked at Horace incredulously. Horace had loosened off the bars in the window and created a perfectly acceptable gap through which he could escape. The window was fifty yards from the forest and although the German guards routinely patrolled the perimeter of the camp, Flapper admitted escape was not difficult. The difficulty lay in what was beyond and as the two men faced each other, one with a stupid grin on his face, the other with a look of dismay, Garwood knew, just knew, that his friend from Leicestershire would be out through the window that night.

THE FOOD RUN

'See, Jim, all of the villagers keep a vegetable garden.' Horace peered out over the well cultivated land. He could see the tops of turnips and winter swedes and a few bushes of sprouts.

'And Jim, some keep livestock.' She grinned as she pointed to several rabbit hutches and hen huts. 'We need to get some more meat into you, Jim Greasley.'

At first they collected sprouts and a few carrots and as many small swedes as Horace could squeeze into his pockets.

'Next time you should bring a bag, Rose. I'll be able to get a few turnips, too.'

'I will. But now, darling, it's time for meat.'

Horace pointed to a hen house ten yards from the nearest back wall of a small cottage. 'Over there. You keep watch and give me a little whistle if you notice a light going on or a curtain moving.'

He was just about to set off when she grabbed at his trouser leg. 'Are you mad, Jim? Haven't you heard the noise a hen makes when it's in danger? Go for the rabbits - they are silent.'

Horace lifted his hand and stroked her cheek. 'You're right, Rose, not just a pretty face.'

'I have my uses, Jim.' She winked as Horace set off slowly on his hands and knees, taking care to keep his head down. The hutches weren't locked, the wire meshed gates were simply held together with twine. The rabbits reminded Horace of the prisoners back at the camp. Escape would have been easy for the rabbits by simply gnawing through the rope. But the rabbits weren't going anywhere - why should they? They had a warm bed and they were fed regularly - why should they venture out into the great unknown?

And as he reached in and grabbed the first rabbit he wondered whether this poor creature ever had any inclination of escape, ever thought for one moment to start chewing at the twine. He dispatched the rabbit with an all too familiar pull and twist at the back of its neck. The third and fourth vertebrae and the spinal column separated with little effort and the life left the small creature immediately, right there and then outside its home.

He returned to Rose, all smiles.

'We'll be eating well tomorrow, Rose – rabbit stew.'

He had a rabbit tied down the trouser of each leg. He thanked his lucky stars that the uniform of the Russian officer he'd been given to wear belonged to a man far bigger than him.

The trousers were held up by string and the dead creatures fitted quite comfortably down each leg with enough room to manoeuvre himself through the bars. He made an undignified entrance, the extra weight causing him to lose his balance and crash to the floor.

'Fucking hell, Jim,' It was Flapper.

'Wait till you see what I've got, lads.'

Jock Strain struck a match and lit the candle underneath his bed.

Horace felt for the ears of the rabbit down his right leg. And like a magician at the London Palladium, he produced the rabbit right on cue, with perfect timing. 'Hey presto!' he cried out.

Jock Strain, the prisoners' resident chef, was fully awake now, clearly interested in the additional supplies for the early evening recipe. 'Where the hell did you get that?'

Horace didn't answer and instead pulled out its mate from the other leg. He stood with the two creatures held aloft in triumph. 'Once a hunter, always a hunter,' he exclaimed. He didn't have the heart to tell the men they were domesticated rabbits he'd simply lifted from a hutch.

'Holy mother of God!'

'Rabbit stew.'

'Magic, Jim - bloody magic. What a stew we're going to have today! If only we had a few more vegetables to pack it out a bit.'

And suddenly Horace remembered about the swedes and carrots and winter sprouts and a big smile beamed across his face.

'What? What is it now?' Jock asked.

Jock Strain cooked for just over ninety five men. The Germans normally supplied the provisions early in the morning with the chef preparing the vegetables, meat and stock during the course of the day. They'd talked long and hard about saving one of the rabbits for another day but Horace had boasted there were plenty more where that had come from. He felt he owed the men something for helping him with his escape plan every time he broke out and he felt it was the least he could do. He vowed to bring a little something back each time, even if it was just a few extra vegetables.

No, the men had voted for a feast. Nothing had been wasted. Every single last morsel of flesh from the two rabbits went into the stew. Brains, heart, liver, kidney, lungs - even the genitals from the male rabbit. The carcasses had been left in the pot until the very last minute so that every ounce of goodness had soaked into the stew.

BBC RADIO

'Can you get me a radio, Rose?'

'A what?'

'A radio.'

'I heard you, Jim. I heard you the first time.'

'Well, can you?'

Rose reached across for her underwear and began to dress herself. Horace followed suit as he pulled his trousers from the back of the pew.

Rose was thinking; he didn't want to interrupt her thoughts. After a few minutes she spoke.

'Impossible, Jim.'

Horace's face fell. 'But why?'

Rose pulled a light cotton dress up over her thighs and began fastening the buttons. His eyes were drawn to her firm young breasts.

'The Germans confiscated every radio in the village nearly a year ago.'

'But your father has one, you listen, you bring me ...'

'Yes. It's in the attic of our house, Jim, and it's the size of a small horse, built into an old dresser. It's not as if it will fit in my purse.'

The two lovers dressed and walked into the forest hand in hand in the direction of the village. The roof of the forest gradually disappeared as they neared the village and the stars that hung high in the sky illuminated their way like tiny seeds of light.

Jimmy White wagged a finger in the air. 'I've heard the stories; you escape from the camp at night and raid the villages, pinching the rabbits and the hens; you're a fucking nutter Greasley. And now you want to build a bloody radio.'

'That's right. I'll get you the parts.'

Jimmy White began pacing the room. 'Impossible; it's just not possible, I'm afraid.'

'Anything's possible,' stated Horace. They said it was impossible to break out of here but I've managed it over a hundred times.'

Jimmy White shook his head. 'You don't understand, Jim. I'd need valves and a transistor, a capacitor and a resister, an amplifier and primary and secondary winding units and earphones. Then I'd need some solder and some wiring and if it were humanely possible to get all that in here, where would we put it and more importantly, when and where would we listen to it?'

Horace spoke. 'Write me a list. You're to move into the prison staff quarters tomorrow night; Colin Jones has agreed to swap with you. Impressive, isn't it?'

'I'll say,' said Flapper.

'Think it will work?'

'We'll soon find out.'

Horace didn't hang around and within a minute had connected the radio to the power surge. The tiny red light beside the winder sparked

226

into life, emitting a faint glow. The two men smiled. As Horace reached for the headphones, Flapper placed a hand on his arm and Jimmy White lay patiently on the bunk alongside.

Five minutes passed.

'All I can hear is fucking static, I haven't heard one voice. Surely I should have heard a voice? I don't want to hear Churchill or the fucking Queen, I just want to hear a voice. Hitler would have been nice, for once I wouldn't have minded if I'd heard Hitler speaking or even Musso fucking lini, but no, I've heard nothing.'

Jimmy rolled over onto his stomach. 'It might be wired up wrong. I'll take a look at it tomorrow.'

Flapper chipped in. 'Give me a go, Jim.'

Horace handed him the earphones. 'Be my guest.'

Despite his best intentions Flapper didn't have the delicate fingers or the patience to participate in such an exercise. After ten minutes he cast the earphones back onto the bed. 'I'm going to kip. Chalky is right - we can take a look at it tomorrow.'

Jimmy White eased himself from Horace's bunk and walked gingerly over to his bunk. Horace replaced the false wooden panel with a sigh and wandered over to help Garwood replace the chimney and the iron plate. At least they'd achieved something, he thought to himself. The radio was wired up and ready for a little fine tuning tomorrow. It might take a day or two, he thought, but they'd get there.

Sleep didn't come easy. He dozed but didn't really fall into a deep slumber.

Unbeknown to Horace, Jock Strain hadn't either. He took a glance at his watch by the moonlight shining in through the window. It was 3.10 in the morning and he wondered just what the hell Jim Greasley was doing removing the panel above his shelf again. He eased himself from his bunk and crept over towards him.

'What the fuck are you up to?' he asked. 'Do you know what time it is?'

'I can't sleep, Jock. I thought I'd give it another go.'

Horace sat on one end of the bunk and Jock sat on the other. They sat in silence for almost an hour while Horace tried every combination. He sensed when the winding units came to an end then changed direction and went the other way, slowly, carefully, like a safe cracker on the combination wheel of a safe. And then after about twenty minutes when he was sure the winders had come to the end of the line, he would change direction and start all over again.

Each time he tried to go slower and slower. He'd heard voices the last couple of times – or was that his imagination? He wanted to hear voices – was his mind playing tricks on him? No, he'd definitely heard something.

He sighed, looked across at Jock. Miraculously he was still awake.

'One more go, Haggis, eh? Then we can turn in; get Jimmy to take a look tomorrow.'

Jock Strain nodded, rubbing at his eyes.

Horace took a deep breath and started again. Five minutes into the repeat performance Horace paused. There was no mistaking it this time, he'd definitely heard something.

The Scot sensed it too, noticed a spark of interest in the face that had showed no emotion whatsoever for nearly two hours. 'What is it, Jim?'

Horace held up a hand, lightened his grip on the winding wheel. 'I dunno, Jock, it's just that I thought I heard a drumbeat.'

The blood in Jock Strain's body turned to ice. 'Describe it, Jim.'

Horace shrugged his shoulders. 'Describe a drumbeat, mate? What do you mean? It was a drumbeat, how do you describe that? It just went boom... boom... boom. You know? Like a drumbeat.'

'Drum radio,' Jock whispered to himself in a voice that Horace couldn't hear through the earphones. 'Drum radio,' he repeated a little louder.

'What, Jock? What did you say?'

Jock leapt to his feet. He positioned himself on his knees next to the radio set. 'Just you keep that bloody winder where it is, Jim, you might have something.'

'Have something? What do you mean? Some bugger bashing away on a skin drum.

Sorry, Jock, but that wasn't exactly what I had in mind when we rigged this little beauty up. I had more –'

'Drum radio, Jim.'

'Drum what?'

'Drum radio, a BBC channel brought out a few weeks after you were captured in France. You've never heard of it, have you?'

Horace shook his head.

'It's a news channel. I caught a couple of broadcasts before I left for France. I came into the war a little after you, remember?'

'A BBC station?'

Jock grinned. Horace repositioned his earphones as his fingers barely came into contact with the winder. Ever so delicately he eased the wheels to the right and left, taking care not to take them too far in either direction. He stopped breathing, his skin tingled, shivers ran the length of his spine. The unmistakable public school tones of a BBC news reader burst into his eardrums.

Horace took his fingers from the wheel and breathed deeply. He held up a hand and then a thumb and a smile as wide as the mouth of the Thames burst across his face as he shouted to his friend kneeling on the floor. 'We've got the news, Jock! We've got the fucking BBC news!'

Horace burst into tears and Jock quickly followed suit, all too aware of the contagious effect a man crying had on him. Jimmy White heard the commotion and rose from his sick bed.

'Shut the fuck up, you two, you'll have Jerry in here.'

The sight of his two friends hugging each other with tears rolling down their cheeks astounded the radio ham.

It meant only one thing.

'It's working, isn't it?' Jimmy asked in utter disbelief.

Horace was sobbing as he rose to greet him.

'We've got the BBC news, Chalky. You're a bloody genius, man!'

More men rose from their beds now. Freddie Rogers and Dave Crump came over too. By this time Horace was back on the earphones with the same, silly grin on his face listening to a report from Tunisia in North Africa. The Allies it seemed were heading for another victory and had full control of North Africa.

The smiling yet tearful faces of Flapper Garwood, Jock and now Jimmy White left the other men in the staff working quarters at Freiwaldau in German occupied Silesia under no illusion as to what had been achieved. The men were slapping Horace on the back; some were shaking Jimmy White's hand and one of the lads planted a big wet kiss on his cheek.

They were heroes. Heroes in the same sense as the VC winner taking out a German machine gun post, or the scheming general whose cunning plans swung the battle against all the odds. They were Montgomery, Churchill, General McArthur and Douglas Bader rolled into one.

Against all odds Joseph Horace Greasley Rosa and Jimmy White had built a radio capable of picking up a BBC news channel under the noses of their German captors.

It was simply monumental ... a triumph that would rank up there with anything Horace had achieved so far. It was yet another personal victory for Horace and at that very moment, his moment of conquest, he thought back to the woman who had made it all possible.

The woman he loved with all his heart.

THE BEGINNING OF THE END

He had been trying to make her see sense for many weeks. Rose was different that evening. Horace was adamant he wouldn't break out of the camp again. He knew she would not join the exodus as long as he continued to meet her. This was their last meeting and Rose knew it.

'I will go,' she announced, just a few minutes into their meeting. 'I will run to the Americans, but only if you come with me.

'No, Rose, no!' he cried, 'It's too dangerous, the place is teaming with German soldiers on the run making their way back to Berlin, Hamburg and Düsseldorf. If we are caught together we'll be shot on the spot. You must take your chance alone. You can –'

She was crying again as she interrupted. 'But we can help each other, we can –'

'No, Rose, as soon as a German hears me speak he'll know I'm an escapee and he'll think nothing of putting a bullet into me. Is that what you want?'

It was a cruel but necessary blow, anything that would make her see sense. Horace knew if they were caught together it would mean a bullet for the escapee and one for the collaborator after the Germans had had their fun with her. He wanted so much to take his chance with her, felt sure between them they'd probably make it. But probably wasn't good enough. On their own they'd stand a better chance.

He held her shoulders, tried to make eye contact. 'Look at me, Rose. I won't meet you again, do you hear? You must go to the Americans ... please ... tell me you'll go the Americans.'

It was barely a nod – hard to distinguish between the trembling and the sobbing – nevertheless it was a slight nod of the head.

Horace lifted her forcibly from the ground as he wrapped his arms tightly around her. He was so relieved. They kissed and hugged and sobbed as the two of them broke down and the tears fell to the forest floor.

There was no going back. The decision had been made.

'It's for the best,' he explained as he handed her a note with his address in Ibstock. 'As soon as you can, write and tell me where you are.'

'We can be together, Jim?'

'Yes, of course we can. The war will be over in weeks and I'll come for you.'

'But you do not know where I will be.'

'You'll tell me.'

Rose nodded, 'Yes, I will tell you where I am.' Then she hesitated. 'You will come, Jim, won't you?'

Horace leaned forward and kissed her gently on the forehead. 'I will come for you, my English Rose. Wherever you are I will come ... even if I have to walk there bare footed over broken glass.'

LAURENCE CHARLES BARNES

Kings Royal Rifle Corps

By Lesley Margaret Jones née Barnes

Lersley lives in Sydney, Australia with her partner and family. She is a Registered Nurse and Midwife, currently working with her Partner Steve in a training business, training health care and First Aid.

She has managed Aged Care Facilities after graduating from UNI with a Bachelor of Health Science. Dad attended her first graduation just before he passed away.

In a letter to my mother Ruby, then still Dad's girlfriend, he wrote, 'One day I'll write to you in German as I am now qualified interpreter for this camp, brains coming out at last!' This I was told earned him extra black bread rations.

232

As interpreter Dad was also allowed to go with a guard to the local village to buy camp supplies. This enabled him to open a bank account to deposit card money he had won playing with other POWs and guards. The receipt for this money was kept in his top pocket and handed in on return to England. It went to Whitehall and was honoured as it was unheard of a POW banking money.

Relationships with some of the guards were good as they traded with them sugar stolen from the sugar factory. When asked how he managed to get the sugar out he replied, 'It was always hot so we took off our jackets and slung them over our shoulders. There was always two of us working together in the hot area so at the end of our shift we walked out towards the gates that were always guarded. As we were searched, we casually held the jackets out at arm's length and our body was searched each time. They never touched our jacket pockets or found the sugar. The sugar was valuable as we distilled it to make alcohol and to trade with guards as their families were on strict rations. You know they were deprived and frightened of the things that were happening. The German families also suffered.'

When talking to Dad about his conversations with the German guards he was very clear in his reply. 'You listened,' he said, 'I was lucky my schoolboy German language skills soon improved to listen to and understand what they were saying to each other and to us. I was able to interpret on a professional basis because I soon picked up my language skills, but also on a survival basis to let other POWs know who was okay and who not to trust.

'I remember the day I had won a whole lot or Deutschmarks at cards playing with one of our usual guards and the hut mates. There were two Australians, a Kiwi New Zealander and Alec, a Scot. As I was the only Englishman and subject to continual teasing, I felt I needed to guard my winnings carefully. I spoke with our friendly guard about my dilemma and he came up with the idea of me applying for the job of sourcing camp supplies from the local village. I thought that was good and as I already had just got the job of camp interpreter thought I had a good chance. I applied with my guard's recommendation and got the job, another escape from boredom. The guard then suggested I open a bank account in the village.

233

'I believe a local shop was like a sub post office and you could use it to deposit money for a bank in Dresden. I stated I was unable to write in German although fluent in speech. I was given time to practise with his help.'

Dad stated he thought the guard was helping him because he felt it was a good thing and because the extra sugar supplies made his wife happy!

There was the issue of prison clothes, so the guard assisted dad with a change of clothes and gave him time to deposit his money, change back, and return to the camp.

The banking went as planned with no hiccups. The slip was a receipt and Dad kept it safe in his top pocket on the Long March and cashed it in when demobbed at Dover. The money paid for his wedding reception feast on the black market in 1946.

Working parties and jobs my dad did as POW included breaking rocks for a railway, that was soul destroying work. I also vaguely remember him talking about a timber mill. There was also the work in the sugar factory, which was very hot and guarded at the gates. Dad was also a motor mechanic, and he enjoyed working on the cars that were at the camp. He wrote about this job in his letters to Mum.

The camp interpreter allowed him to know what was going on and warn others, it was one of the most important jobs. He also shopped for supplies in the village, he always enjoyed that!

Boredom was a constant theme in his letters. They were always looking for ways to combat it. In one letter he complained that it was noisy as he was writing in a barracks with 21 others, a jazz band playing; they had a mouth organ, two flutes, a guitar, combs and paper bits of stick army boots and tin mugs. He remarked, 'They are now playing Christmas carols! I give up!'

On 25 October 1942 Dad proposed to Mum by proxy in a letter and they became engaged. His parents bought the ring for her and he reimbursed them when he got home.

Reading Dad's letters it is clear that he was desperate to receive letters from her and frustrated when he had to wait months and then a pile would arrive at the same time. He tried different ways to suggest how she should send them.

Red Cross parcels were life savers and all the chaps loved them.

In one letter Dad tried to set up a camp mate with mum's friend, Ruth (my godmother). He enclosed the letter, which gave the POWs name and number for reference: 'R.L Osler C.Q.M S POW no17 Stalag VIII-B. "He's a great pal of mine. Likes beautiful women and fast cars ... this chap saw a photo of you and wanted one just like it!"'

For many years Dad did not talk about the war, occasionally Mum would say how hard it was in London during the Blitz to which Dad always replied, 'Nothing like what our boys did to Dresden.' He said he was on a train watching streets lift up intact.

I was able to get more information when he was helping me through darker periods in my life I then realised what he went through, eating rats, smoking the pages of the bible, feeling cold and hungry. He talked a little about the Long March, the cold, the foot sores and decent boots were a godsend if you could find them.

He was liberated by the Russians and was bitter. They kept them from being handed over, many died then as food was very short. The Russian women would shoot first if there was not enough food to go around. Dad once said: 'My God, those Russian women officers were tough sitting on their tanks riding through the villages. Far worse than the Germans. They marched us in the cold for no reason, we became disorientated, chaps died in large numbers by the roadside.'

Dad was eventually returned to Allied Forces and came home with his friend Alec, weighing five stone.

I was born in 1956 and when I was a child Dad eventually decided to go to technical college to learn written German. His teacher was a man named Heinke, a U-boat commander and British POW who stayed in England and married an English girl. They became great friends and Dad was able to speak German once more.

There was always empathy for the poor German families, the Polish farmers who hid him on one escape and the anger that the war lasted so long while he was a young man.

There was no debriefing or counselling in those days and in later years Dad's anger turned into silence and wanting to forget it all. He and Mum followed me to Australia and he died young, but happy, with his grandchildren around him. I am thankful for his resilience and strength to keep going in difficult times. I met Uncle Alec and his wife Auntie Margaret as a child but have lost touch since.

Dad left me with wise words. 'Given enough power even the best people will turn on each other. We fought for you to live in a free world. Don't let them ever take it from you.'

GUNNER ROBERT SAINSBURY

26th Battery New Zealand Army (NZA)
2nd New Zealand Expeditionary Force (NZEF)

By Peter Sainsbury

Peter Sainsbury grew up in Wellington, New Zealand, the youngest of six boys. After trying various careers, he trained and worked as a journalist before heading overseas. He spent nearly ten years working in Asia mainly based in Cambodia where he covered the end of the Khmer Rouge's war with the Government and the death of Pol Pot.

He also worked in Africa, the UK and USA, sometimes as a journalist but also as a human rights worker and researcher.

These days he runs a business restoring Austin Healey Sprites and antique steam engines.

He is married to Dr. Sophie Richardson. They have one son, Osborn (16). On his 40th wedding anniversary Robert, or Bob as he was known to his friends, was asked by his six sons if he and his wife, Dulcie would like to have a holiday in Europe as an anniversary gift.

He thought for a moment, laughed and said. 'Thank you, but I walked across it once, I don't need to see it again,' referring to the Long March at the end of the war.

As the bearer of the offer, the youngest in the family and the most clueless, I then half-jokingly asked if in truth it was really because he was still angry with the Germans.

Dad's response showed how he could communicate a great deal of information in a few words and a brief look. He gave a long drawn out, almost nasal, 'No', which, together with a sideways glance, translated as, 'Who put a 50-cent piece in this bloody idiot and pushed the start button?'

Usually the conversation would have ended there; he rarely spoke about his war experiences and when he did the comments were typically short, but this time he kept talking. His demeanour changed, usually a quick witted and good humoured man he became more serious. 'I don't hate the Germans. I was 22 years old, I joined up because it was the right thing to do. When I got to the camp, what did I find but a bunch of 22-year-olds in German uniforms most of whom had not even been given the choice about joining up.'

He said the greatest mistake many people made before, during and after the war was to conflate an ideology with a race or nation. 'Not all Germans were Nazis,' he said, 'and not all Nazis were German, look at Lord Haw-Haw or Oswald Mosely, and their upper class English mates.

'The people who made me angry were the politicians who created the mess and those who made money from the war.'

It was not a long conversation but it was the first of several that became longer as he grew older, the longest being just before he died.

This openness late in life was a marked contrast to what my older brothers, who grew up in the early 1950s, experienced.

'What I remember is how raw it all was and how careful even as a very young child you had to be,' said one of them. 'You could touch a nerve by asking the wrong question – I had a few very bad experiences.'

From Bob's letters to his parents and another from his battery sergeant major, it was clear why these things would have been raw only a few years after the events.

Bob, like most of the 2nd NZEF, was not a professional soldier. These men were farmers, clerks, drivers – ordinary young New Zealand men who, with little preparation or even worldly experience, were thrown into the heat of battle. It was an awakening.

Bob's ebullient manner, and always ready with a joke, belied his underlying deep sense of purpose, courage and responsibility as attested by BSM V M Rowland in a letter to Bob's parents dated 22 July 1941. 'I would like to tell you that in Greece our Bob did a magnificent job. E Troop was in the thickest of it from the start. On their first day they fought from mid-morning till nearly nine in the evening without any of their own troops in front and inflicted colossal damage and terrific casualties among the enemy ... and then about midnight they had to contend with the complications of parachute troops who landed at dusk, some miles to their rear. It is a miracle that any man came out alive from that position.

'We were bombed and machine gunned from the air for up to ninety minutes at a time, shelled all day long, plastered towards evening with mortars, peppered by machine guns and sniped at from both flanks. During all that time Bob and young Belworthy from Dunedin ... kept the fire orders [going] steadily through to the guns.

'That day there were technical difficulties enough with wires being cut and blown, radio interference and jamming by high powered Hun stations, yet the orders were always passed through. Bob's real efficiency and quiet cool courage was an inspiration.

... few of the old are missed more than Bob with his pungent quips and wise-cracks.'

It is interesting to contrast this with Bob's more colloquial account of those days. He gave the letter to a friend who was being evacuated from Crete and it was obviously posted in New Zealand because it had not been censored. 'As soon as it was light the next morning, we started to plaster their infantry up 'hill and down dale'. Everybody thought it was a great war, sitting back blowing Huns up. We were very shortly to get a rude shock.

'Before I go any further, a word or two about the German infantry. When they advance, they formed up in their companies and just moved forward in one body. We would plonk a shell into them, the machine guns would mow them down. It would make no difference, another lot would take their place and so on. But they don't like the bayonet, it must have cost them thousands of men, it was like a butcher's picnic, the only trouble was, we were outnumbered ten to one, and the weight of numbers told. I think the Hun is either mad or drunk.'

One area that was rarely touched on were his comrades, particularly those who never returned. One of the saddest documents found while researching this chapter was a letter from his mother to the parents of his best friend, 'Ken', dated 4 May1943. 'I feel I must write and tell you how delighted I was to see your son's name in the *Dominion* today listed as a prisoner of war,' she wrote. 'Robert will be delighted to hear about Ken, he was distressed when we wrote about him, and said he was his best friend, so it will be lovely to be able to give him the good news.

I wonder if Ken is in Stalag VIII-B, Robert is there but as there are 20 000 men there, he has not even seen many of the boys who were taken prisoner when he was, but they write to each other.'

Tragically it was a mistake. Ken was last heard from in 1941 and is believed to have been killed in action.

Bob never spoke of him.

From Greece Bob was evacuated to Crete about which he said little, other than with his unit scattered, he was with a pool of similarly placed soldiers. He said the invasion was well telegraphed with continual bombing for the preceding three days. He was given a Bren Gun and told to take up a position above the Maleme Airfield and try and shoot down any German aircraft that came over.

Given the lack of air cover and anti-aircraft equipment on Crete the German bombers came over low enough to actually see the pilots. And, of more consequence for Bob, they spotted him. 'They soon knew I was there, I would shelter behind a rock and then have a go at them,' he said. 'After that, as they came over they would give me a tickle up with a machine gun. I didn't like that much.'

Bob nearly made it to the evacuation area where soldiers who were married or had no weapon were given priority. Bob, not having a weapon at this point, was in line to embark when a friend came up to him gave him his rifle and ran off for the ship at which point Bob was put in the group to remain.

This story came about when at a family birthday, probably about 1980, the phone went and Dad answered it to find it was the man who have given him his gun and run off. They talked for a while then Dad returned to the dinner table told us the story and finished by wryly saying, 'I could have done without ever hearing from him again.'

Although not without incident, Bob's time in Lamsdorf was anti-climactic when compared to the journey from New Zealand, arrival in Egypt where they trained and went sightseeing, the battles he had been through in Greece and Crete, even the staging camps before his move to Lamsdorf. In the staging camps, he said, they would crawl out under the wire of an evening and barter for food or whatever with the locals, many of whom were sympathetic though occasionally deals did not go as planned.

'I took out some old boots and other rubbish and came back with a bottle of Johnnie Walker. I was a hero. We opened the bottle shared it out, tasted it, gagged and spat it back out.' On close examination the bottle, which had been made from celluloid or something similar, had been tampered with. A hot needle had been inserted in the bottom, the whiskey drained out and replaced with retsina, a harsh Greek wine made from pine resin.

From the camps in Greece it was then a journey by train through the Balkans to Lamsdorf. 'We were loaded onto stock wagons and the German guards laughingly pointed out that the doors were not locked so we could jump out whenever we wanted.' It was no secret that the Germans had put a price on prisoner's head (the rest of the body was not necessary in order to collect the reward). Partisans affiliated with Germany were more than happy to follow the train in the hope of picking up some cash for those who unwisely thought of prematurely detraining.

Bob's time in Lamsdorf was a case of making the best of a bad situation. He worked in an iron mine and when asked if he could have opted out, he said: 'It was better to be doing something than nothing otherwise you end up chasing each other round the barracks like some of those English officers.' Working in an iron mine was one thing. Embracing a radical change in lifestyle preference was a step too far.

For leisure, right through the war and captivity Bob was an avid bridge player but after the war, while he continued to play cards he never again played bridge. He said having played every day with the same partner in Lamsdorf for four years meant he had become so proficient the challenge was gone.

241

Bob settled down into a life of routine in the camp, broken up on the downside by occasional bouts of ill health and injury, while on the upside he was with friends and Red Cross parcels started to arrive.

On learning of Bob's safe arrival at Lamsdorf, his parents gave the meat they had planned to have for dinner to the cat and went into town to celebrate the news he was alive and safe.

Working in the iron mines was tough and dangerous work. Bob said one day the prisoner who cut the pit props on a table saw, twisted on one of them as he was pushing it through. The blade shattered and pieces sliced into his head, torso and arms, 'but they stitched him up and he went back to the table saw when he had recovered just the same as he had done before, only with a lot of scars.'

Bob's injuries were more prosaic but still painful and inadequately treated. He said dysentery, a major killer in the war, was treated by a German doctor folding pieces of paper into narrow cones, filling them with charcoal, inserting the larger end in his mouth and blowing the other end as hard as he could.

On another occasion a coffee urn (though he doubts it contained any real coffee), exploded as he went to fill his mug. The hot coffee grindings landed on the back of his hands, severely burning them. Each hand developed one large blister from his fingers to his wrist. He was taken to see the doctor, who looked, said 'um' and 'ah' a few times, took a pair of forceps and pulled the skin off both hands. When asked if it hurt his response was brief: 'Of course it bloody did.'

Red Cross parcels were a great source of joy, including as they did food and letters from home. However on occasion things did not go as planned. Bob told of receiving a Red Cross parcel with items from his parents, including a tinned Xmas pudding. A friend in the barracks had received a parcel with a tin of cream. They whipped up the cream and Dad put the pudding in a pan of water to heat up. They opened it with great anticipation, only to find my grandfather had gone to a local factory and had them fill one of their Christmas pudding tins with cigarettes which he thought would be more welcome.

The food received in the parcels was certainly a welcome change from their usual diet. For the rest of his life, Bob could not face raw cabbage. On the one occasion when coleslaw was served with dinner he actually lost his temper and said 'I lived on the bloody stuff for four years, I am not eating it now.'

The food at Lamsdorf was apparently something of a lottery. On one occasion the cook asked Dad if he had eaten, and Dad said he hadn't, to which the cook replied, 'Stay clear of the meat, it is boiled udder.'

Yet on another occasion, clearly due to a mistake in transportation, a load of fillet steak was delivered to the kitchen. The cook called in Bob and some of the others and explained it was so tender it could be eaten raw and cut pieces for them to try. Bob said it was everything the cook claimed so why he then chose to boil it until it was tough as shoe leather was an eternal mystery to him.

In 1945 with the Russians approaching, the camp was evacuated in groups of about 100. It was a freezing cold winter and they were made to walk to Germany. Many perished along the way. Those that survived endured terrible suffering. Bob weighed 80 pounds at the end of it. And this was a man who, before he left for the war, played senior rugby as a forward.

On returning to England he was hospitalized and then went to stay with his aunt, whose husband was a large shareholder in Bells Distillery. He spent some time travelling in the UK, of which he said little. But it was clear he was letting off steam while there. His most memorable comment was, 'There were a hundred pubs on Princes Street in Edinburgh; I think I got chucked out of most of them.'

Bob returned to New Zealand in August 1945, spent time with his parents in Wairoa and caught up with his four brothers, all of whom served: George, the eldest, a major in the infantry and a trained lawyer, was often called upon to defend at court-martials; Bill was a pilot instructor; Ned served with the Navy in the South Pacific and the youngest, Guy, was in Japan at end of the war and the occupation.

It has been difficult to write this because Bob never kept a diary, many of his letters are missing and he rarely discussed that period of his life in detail, and when he did it was generally to tell a humorous anecdote.

Occasionally his comments were more serious and he seemed to be thinking out loud. On two occasions, shortly before he died, we had a serious discussion about our respective experiences of war. Mine was as a journalist in Cambodia and could not compare to what he had been through; I had only been there to watch. Bob was curious as to what it had been like for me in Cambodia. I explained I saw and did things I never thought I would, to which he replied, 'I know what you mean but don't try talking to people about it if they weren't there, they won't understand.'

I asked him if that was how he felt and why he had been so reticent to talk about war. He replied: 'Of course. Who could you talk to? Unless they were there you couldn't say anything.'

During our discussion he outlined some of his beliefs and attitudes that had always been hinted at or implied but never really set out. For him joining up to fight the Nazis was a clear and obvious moral decision, there was no blood-lust. It was just a job that needed to be done, but he was always careful not to generalize about 'goodies and baddies' in simple nationalistic terms.

His attitude towards those who ran or slavishly embraced the Nazi regime, worked in the concentration camps or were involved in atrocities against civilians and prisoners, was cut and dried. He had no problem with them facing the ultimate punishment, though he did feel it should have been much swifter, without too many legal niceties. This was simply a matter of practicality. He believed that for Germany to rebuild and recover, the worst of the worst needed to be dealt with as quickly as possible.

At the same time, while he was appalled by the Holocaust, he would point out that the concentration camp was a British invention from the Boer war, that the Russians had conducted similar programs against the Jews and other ethnic or religious groups yet remain untouched by history.

But when it came to ordinary soldiers in the heat of battle, Bob was slower to judge. 'If you have not been in a war then you cannot understand what it is like. The chain of command is everything, you have to obey orders and every side committed war crimes. If you put everyone in that boat on trial there would not be a lot of people left.'

This may explain a later conversation about war in which he said: 'If you weren't there then you wouldn't understand and in war you do things you are not always proud of or don't want to think about … I still think about the war but only the good times.'

244

Bob returned to his job with Dalgety's, a large agricultural supply and finance company, qualified as a wool classer and spent the rest of his career as a wool broker.

He was married to Dulcie for more than fifty years before passing away peacefully in May 2000.

He had six sons: Bede, John, Paul, Mark, Noel and Peter.

His funeral was an apt reflection of the man he was. There was a message of condolence from the prime minister and the department of justice allowed several prison inmates to attend on compassionate grounds.

Speaking at his funeral, Noel summed up Bob's life perfectly. 'It could be said he was not an ambitious man but that was not the case. He was not ambitious for wealth or position, though would gladly have accepted anything the lottery or the horse races sent his way. He came back from the war ambitious for a stable, loving family life, something he very successfully achieved.

He rarely said, 'I love you' but that was not necessary, it was a given, never in our lives did we ever have reason to doubt it.

His was a life well lived.'

JOHN WILLIAM PRYKE

Regiment 2nd Battalion Seaforth Highlanders

By Jen Squires

Jen Squires has been happily married to her soulmate for the past 16 years, they have two adult boys who both live in the same town. Jen has been in her current position for 18 years working in the kitchen at a local secondary school. In her spare time she is involved in helping and looking after sick or injured hedgehogs.

My hero and Grandad, John William Pryke, was known as Dick to all his friends. As a boy soldier he was picked up on parade by the inspecting NCO, who that night told him, and the rest of the parade, that he was a right little dirty Dick. It stuck from almost that moment and for the rest of his life he was known as Dick Pryke.

Dick was a corporal in the second battalion of the Seaforth Highlanders. Running away from the orphanage he was brought up in at

246

the age of 14, he lied about his age to join the army, like many boys did in those days.

I remember Grandad had a tattoo of the word 'India' on his left arm, as before the war he had served in India – and that's where he got the tattoo.

Like many, my grandad did not talk much about his time in the war, especially his POW time. The 51st Highlanders had a pretty rough time fighting in Letot and Saint-Sylvain in June 1940, several days after the mass evacuation at Dunkirk.

Thousands of troops, including my grandad, remained on the orders to fight on regardless under the French command. They fought for 10 days against overwhelming odds with very little ammunition, minimum sleep and only scraps of food, desperately trying to keep the Germans away. Eventually they were surrounded at Saint Valery, the fog was so thick, they could hardly see a hand in front of their faces and they were mercilessly bombed from the air as well as the land.

When the word came that the French had raised the white flag, the men from the Seaforth Highlanders had tears in their eyes as they still believed help was coming. Many men fell to their deaths, falling from the cliffs while trying to escape, those who were not shot were captured and endured five long years attending different POW camps.

The prisoners were forced to march hundreds of miles to POW camps in Germany and occupied Poland, where they endured appalling conditions including slave labour and starvation.

Grandad told me of the kindness of the Polish women, who would come out with bread and water for the prisoners who were being force-marched to the different camps, but then the German soldiers would hit them in the face with the butt of the rifle and poured the water away, right in front of the very dehydrated prisoners

Grandad also told me how he managed to get his little toe permanently disfigured when a tank went over his foot on the Long March from Saint Valery to his first camp. He was in a lot of pain but because his toe and foot was broken but he didn't dare stop marching.

When I was a little girl and asked why his little toe was bent over his other toe, he told me, 'During the war I was having a wee and a little worm crawled over my foot.'

I believed him until I was much older.

There was also the story about the camp kitchen staff who managed to feed a bowl of soup laced with liquid paraffin to a German officer. He had great delight in telling me they did not see much of the officer that day.

The men were very loyal to each other and would stick together if one of them got into trouble. The Red Cross would deliver parcels for the POWs. This would give hope and joy to the camp but some of the German soldiers would steal what little things they had, especially the toothpaste that was hard to come by. So some of the prisoners would hide razorblades in the bottom of a tube of toothpaste so the German soldier would slice his thumbs when he pushed the toothpaste up.

Early on in his captivity he realised that he was going to have to make the best of it in order to survive … to do whatever it took. He began to recognise those who were not strong enough to survive and would use the example of two brothers, belonging to the Coleman family of famous Coleman's Mustard fame. Until then, they had lived a life of privilege and simply could not adapt to the rigours of a POW camp. The POWs had one bowl which they ate from and urinated in at nights. The story goes that the Coleman brothers starved to death because they were too proud to eat out of the same bowl that they had to urinate in.

Grandad said that he could see who had neither the inner strength nor who had lost it just by the look in their eyes as they gradually would not even get out of bed if not made to by the Germans.

Grandad had been moved from camp to camp ending up at Lamsdorf for the rest of the war.

'Prisoner of War arrived at Stalag XXI-B on 08.07.1940, coming from Stalag VI-F

Detained in Stalag XXI-B/Z (according to a capture card dated 07.08.1940)

Transferred from Stalag XXI-B/H to Stalag XXI D on 11.04.1940

Transferred from Stalag XXI-D to Stalag VIII-B on 17.08.1944

Detained in Stalag VIII-B, coming from Stalag XXI-D'

Towards the end of the war, as the Russians advanced, POWs were marched from the camps to keep them from being liberated by the Russians, and the Long Walks began. Luckily Dick was marched westwards, away from Lamsdorf, well away from the Russians and was housed in his last camp that was liberated by the Americans.

248

The march had taken its toll on all of the POWs with many simply sitting down and dying. When the Americans liberated Dick he was suffering from typhoid fever and was barely conscious. The dead were being buried in mass graves and Dick was almost put in with them when an orderly noticed his eyes moving. He was transferred to the hospital.

One of my memories visiting my grandad was that he never left anything on his plate, not even a bit of gravy. He used to get a piece of bread and mop up all the gravy so the plate looked like it was clean out the cupboard. When we were children used to say we were starving he would get really upset and tell us we never knew the meaning of the word.

He would tell me and my sister about what little food they had and the soup was more like potato starch water.

It upsets me to this day to see so much food wasted when so many people are starving in the world. We owe so much to our heroes of Lamsdorf.

FURTHER READING
Compiled by KEN SCOTT and PHILIP BAKER

Captivity in British Uniforms: Stalag VIIIB (344) Lamsdorf
By Anna Wickiewicz
Published 2017 by Centralne Muzeum Jeńców Wojennych

Do the Birds Still Sing in Hell?
By Horace Greasley and Ken Scott
Published by Bonnier Books 2012

The Psychiatrist
By John West
Published by Fortis Publishing 2022

Soldier, Prisoner, Hunter, Gatherer
By Don Woods and Ken Scott
Published by Fortis Publishing 2021

A Pacifist's War: Sid's Story
By Sonia Waterfall
Published by FEEDAREAD 2021

Lamsdorf In Their Own Words
Published 2020 by The Online Memorial and Museum
of Prisoner of War

The Long March In Their Own Words
Published 2020 by The Online Memorial and Museum of Prisoner of
War

Against The Wind
By Cyril Rofe
Published in 1956 by Hodder and Stoughton

Sojourn in Silesia
By Arthur Evans
Published in 1995 by Ashford Writers

Thanks for the Memories
By Leighton Bowen
Published in 2011 by Menin House Publishers

The Blue Door
By Lise Kristensen and Ken Scott
Published by Pan Macmillan 2005

Guest of the Führer
By Les Shorrock
Published privately in 2017 and available from Amazon

The Devil Couldn't Break Me
By Laura Aslan and Ken Scott
Published by Andrews UK 2015

The Long Way Home
By John McCallulm
Published 2012 by in Birlinn Ltd

Captives of War:
British Prisoners of War in Europe
in the Second World War
By Clare Makepeace.
Published in 2017 by Cambridge University Press.

Almost a Lifetime
By John McMahon
Published in 1995 by Oolichan Books

Prisoner of War
By Charles Rollings
Published in 2007 by Ebury Press

The Barbed Wire University
By Midge Gillies
Published in 2011 by Aurum Press Ltd

The Last Escape
By John Nichol and Tony Rennel
Published in 2002 by Viking and in 2003 by Penguin

Life Can Be Cruel
The Story of a German POW in Russia.
By HRR Furmanski

The Boys
The Story of 732 Young Concentration Camp Survivors.
By Sir Martin Gilbert

Destined to Survive
A Dieppe Veteran's Story.
By Jack A Poolton and Jayne Poolton-Turvey

252

Printed in Great Britain
by Amazon

79299638R10151